The
Wonder
of
Wisdom

SIGN WONDER

The Wonder of Wisdom

authorHOUSE®

AuthorHouse™ LLC
1663 Liberty Drive
Bloomington, IN 47403
www.authorhouse.com
Phone: 1-800-839-8640

Scripture quotations marked KJV are from the Holy Bible, King James Version (Authorized Version). First published in 1611. Quoted from the KJV Classic Reference Bible, Copyright © *1983 by The HYPERLINK "http://www.zondervan.com/"Zondervan Corporation.*

Scripture quotations marked NKJV are taken from the New King James Version. Copyright © *1982 by HYPERLINK "http://www.thomasnelson.com/"Thomas Nelson, Inc. Used by permission. All rights reserved.*

Published by AuthorHouse 01/21/2014

ISBN: 978-1-4918-5273-6 (sc)
ISBN: 978-1-4918-5278-1 (e)

Library of Congress Control Number: 2014900792

Remembering the poor:

"If there be among you a poor man of one of thy brethren within any of thy gates in thy land which the LORD thy God giveth thee, thou shalt not harden thine heart, nor shut thine hand from thy poor brother: But thou shalt open thine hand wide unto him, and shalt surely lend him sufficient for his need, in that which he wanteth. Beware that there be not a thought in thy wicked heart, saying, The seventh year, the year of release, is at hand; and thine eye be evil against thy poor brother, and thou givest him nought; and he cry unto the LORD against thee, and it be sin unto thee. Thou shalt surely give him, and thine heart shall not be grieved when thou givest unto him: because that for this thing the LORD thy God shall bless thee in all thy works and in all that thou puttest thine hand unto. For the poor shall never cease out of the land: therefore I command thee, saying, Thou shalt open thine hand wide unto thy brother, to thy poor, and to thy needy, in thy land" Deuteronomy 15:7-11

For those who worry about going without in order to satisfy someone else's hunger and thirst, I say to you that it's not in vain that you deny yourself a meal or two. Isaiah 58:6-8 carries a promise from God the Father if these few guidelines and acts of compassion are carried out . . . "Is not this the fast that I have chosen? To lose the bands of wickedness, to undo the heavy burdens, and to let the oppressed go free, and that ye break every yoke? Is it not to deal thy bread to the hungry, and that thou bring the poor that are cast out to thy house? When thou sees the naked, that thou cover him; and that thou hide not thyself from thine own flesh? Then shall thy light break forth as the morning, and thine health shall spring forth speedily: and thy righteousness shall go before thee; the glory of the LORD shall be thy reward." Psalms 41:1 "blessed is he that considers the poor: the LORD will deliver him in time of trouble."

It is my prayer and hope that the contents of these pages will edify, encourage, exhort, restore, renew, build you up in your most Holy faith as you pray in the Holy Ghost and bring comfort to your soul,

CHAPTER 1

"Where there is no vision, the people perish:" (Proverbs 29:18)

"I will stand on my watch, and set me on the tower, and I will watch to see what he will say to me, and what I shall answer when I am reproved. And the LORD answered me, and said, _write the vision, and make it plain_ on tables, that he may run that reads it. For the vision is yet for an appointed time, but at the end it shall speak, and not lie: though it tarry, wait for it; because it will surely come, it will not tarry" Habakkuk 2:1-3.

This is what we are projecting and working towards!

"Pure religion and undefiled before God and the Father is this, _to visit the fatherless and widows in their affliction_, and to keep himself unspotted from the world" James 1:27. If we claim to be who we are without the works, the fruits, then our work becomes futile, in vain and without value. We are commanded to "learn to do good; Seek justice, Reprove the ruthless, Defend the orphan, Plead for the widow" Isaiah 1:17 because "the LORD protects the strangers; He supports the fatherless and the widow, But He thwarts the way of the wicked" Psalm 146:9.

Since ". . . the poor shall never cease out of the land: therefore I command you, saying, you shall _open your hand wide to your brother, to your poor, and to your needy, in your land_" Deuteronomy 15:11. "When you cut down your harvest in your field, and have forgotten a sheaf in the field, you shall not go again to fetch it: it shall be for the stranger, for the fatherless, and for the widow: that the LORD your God may bless you in all the work of your hands" Deuteronomy 24:19. "And when ye reap the harvest of your land, thou shalt not

1

wholly reap the corners of thy field; neither shalt thou gather the gleanings of thy harvest. And you shall not glean your vineyard, neither shall you gather every grape of your vineyard; you shall leave them for the poor and stranger: I am the LORD your God" Leviticus 19:9-10.

The Purpose of giving a tenth part of your income (the tithe) in support of The Work of God has always been to have *the Levite* taken care of because they "have no inheritance" among the Israelites, the tithe was given to them "for an inheritance, for their service which they serve, even the service of the tabernacle of the congregation." (Numbers 18:21, 31). "And if **a stranger** (alien/refugee/immigrant) dwells with you in your land, you shall not mistreat him. The stranger (alien/refugee/immigrant) who dwells among you shall be to you as one born among you, and you shall love him as yourself; *for you were strangers (aliens/refugees/immigrants) in the land of Egypt*: I am the LORD your God" Leviticus 19:33-34. He is "*a Father of the fatherless* and a judge for the widows, Is God in His holy habitation" Psalm 68:5. Therefore "*You shall not afflict any widow or orphan. If thou afflict them in any wise, and they cry at all unto me, I will surely hear their cry; and my wrath shall wax hot, and I will kill you with the sword; and your wives shall be widows, and your children fatherless.*" Exodus 22:22-24.

This is God's attitude toward the widow. Even though not often practiced today due to the "evolution of the mind," modern culture and civilization. "If brethren dwell together, and one of them die, and have no child, *the wife of the dead shall not marry without unto a stranger*: her husband's brother shall go in unto her (gross), and take her to him to wife, and perform the duty of an husband's brother unto her. And it shall be, that the firstborn which she beareth shall succeed in the name of his brother which is dead, that his name be not put out of Israel. And if the man like not to take his brother's wife, then let his brother's wife go up to the gate unto the elders, and say, My husband's brother refuseth to raise up unto his brother a name in Israel, he will not perform the duty of my husband's brother. Then the elders of his city shall call him, and speak unto him: and if he stand to it, and say, I like not to take her; Then shall his brother's wife come unto him in the presence of the elders, and loose his shoe from off his foot, and spit in his face, and shall answer and say, So shall it be done unto that man that will not build up his brother's house. And his name shall be called in Israel, The house of him that hath his shoe loosed" Deuteronomy 25:5-10.

"When you have finished laying aside all the tithe of your increase in the third year—the year of tithing—and have given *it* to the Levite, the stranger, the fatherless, and the widow, so that they may eat within your gates and be filled, then you shall say before the LORD your God: 'I have removed the holy *tithe* from *my* house, and also have given them to the Levite, the stranger, the fatherless, and the widow, according to all Your commandments which You have commanded me; I have not transgressed Your commandments, nor have I forgotten *them*. I have not eaten any of it when in mourning, nor have I removed *any* of it for an unclean *use*, nor given *any* of it for the dead. I have obeyed the voice of the LORD my God, and have done according to all that You have commanded me. Look down from Your holy habitation, from heaven, and bless Your people Israel and the land which You have given us, just as You swore to our fathers, "a land flowing with milk and honey" Deutoronomy 26:12-15.

"For who hath despised the day of small things? for they shall rejoice, and shall see the plummet in the hand of Zerubbabel with those seven; they are the eyes of the LORD, which run to and fro through the whole earth" Zechariah 4:10. "Though your beginning was small, yet your latter end should greatly increase" Job 8:7. Our ministry is geared towards the people. There cannot be a ministry without the people. The reason why this nation has been blessed is because of the care she has projected to the needy, the poor or disadvantaged. We model what the Word of God says and with all our might we are looking to do the same. Bring relief to those in need both here and abroad. Suffering is eminent and when defenseless children become victims it is the responsibility of those who are able to relieve the oppressed and defend the cause of the stranger, the orphan and the widow. This is our greatest motivation.

In addition to helping those in need because of circumstances beyond their control, Jesus gave a commission in ". . . All authority in heaven and on earth has been given to me. Therefore *go and make disciples of all nations, *baptizing them in the name of the Father and of the Son and of the Holy Spirit,* and *teaching them to obey* *everything I have commanded you*. And surely I am with you always, to the very end of the age" Matthew 28:18. "For it is precept upon precept, precept upon precept, line upon line, line upon line, here a little, there a little" Isaiah 28:8. Every good leader is known for his ability to duplicate himself; Reproduction, It's a numbers game as some sales experts would say. "The fruit of the righteous is a tree of life; and *he that wins souls is wise*" Proverbs 11:30. Growth and stability is evident in the fruit/s one is able to bear. No matter where we start, or how small the beginning may seem, being consistent is what will bring us the results we so desire. Not forgetting that there is a reward at the end, "if we faint not." This is the consequence of laying down our lives for others but the work must go on: "You/ we will be hated by all because of My name, but it is the one who has endured to the end who will be saved" Matthew 10:22. "For consider Him who has endured such hostility by sinners against Himself, so that you/we will not grow weary and lose heart" Hebrews 12:3. For His name sake we know that we will suffer rejection and hatred but God has promised a reward. "Therefore, since we have this ministry, *as we received mercy*, we do not lose heart," II Corinthians 4:1. "Therefore, my beloved brethren, be steadfast, immovable, always abounding in the work of the Lord, knowing that your toil is not in vain in the Lord" 1 Corinthians 15:58. ". . . being patient, brethren, until the coming of the Lord, the farmer waits for the precious produce of the soil, being patient about it, until it gets the early and late rains" James 5:7. ". . . let us not be weary in well doing: for in due season we shall reap, if we faint not" Galatians 6:9.

CHAPTER 2

The Three C's To The Three W's: Woneness (Oneness), Wholeness, Wellness eluding Wantonness!

"If there be therefore any Consolation IN Christ, if any Comfort of Love (Agape), if any Communion of the Spirit" Philippians 2:1. Until I read this recently . . . again, it really hadn't hit me that what we've been doing as Body has been deficient of the three C's that bring healing to it. If we as a family really meditated on those things and let these words marinade in our Spirit, there wouldn't be as big a mess as we see in the church today. Breaking it down we know that we ought to be One with Christ but really haven't grasped the real meaning of at-one-ment with Christ which brings about complete health and healing . . . This portion of scripture alone describes the communion and correlation between God the Father, The Son and The Holy Spirit without getting into detail about how embedded they are and intertwinned.

The Love of God for this world was the driving force behind the reconciliation between Him and His creation ". . . God demonstrates his own love for us in this when we were yet sinners, Christ died for us," Romans 5:8. Therefore Jesus Christ came in the picture conquered death hell and the grave, the factors that threatened our place in Him, bringing Comfort of His Love to us and Him and through Christ we have this Consolation that everything is alright in spite of turbulent circumstances. Because of Jesus Christ we are able to enjoy Communion with His Holy Spirit whom God sent after Jesus returned to the Father. "It is expedient for you that I go away (Jesus said): for if I go not away, the Comforter will not come to you; but if I depart, I will send him to you" John 16:7 . . . "But the Helper, the Holy Spirit, whom the Father will send in My name, He will teach you all things, and bring to your remembrance all that I said to you" John 14:26.

Like-mindedness, the same Love, being on One Accord and of One mind are the components that bring about the joy (fruit of the Spirit), which is our strength which brings about the "togetherness"—united we stand, divided we fall; an American motto. The moment we deviate we from this "like-mindedness, unity", strife and vain glory begin to rule in our hearts bringing division, disintegration and disentanglement and later we experience the absence of joy which weakens us as believers and takes away our strength. Unity, lowliness of mind, humility and the state of being One with God and the Body is what brings about the fulfillment of this joy which is our strength. Letting each esteeming each other better than themselves and having a spirit of servitude; being mindful of each other and not letting oneself seek "his own things" but on the things of others. Serving one another eliminates pride, arrogance and division.

High-mindedness brings about division and solitude (Philippians 2:1-4). It has never been the will of God for anyone to walk alone. "For as we have many members in one body, and all members have not the same office: So we, being many, are one body in Christ, and every one members one of another. Having then gifts differing according to the grace that is given to us, whether prophecy, let us prophesy according to the proportion of faith; Or ministry, let us wait on our ministering: or he that teacheth, on teaching; Or he that exhorteth, on exhortation: he that giveth, let him do it with simplicity; he that ruleth, with diligence; he that sheweth mercy, with cheerfulness" Romans 12:4-8.

So "let this mind be in you, which was also in Christ Jesus: Who, being in the form of God, thought it not robbery to be equal with God: But made himself of no reputation, and took upon him the form of a servant, and was made in the likeness of men: And being found in fashion as a man, (because) He humbled himself, and became obedient unto death, even the death of the cross" Philippians 2:5-8. Christ as our model to this Oneness with the Creator, took upon Himself to become "the curse" so that we

His creation could be free from the curse of sin death and hell (Galatians 3:13). He became us that we might become like Him (Likeminded with Christ). Reuniting us God, through Christ we now have this Consolation and Comfort of God's Love and the Communion with His Holy Spirit. In commemoration of Christ's life, death, burial and resurrection we ought to re-member, re-unite ourselves and re-commune ourselves with the Godhead, and only then will we experience the joy unspeakable, the peace (like a river), the Love that can only come from our re-connection with God, and the togetherness that is so needful for survival. Being One with God and One with the Body is the only way to birth those bowels of compassion and mercy (Philippians 2:1) that will bring about change to the ministry of Christ and His work.

Therefore "let love be without dissimulation. Abhor that which is evil; cleave to that which is good. Be kindly affectioned one to another with brotherly love; in honor preferring one another; not slothful in business; fervent in spirit; serving the Lord; rejoicing in hope; patient in tribulation; continuing instant in prayer; distributing to the necessity of saints; given to hospitality. Bless them which persecute you: bless, and curse not. Rejoice with them that do rejoice, and weep with them that weep. Be of the same mind one toward another. Mind not high things, but condescend to men of low estate. Be not wise in your own conceits. Recompense to no man evil for evil. Provide things honest in the sight of all men. If it be possible, as much as lieth in you, live peaceably with all men.

Dearly beloved, avenge not yourselves, but rather give place unto wrath: for it is written, Vengeance is mine; I will repay, saith the Lord. Therefore if thine enemy hunger, feed him; if he thirst, give him drink: for in so doing thou shalt heap coals of fire on his head. Be not overcome of evil, but overcome evil with good" Romans 12:9-21. This wraps it up. Our joy becomes full when we become One with God and the body. We are then enabled to succumb to His will without resistance and enabled to fulfill His will for our lives without fear or doubt because "there is no fear in Love but perfect Love casts out fear" 1 John 4:18.

So ". . . work out your own salvation with fear and trembling. For it is God which worketh in you both to will and to do of his good pleasure. Do all things without murmurings and disputings:

That ye may be blameless and harmless, the sons of God, without rebuke, in the midst of a crooked and perverse nation, among whom ye shine as lights in the world; holding forth the word of life; that I may rejoice in the day of Christ, that I have not run in vain, neither labored in vain. Yea, and if I be offered upon the sacrifice and service of your faith, I joy, and rejoice with you all. For the same cause also do ye joy, and rejoice with me" Phillipians 2:12-18. It all begins with Him and ends with Him.

First we have to be regrafted in if we lost our Consolation IN Christ, our Comfort of Love and our Communion of His Holy Spirit. And if we have never experienced either one of these then we have to be grafted in. Declare and be committed to the One who would unite or reunite you. "For he saith, I have heard thee in a time accepted, and in the day of salvation have I succored thee: behold, now is the accepted time; behold, now is the day of salvation" II Corinthians 6:2.

"Jesus answered him, "Truly, truly, I say to you, unless one is born again he cannot see the kingdom of God." Nicodemus said to him, "How can a man be born when he is old? Can he enter a second time into his mother's womb and be born?" Jesus answered, "Truly, truly, I say to you, unless one is born of water and the Spirit (water baptism by emulsion and the baptism of the Holy Spirit), he cannot enter the kingdom of God. That which is born of the flesh is flesh and that which is born of the Spirit is spirit" John 3:3-6. "However, you are not in the flesh but in the Spirit, if indeed the Spirit of God dwells in you. But if anyone does not have the Spirit of Christ, he does not belong to Him. And if Christ be in you, the body is dead because of sin; but the Spirit is life because of righteousness. And if the Spirit of him that raised up Jesus from the dead dwell in you, he that rose up Christ from the dead shall also quicken your mortal bodies by his Spirit that dwells in you." Romans 8:9-11

Secondly "not forsaking the assembling of ourselves together, as the manner of some is; but exhorting one another: and so much the more, as you see the day approaching" Hebrews 10:25, "but encourage one another day after day, as long as it is still called "Today," so that none of you will be hardened by the deceitfulness of sin" Hebrews 3:13. Getting into a local church for spiritual growth and nourishment is essential. We ought to "obey them that have the rule over you (talking about spiritual authority), and submit yourselves: for they watch for your souls, as they that must give account, that they may do it with joy, and not with grief: for that is unprofitable for you" Hebrews 13:17. These Spiritual Leaders have to "Be on guard for themselves and for all the flock, among which the Holy Spirit has made them overseers, to shepherd the church of God which He purchased with His own blood" Acts 20:28 . . . "that you also be in subjection to such (spiritual) men and to everyone who helps in the work and labors" I Corinthians 16:16, and "remember those who led you, who spoke the word of God to you; and considering the result of their conduct, imitate their faith" Hebrews 13:7.

Thirdly, partaking of His BODY in remembrance and commemoration of His death, burial and resurrection. ". . . the Lord Jesus in the night in which He was betrayed took bread; And when he had given thanks, he broke it, and said, Take, eat: this is my body, which is broken for you: this do in remembrance of me. In the same way He took the cup also after supper, saying, "This cup is the new covenant in My blood; do this, as often as you drink it, in remembrance of Me. For as often as you eat this bread, and drink this cup, you do show the Lord's death till he come. But whoever shall eat this bread, and drink this cup of the Lord, unworthily, shall be guilty of the body and blood of the Lord. So let a man examine himself, and let him eat of that bread, and drink of that cup. For he that eats and drinks unworthily, eats and drinks damnation to himself, not discerning the Lord's body." 1 Corinthians 11:23-29.

It is expedient to have undergone the first two steps described above. Commemorating His Body is only for those who've been grafted in and whose hearts are pure before Him, who've made a conscious decision that Jesus Christ is their Lord and savior and committed their hearts and lives to Him and His work. Not everyone is acceptable or accepted to partake of His Body. But according to the words of Jesus, we have no life (Zoe, the God kind of life) in us unless we partake of His body and blood as written: ". . . Jesus said to them, truly, I say to you, except you eat the flesh of the Son of man, and drink his blood, you have no life in you" John 6:53. So we MUST partake of His Body and His Blood. This is the heart and soul of this ministry, the life and the work He did for us to attain eternal life. Neglecting this would mean rejecting Him.

To continue with the Consolation we have IN Christ, the Comfort of His Love and the Communion of His Holy Spirit, we have to pray without ceasing;"1 Thessalonians 5:17, and with all prayer and petition, pray at all times, in the Spirit, and with this in view, be on alert with all perseverance and petitions for all the saints" Ephesians 6:18. This may sound and seem overwhelming but you are not required or expected to know how or what to pray . . . "Likewise the Spirit also helps our infirmities: for we know not what we should pray for as we ought: but the Spirit Himself makes intercession for us with groanings which cannot be uttered" Romans 8:26. God by His Spirit assists us in prayer because we do not know what or how we should pray. Even after Jesus' disciples had spent months with Him and watched Him and heard Him, they still didn't know how to pray.

"And it came to pass, that, as he was praying in a certain place, when he ceased, one of his disciples said unto him, Lord, teach us to pray, as John also taught his disciples. And he said unto them, When ye pray, say, Our Father who art in heaven, Hallowed be thy name, Thy kingdom come, Thy will be done on earth, as in heaven. Give us day by day our daily bread. And forgive us our sins; for we also forgive every one that is indebted to us. And lead us not into temptation; but deliver us from evil" Luke 11:1-4. Jesus continued to teach about prayer and said "and I say unto you, ask, and it shall be given you; seek, and ye shall find; knock, and it shall be opened unto you. For every one that asketh receiveth; and he that seeketh findeth; and to him that knocketh it shall be opened. If a son shall ask bread of any of you that is a father, will he give him a stone? or if he ask a fish, will he for a fish give him a serpent? Or if he shall ask an egg, will he offer him a scorpion? If ye then, being evil, know how to give good gifts unto your children: how much more shall your heavenly Father give the Holy Spirit to them that ask him?" Luke 11:9-13. "Be anxious for nothing, but in everything by prayer and supplication with thanksgiving let your requests be made known to God" Philippians 4:6. So for those familiar with prayer "then, I urge that entreaties and prayers, petitions and thanksgivings, be made on behalf of all men, 1 Timothy 2:1.

This is the root to Spiritual growth and maturity. Without knowledge we perish as recorded here that "My people are destroyed for lack of knowledge: because thou hast rejected knowledge, I will also reject thee, that thou shalt be no priest to me: seeing thou hast forgotten the law of thy God, I also will forget thy children" Hosea 4:6. It is the knowledge of God that sustains this Consolation we have IN Christ, His Comfort of Love and the Communion we have in His Holy Spirit. Without knowing how can we pursue His heart, life and love. "Therefore My people go into exile for their lack of knowledge;" Isaiah 5:13. This is where the knowledge of God begins . . . "For the lips of a priest should preserve knowledge, and men should seek instruction from his mouth; for he is the messenger of the LORD of hosts" Malachi 2:7.

Where to begin? start to read a little at a time, "For precept must be on precept, precept on precept; line on line, line on line; here a little, and there a little:" Isaiah 28:10, this way you won't have to feel overwhelmed at the task of acquiring all the information you need from the scriptures at one time. Once you have begun to grasp, ". . . keep the words of this covenant to do them, that you may prosper in all that you do" Deuteronomy 29:9, and "let not this book of the law depart from your mouth but you shall meditate therein day and night, that you may observe to do according to all that is written therein: for then you shall make your way prosperous, and then you shall have good success" Joshua 1:8.

Now we are not under law but under grace. Mastering Grace which is given freely begins with knowledge of His WORD so that if and when you slip up, "there is therefore now no condemnation to them which are in Christ Jesus, who do not walk after the flesh, but after the Spirit" Romans 8:1 and "who is the one who condemns? Christ Jesus is He who died, yes, rather who was raised, who is at the right hand of God, who also intercedes for us" Romans 8:34. So no one can point a finger at you, I don't care who they are, as it is written, "there is none good or righteous, no not one, there is none that understands, there is none that seeks after God. ALL HAVE TURNED ASIDE, TOGETHER THEY HAVE BECOME USELESS; THERE IS NONE WHO DOES GOOD, THERE IS NOT EVEN ONE" Romans 3:10-12. So no one has the right to condemn you. It is Christ that died for you, and ". . . you are bought with a price: therefore glorify God in your body, and in your spirit, which are God's" 1 Corinthians 6:20. So in your quest to attain this Consolation we have IN Christ, His Comfort of Love and Communion of His Holy Spirit,

. . . Be Reunited and Celebrate the AT-One-Ment with God.

CHAPTER 3

Angels in waiting

Since the day we were born, there have been assigned us an angel to watch over us and guide us in the way that we should go. In this predestination that God set for us since the foundations of the world, HE assigned everyone a guide, a guardian someone to watch over HIS word. "Take heed that ye despise not one of these little ones; for I say unto you, that in heaven their angels do always behold the face of my Father which is in heaven" Matthew 18:10. The gifts, talents and callings inside of you that are without repentance according to Romans 11:29. They were preordained by God since birth for HIS pleasure and His glory Revelation 4:11. God already had an assignment for us and designated a path, originated for all of us. God put the potential inside of us and since we're made in HIS image Genesis 1:26 expects greatness because HE is God. It's a sin I'd say that not everyone lives out to their fullest potential as planned and orchestrated by God. Thanks to the will God gave to us.

Fatal if misdirected and if we allow the enemy of our destiny to beguile, tempt or mislead. If we don't use this powerful gift to work for us for our good, there's a penalty for that as Jesus Himself described in Matthew 25:14-30. Being unproductive can be fatal. Jesus gave a parable to His listeners about the good (productive) servants and the evil (unproductive) lazy servants. In this parable He narrates that at the end of their toil and journey there were consequences based on their actions. Nothing done goes unrewarded or unpunished. It's either or and not both ways. These angels also cannot work without our effort. They are sent to protect for the good of us but it's entirely up to us to ensure God's work is accomplished and if not efforts be made towards the work designed for us.

The bible records that "foolishness is bound up in the heart of the child" Proverbs 22:15. These angels that have been assigned to us only do the will of the Father for our lives and that's why many of us never make it to our destination. The will of God for our lives is not complicated to unravel. It doesn't take a visit to a psychic to tell us what the future holds. Our future is hidden in God and only God can reveal to us our destiny. The reason why GOD has hidden this future is because of the enemy of our souls. The Bible records that I (HE) said, "You are gods, And all of you are sons of the Most High" Psalm 82:6, but often act and do contrary to Him and His ways making it harder sometimes impossible to find that path created just for you because we yield to the enemy when we act contrary to HIS way.

The best example that I could give are the children of Israel. Many of their carcasses fell in the wilderness because God wanted to take them to a place that belonged to them but that generation that left Egypt never lived to see it save Joshua and Caleb. Moses didn't even get the opportunity as their leader because of "walking contrary" to HIS way and instructions. Their children after them inherited their promise even though the promise belonged to those that fell in the wilderness as well. "Therefore, as the Holy Spirit says: "Today, if you will hear His voice, do not harden your hearts as in the rebellion, in the day of trial in the wilderness, where your fathers tested Me, tried Me, and saw My works forty years. Therefore I was angry with that generation, and said, 'they always go astray in their heart, and they have not known My ways.' So I swore in My wrath, 'they shall not enter My rest.' "Beware, brethren, lest there be in any of you an evil heart of unbelief in departing from the living God; but exhort one another daily, while it is called "Today," lest any of you be hardened through the deceitfulness of sin. For we have become partakers of Christ if we hold the beginning of our confidence steadfast to the end, while it is said: "Today, if you will hear His voice, Do not harden your hearts as in the rebellion." Hebrews 3:7-15, for Christ "Who is gone into heaven, and is on the right hand of God; angels and authorities and powers being made subject unto him" 1 Peter 3:22 and obedient unto Him. That same authority over the angels has been given us.

This is the promise of God about guidance: "Behold, I am going to send an angel before you to guard you along the way and to bring you into the place which I have prepared. Be on your guard before him and obey his voice; do not be rebellious toward him, for he will not pardon your transgression, since My name is in him. But if you truly obey his voice and do all that I say, then I will be an enemy to your enemies and an adversary to your adversaries. For My angel will go before you and bring you in to the land of the Amorites, the Hittites, the Perizzites, the Canaanites, the Hivites and the Jebusites; and I will completely destroy them" Exodus 23:20-23.

This not only speaks collectively as a family but as individuals. God has promised that, ". . . He shall give His angels charge over you, to keep you in all your ways. They shall bear thee up in their hands, lest thou dash thy foot against a stone" Psalm 91:11-12. These angels are there to serve, protect, fight our battles and guide us to bring us to the place that we were ordained to be; (the person you were supposed to become). The place to be and the person to become go hand in hand. There has to be regeneration and a renewal of the mind, a process and a growth to accommodate our new place of destiny. A metamorphosis has to have occurred inorder to function orderly at our place of destiny otherwise there would be disorder and dysfunction. "Bless the LORD, ye his angels, which excel in strength, that do his commandments, hearkening unto the voice of his word" Psalm 103:20.

It is never obvious without the knowledge of angels and their assignment unless God reveals them to us, doesn't just happen by chance or coincidence but assignment of angels happens on purpose and according to GOD's will. God has protected us, "Thou hast beset (hedged) me behind and before, and laid Your hand upon me. Such knowledge is too wonderful for me; it is high, I cannot attain unto it" Psalm 139:5-6. Preparation of the mind and spirit has to take place for this type of knowledge otherwise He wouldn't reveal Himself if preparation hadn't taken place for a reception. Look at the story of Moses; he had to have been prepared at the palace by his own mother and the knowledge that was imparted while growing up as Pharaohs son prepared him for his real job in life, ref the book of Exodus. This is the reason why some have had encounters with angels and others haven't.

". . . when Herod was about to bring him out, that night Peter was sleeping, bound with two chains between two soldiers; and the guards before the door were keeping the prison. Now behold, an angel of the Lord stood by him, and a light shone in the prison; and he struck Peter on the side and raised him up, saying, "Arise quickly!" And his chains fell off his hands. Then the angel said to him, "Gird yourself and tie on your sandals"; and so he did. And he said to him, "Put on your garment and follow me." So he went out and followed him, and did not know that what was done by the angel was real, but thought he was seeing a vision. When they were past the first and the second guard posts, they came to the iron gate that leads to the city, which opened to them of its own accord; and they went out and went down one street, and immediately the angel departed from him" Acts 12:6-10. Peter had been prepared for his journey and his latter years and GOD sent Christ to be HIS teacher to prepare him for the remaining years of his life.

On occasion when facing difficulty and impossibilities in our lives sometimes life threatening, there are angels assigned to fight our battles. One example is Elisha in his time. According to the following passage it is written "Therefore he (King of Syria Israel's enemies) sent horses and chariots and a great army there, and they came by night and surrounded the city. And when the servant of the man of God arose early and went out, there was an army, surrounding the city with horses and chariots. And his servant said to him, "Alas, my master! What shall we do?" So he answered, "Do not fear, for those who are with us are more than those who are with them." And Elisha prayed, and said, "LORD, I pray, open his eyes that he may see." Then the LORD opened the eyes of the young man, and he saw. And behold, the mountain was full of horses and chariots of fire all around Elisha. So when the Syrians came down to him, Elisha prayed to the LORD, and said, "Strike this people, I pray, with blindness." And He struck them with blindness according to the word of Elisha." 2 Kings 6:14-18.

This is why we ought not to fear or be dismayed. Because those that are for us are more and greater than those that are against us. "Ye are of God, little children, and have overcome them: greater is he that is in you, than he that is in the world" 1 John 4:4. Even though there are different assignments of angels and the fact that angels have designated duties, some are called to serve at the mercy seat, who are also archangels and these are mightier and stronger and others are called to guide. There are tidings/message angels sent from God with messages, there are warring angels and judgment angels who execute judgment on the earth as seen in the latter book of Revelations. They also excel in strength and only carry out the Will of God, they oppose evil and fight you if you do not comply to God's will.

If an "angel" is sent or assigned to you to oppose God's will for your life and guides you in a destructive path, know that that is no angel but a demonic spirit sent by the angel of light. We are warned in the bible "Beloved, believe not every spirit, but try the spirits whether they are of God: because many false prophets are gone out into the world. Hereby know ye the Spirit of God: Every spirit that confesseth that Jesus Christ is come in the flesh is of God: And every spirit that confesseth not that Jesus Christ is come in the flesh is not of God: and this is that spirit of antichrist, whereof ye have heard that it should come; and even now already is it in the world" 1 John 4:1-3. Angels are spirit beings as noted here "Bless the LORD, O my soul. O LORD my God, thou art very great; thou art clothed with honor and majesty . . . Who maketh his angels spirits; his ministers a flaming fire:" Psalm 104:1,4.

We ought to know who's real and who's not. Satan fell with a third of God's angels. He and the third of the angels remain God's angels who are doomed for eternal destruction. "All things were made by HIM and without HIM was nothing made that was made" Colossians 1:16; John 1:3. They are God's and God will do to them as He pleases as written: "Then another sign appeared in heaven: an enormous red dragon with seven heads and ten horns and seven crowns on his heads. His tail swept a third of the stars out of the sky and flung them to the earth (stars also mean angels, God also calls His angels sons—Job 38:7) . . . And there was war in heaven. Michael and his angels fought against the dragon, and the dragon and his angels fought back. But he was not strong enough, and they lost their place in heaven. The great dragon was hurled down— that ancient serpent called the devil, or Satan, who leads the whole world astray. He was hurled to the earth and his angels with him" Revelation 12:3-4; 12:7-9.

"Behold, he put no trust in his servants; and his angels he charged with folly:" Job 4:18; ". . ., He puts no trust in His holy ones, and the heavens are not pure in His sight;" Job 15:15; "And no marvel; for Satan himself is transformed into an angel of light" II Corinthians 11:14. He comes to steal kill and destroy (John 10:10). Therefore "Let no man beguile you of your reward in a voluntary humility and worshipping of angels, intruding into those things which he hath not seen, vainly puffed up by his fleshly mind" Colossians 2:18. We are not to pray to angels, angels are not God!! Even though great power has been bestowed upon them and they carry out the will of God, they are still subject to Sovereignty and are not supreme. Only God is!!! This knowledge of Him will make it easier for us to distinguish between the true angel and the angel of light. It is He (Elohim) who truly cares about us and wants to lead us to "the place" if we let him. He will lead, guide and keep us here and after. He already assigned His angels to be with us at all times and guide us in all our ways, that's how much He cares for us. "The angel of the LORD encamps round about them that fear him, and delivers them" Psalm 34:7. Just keep His way and make our path straight and we will live to see His goodness . . .

. . . and let His angels guide you . . .

CHAPTER 4

Integrity In Question! Honoring our Father's commandment: will you be found true???

First Example; illustrations and recorded facts have been written in the bible and other books as a format and a model for us to use as a universal family. Integrity has always been held in high esteem and has a role to play as some defiant sons and daughters were put on display and found wanting when put on a balance. Examples Belshazar, king of Babylon found in Daniel 5:1-30. He was the wicked king who didn't learn from his father king Nebuchadnezzar, Daniel 5:17-22, emphasis on verse 22, who was driven from civilization and sent to the wild to live like an animal for seven years until he acknowledged that power did not belong to him but God. At the end of the seventh year, understanding returned to him and his eyes were opened and he magnified God. King Nebuchadnezzar had been warned by the prophet Daniel that these things would occur to him as a result of pride and arrogance and his refusal to acknowledge GOD as the source behind his and the kingdom's greatness.

Here's the story; Reference? the book of Daniel 4 from verse 29: "Twelve months later, (after he had received the prophesy from Daniel), as the king (Nebuchadnezzar) was walking on the roof of the royal palace of Babylon, he said, "Is not this the great Babylon I have built as the royal residence, by my mighty power and for the glory of my majesty?" The words were still on his lips when a voice came from heaven, "This is what is decreed for you, King Nebuchadnezzar: Your royal authority has been taken from you. You will be driven away from people and will live with the wild animals; you will eat grass like cattle. Seven times will pass by for you until you acknowledge that the Most High is sovereign over the kingdoms of men and gives them to anyone he wishes." Immediately what had been said about Nebuchadnezzar was fulfilled. He was driven away from people and ate grass like cattle. His body was drenched with the dew of heaven until his hair grew like the feathers of an eagle and his nails like the claws of a bird. At the end of that time, I, Nebuchadnezzar, raised my eyes toward heaven, and my sanity was restored. Then I praised the Most High; I honored and glorified him who lives forever. His dominion is an eternal dominion; his kingdom endures from generation to generation" Daniel 4:29-34.

Second Example: "Now behold, there came a man of God from Judah to Bethel by the word of the LORD, while Jeroboam was standing by the altar to burn incense. He cried against the altar by the word of the LORD, and said, "O altar, altar, thus says the LORD, 'Behold, a son shall be born to the house of David, Josiah by name; and on you he shall sacrifice the priests of the high places who burn incense on you, and human bones shall be burned on you.'" Then he gave a sign the same day, saying, "This is the sign which the LORD has spoken, 'Behold, the altar shall be split apart and the ashes which are on it shall be poured out.'" Now when the king heard the saying of the man of God, which he cried against the altar in Bethel, Jeroboam stretched out his hand from the altar, saying, "Seize him." But his hand which he stretched out against him dried up, so that he could not draw it back to himself. The altar also was split apart and the ashes were poured out from the altar, according to the sign which the man of God had given by the word of the LORD. The king said to the man of God, "Please entreat the LORD your God, and pray for me, that my hand may be restored to me." So the man of God entreated the LORD, and the king's hand was restored to him, and it became as it was before. Then the king said to the man of God, "Come home with me and refresh yourself, and I will give you a reward." But the man of God said to the king, "If you were to give me half your house I would not go with you, nor would I eat bread or drink water in this place. "For so it was commanded me by the word of the LORD, saying, 'You shall eat no bread, nor drink water, nor return by the way which you came.' So he went another way and did not return by the way which he came to Bethel." 1 Kings 13:1-10.

"Now an old prophet was living in Bethel; and his sons came and told him all the deeds which the man of God had done that day in Bethel; the words which he had spoken to the king, these also they related to their father. Their father said to them, "Which way did he go?" Now his sons had seen the way which the man of God who came from Judah had gone. Then he said to his sons, "Saddle the donkey for me." So they saddled the donkey for him and he rode away on it. So he went after the man of God and found him sitting under an oak; and he said to him, "Are you the man of God who came from Judah?" And he said, "I am." Then he said to him, "Come home with me and eat bread." He said, "I cannot return with you, nor go with you, nor will I eat bread or drink water with you in this place. "For a command came to me by the word of the LORD, 'you shall eat no bread, nor drink water there; do not return by going the way which you came.'" He said to him, "I also am a prophet like you, and an angel spoke to me by the word of the LORD, saying, 'Bring him back with you to your house, that he may eat bread and drink water'" But he lied to him. So he went back with him, and ate bread in his house and drank water. Now it came about, as they were sitting down at the table, that the word of the LORD came to the prophet who had brought him back; and he cried to the man of God who came from Judah, saying, "Thus says the LORD, 'Because you have disobeyed the command of the LORD, and have not observed the commandment which the LORD your God commanded you, but have returned and eaten bread and drunk water in the place of which He said to you, "Eat no bread and drink no water"; your body shall not come to the grave of your fathers." It came about after he had eaten bread and after he had drunk, that he saddled the donkey for him, for the prophet whom he had brought back. Now when he had gone, a lion met him on the way and killed him, and his body was thrown on the road, with the donkey standing beside it; the lion also was standing beside the body" 1 Kings 13:11-24.

The old prophet lied and seduced the young prophet into disobeying God. What the young prophet should have realized God hardly changes His mind and if God changed His mind, him being a prophet should have been informed by God Himself. It is written "Surely the Lord GOD does nothing Unless He reveals His secret counsel to His servants the prophets" Amos 3:7. It cost him his life and he paid the consequences of disobeying God.

The Third Example: "The word which came to Jeremiah from the LORD in the days of Jehoiakim the son of Josiah, king of Judah, saying, "Go to the house of the Rechabites, speak to them, and bring them into the house of the LORD, into one of the chambers, and give them wine to drink" Jeremiah 35:1. Remember the laws of the priests or one set aside to be in the temple continually. "Then the LORD spoke to Aaron, saying: "Do not drink wine or intoxicating drink, you, nor your sons with you, when you go into the tabernacle of meeting, lest you die. It shall be a statute forever throughout your generations, that you may distinguish between holy and unholy, and between unclean and clean, and that you may teach the children of Israel all the statutes which the LORD has spoken to them by the hand of Moses" Leviticus 10:8-11; "The priests, the Levites—all the tribe of Levi— shall have no part nor inheritance with Israel; they shall eat the offerings of the LORD made by fire, and His portion. Therefore they shall have no inheritance among their brethren; the LORD is their inheritance, as He said to them" Deuteronomy 18:1,2. This was a test from God to see if they would obey. God already knew if they would pass or fail the test but His message was to the Jewish community through the prophet Jeremiah.

"Then I took Jaazaniah the son of Jeremiah, the son of Habazziniah, his brothers and all his sons, and the whole house of the Rechabites, and I brought them into the house of the LORD, into the chamber of the sons of Hanan the son of Igdaliah, a man of God, which was by the chamber of the princes, above the chamber of Maaseiah the son of Shallum, the keeper of the door. Then I set before the sons of the house of the Rechabites bowls full of wine, and cups; and I said to them, "Drink wine." But they said, "We will drink no wine, for Jonadab the son of Rechab, our father, commanded us, saying, 'You shall drink no wine, you nor your sons, forever. You shall not build a house, sow seed, plant a vineyard, nor have any of these; but all your days you shall dwell in tents, that you may live many days in the land where you are sojourners.' Thus we have obeyed the voice of Jonadab the son of Rechab, our father, fin all that he charged us, to drink no wine all our days, we, our wives, our sons, or our daughters, nor to build ourselves houses to dwell in; nor do we have vineyard, field, or seed. But we have dwelt in tents, and have obeyed and done according to all that Jonadab our father commanded us" Jeremiah 35:3-10. They were laid on the balance, tested, tried and found true and worthy to receive the blessing and the promise that came afterwards . . . "Surely the sons of Jonadab the son of Rechab have performed the commandment of their father, which he commanded them, but this people has not obeyed Me" Jeremiah 35:16 . . . and Jeremiah said to the house of the Rechabites, "Thus says the LORD of hosts, the God of Israel: 'Because you have obeyed the commandment of Jonadab your father, and kept all his precepts and done according to all that he commanded you, therefore thus says the LORD of hosts, the God of Israel: "Jonadab the son of Rechab shall not lack a man to stand before Me forever" Jeremiah 35:18:19.

The Fourth Example is that of Job. The bible describes him as a close to perfect man, "that man was blameless and upright, and one who feared God and shunned evil" Job 1:1, that God Himself recommended him to Satan as recorded in this text. "Now there was a day when the sons of God came to present themselves before the LORD, and Satan also came among them. And the LORD said to Satan, "From where do you come?" So Satan answered the LORD and said, "From going to and fro on the earth, and from walking back and forth on it." Then the LORD said to Satan, "Have you considered My servant Job, that there is none like him on the earth, a blameless and upright man, one who fears God and shuns evil?" Job 1:6-8. After all that happened to Him from Job 1:9-18, ". . . Job arose, tore his robe, and shaved his head; and he fell to the ground and worshiped. And he said: "Naked I came from my mother's womb, And naked shall I return there. The LORD gave, and the LORD has taken away; Blessed be the name of the LORD." In all this Job did not sin nor charge God with wrong" Job 1:20-22. His adversity was so great and severe that as recorded in the text ". . . when Job's three friends heard of all this adversity that had come upon him, each one came from his own place—Eliphaz the

Temanite, Bildad the Shuhite, and Zophar the Naamathite. For they had made an appointment together to come and mourn with him, and to comfort him. And when they raised their eyes from afar, and did not recognize him, they lifted their voices and wept; and each one tore his robe and sprinkled dust on his head toward heaven. So they sat down with him on the ground seven days and seven nights, and no one spoke a word to him, for they saw that his grief was very great" Job 2:11-13. "Then said his wife (Job's wife) to him, do you still retain your integrity? Curse God, and die. But he said to her, "You speak as one of the foolish women speaks. Shall we indeed accept good from God and not accept adversity?" In all this Job did not sin with his lips." Job 2:9-10.

The Fifth Example: Joseph and Potiphar's wife. A brief description of what he looked like is found in this passage; "Now Joseph was well-built and handsome," Genesis 39:6 "Joseph had been taken down to Egypt. Potiphar, an Egyptian who was one of Pharaoh's officials, the captain of the guard, bought him from the Ishmaelites who had taken him there. The LORD was with Joseph and he prospered, and he lived in the house of his Egyptian master. When his master saw that the LORD was with him and that the LORD gave him success in everything he did, Joseph found favor in his eyes and became his attendant. Potiphar put him in charge of his household, and he entrusted to his care everything he owned. From the time he put him in charge of his household and of all that he owned, the LORD blessed the household of the Egyptian because of Joseph. The blessing of the LORD was on everything Potiphar had, both in the house and in the field. So he left in Joseph's care everything he had; with Joseph in charge, he did not concern himself with anything except the food he ate" Genesis 39:1-6. And because Joseph was a cutie and was well built and handsome, ". . . after a while his master's wife took notice of Joseph and said, "Come to bed with me!" But he refused. "With me in charge," he told her, "my master does not concern himself with anything in the house; everything he owns he has entrusted to my care. No one is greater in this house than I am. My master has withheld nothing from me except you, because you are his wife. How then could I do such a wicked thing and sin against God?" And though she spoke to Joseph day after day, he refused to go to bed with her or even be with her.

One day he went into the house to attend to his duties, and none of the household servants was inside. She caught him by his cloak and said, "Come to bed with me!" But he left his cloak in her hand and ran out of the house." Genesis 39:7-12.

"When his master heard the story his wife told him, saying, "This is how your slave treated me," he burned with anger. Joseph's master took him and put him in prison, the place where the king's prisoners were confined. But while Joseph was there in the prison, the LORD was with him; he showed him kindness and granted him favor in the eyes of the prison warden. So the warden put Joseph in charge of all those held in the prison, and he was made responsible for all that was done there. The warden paid no attention to anything under Joseph's care, because the LORD was with Joseph and gave him success in whatever he did. Genesis 39:19-23. Long story short, Potiphar's wife set him up, lied on him (sounds very familiar to me) and Joseph was cast in prison and for two years he remained there until an opportunity arose and the Pharaoh needed Joseph again. The moral of the story is Joseph remained faithful, though tested and tried, laid on the balance, he came through and God blessed him and put him in charge of Egypt. He became second in command in all of Egypt because he honored His Father's commandment as written in the text. "Then Pharaoh said to Joseph, "Since God has made all this known to you, there is no one so discerning and wise as you. You shall be in charge of my palace, and all my people are to submit to your orders. Only with respect to the throne will I be greater than you. So Pharaoh said to Joseph, "I hereby put you in charge of the whole land of Egypt." Then Pharaoh took his signet ring from his finger and put it on Joseph's finger. He dressed him in robes of fine linen and put a gold chain around his neck. He had him ride in a chariot as his second-in-command, and men shouted before him, "Make way!" Thus he put him in charge of the whole land of Egypt. "Genesis 41:39-43. But that didn't just happen, it was "When two full years had passed," Genesis 41:1. So all that time he remained in prison until his time of visitation.

The Sixth Example: Shadrack, Meshack and Abednego. "Nebuchadnezzar the king made an image of gold, whose height was sixty cubits and its width six cubits. He set it up in the plain of Dura, in the province of Babylon. And King Nebuchadnezzar sent word to gather together the satraps, the administrators, the governors, the counselors, the treasurers, the judges, the magistrates, and all the officials of the provinces, to come to the dedication of the image which King Nebuchadnezzar had set up. So the satraps, the administrators, the governors, the counselors, the treasurers, the judges, the magistrates, and all the officials of the provinces gathered together for the dedication of the image that King Nebuchadnezzar had set up; and they stood before the image that Nebuchadnezzar had set up. Then a herald cried aloud: "To you it is commanded, O peoples, nations, and languages, that at the time you hear the sound of the horn, flute, harp, lyre, and psaltery, in symphony with all kinds of music, you shall fall down and worship the gold image that King Nebuchadnezzar has set up; and whoever does not fall down and worship shall be cast immediately into the midst of a burning fiery furnace." So at that time, when all the people heard the sound of the horn, flute, harp, and lyre, in symphony with all kinds of music, all the people, nations, and languages fell down and worshiped the gold image which King Nebuchadnezzar had set up" Daniel 3:1-7.

"Therefore at that time certain Chaldeans came forward and accused the Jews. They spoke and said to King Nebuchadnezzar, "O king, live forever! You, O king, have made a decree that everyone who hears the sound of the horn, flute, harp, lyre, and psaltery, in symphony with all kinds of music, shall fall down and worship the gold image; and whoever does not fall down and worship shall be cast into the midst of a burning fiery furnace. There are certain Jews whom you have set over the affairs of the province of Babylon: Shadrach, Meshach, and Abed-Nego; these men, O king, have not paid due regard to you: (Pressure has been mounting in the middle east for Israel to give up Jerusalem and our precious government has been pressuring Israel to submit and give up their land of promise to the Arabs but God gave Jerusalem to the Jews and the land belongs to the Jews and will always belong to the Jews). They do not serve your gods or worship the gold image which you have set up. Then Nebuchadnezzar, in rage and fury, gave the command to bring Shadrach, Meshach, and Abed-Nego. So they brought these men before the king. Nebuchadnezzar spoke, saying to them, "Is it true, Shadrach, Meshach, and Abed-Nego, that you do not serve my gods or worship the gold image which I have set up? Now if you are ready at the time you hear the sound of the horn, flute, harp, lyre, and psaltery, in symphony with all kinds of music, and you fall down and worship the image which I have made, good! But if you do not worship, you shall be cast immediately into the midst of a burning fiery furnace. And who is the god who will deliver you from my hands?" Daniel 3:8-15. This paragraph is parallel to what is going on today with the U.S. government pressuring Israel to give up their land of promise to the Arabs or else . . . God knows what. Jerusalem was promised to the Jews and will remain in the hands of the Jews because God said so!!

"Shadrach, Meshach, and Abed-Nego answered and said to the king, "O Nebuchadnezzar, we have no need to answer you in this matter. If that is the case, our God whom we serve is able to deliver us from the burning fiery furnace, and He will deliver us from your hand, O king. But if not, let it be known to you, O king, that we do not serve your gods, nor will we worship the gold image which you have set up. Then Nebuchadnezzar was full of fury, and the expression on his face changed toward Shadrach, Meshach, and Abed-Nego. He spoke and commanded that they heat the furnace seven times more than it was usually heated. And he commanded certain mighty men of valor who were in his army to bind Shadrach, Meshach, and Abed-Nego, and cast them into the burning fiery furnace. Then these men were bound in their coats, their trousers, their turbans, and their other garments, and was cast into the midst of the burning fiery furnace. Therefore, because the king's command was urgent, and the furnace exceedingly hot, the flame of the fire killed those men who took up Shadrach, Meshach, and Abed-Nego. And these three men, Shadrach, Meshach, and Abed-Nego, fell down bound into the midst of the burning fiery furnace." Daniel 3:16-23.

"Then King Nebuchadnezzar was astonished; and he rose in haste and spoke, saying to his counselors, "Did we not cast three men bound into the midst of the fire?" They answered and said to the king, "True, O king." "Look!" he answered, "I see four men loose, walking in the midst of the fire; and they are not hurt, and the form of the fourth is like the Son of God. Then

Nebuchadnezzar went near the mouth of the burning fiery furnace and spoke, saying, "Shadrach, Meshach, and Abed-Nego, servants of the Most High God, come out, and come here." Then Shadrach, Meshach, and Abed-Nego came from the midst of the fire. And the satraps, administrators, governors, and the king's counselors gathered together, and they saw these men on whose bodies the fire had no power; the hair of their head was not singed nor were their garments affected, and the smell of fire was not on them. Nebuchadnezzar spoke, saying, "Blessed be the God of Shadrach, Meshach, and Abed-Nego, who sent His Angel and delivered His servants who trusted in Him, and they have frustrated the king's word, and yielded their bodies, that they should not serve nor worship any god except their own God! Therefore I make a decree that any people, nation, or language which speaks anything amiss against the God of Shadrach, Meshach, and Abed-Nego shall be cut in pieces, and their houses shall be made an ash heap; because there is no other God who can deliver like this." Then the king promoted Shadrach, Meshach, and Abed-Nego in the province of Babylon." Daniel 3:24-30. There is no need for me to expound. This is so profound, so self-explanatory. These men remained faithful in spite of the consequences and God came through yet again.

The Seventh Example: Our King Jesus Christ. In the text, Jesus, full of the Holy Spirit, returned from the Jordan and was led by the Spirit in the desert, where for forty days he was tempted by the devil. He ate nothing during those days, and at the end of them he was hungry. (i)The devil said to him, "If you are the Son of God, tell this stone to become bread." Jesus answered, "It is written: 'Man does not live on bread alone.' The devil led him up to a high place and showed him in an instant all the kingdoms of the world. And he said to him, (ii)"I will give you all their authority and splendor, for it has been given to me, and I can give it to anyone I want to. So if you worship me, it will all be yours." Jesus answered, "It is written: 'Worship the Lord your God and serve him only.' The devil led him to Jerusalem and had him stand on the highest point of the temple. "If you are the Son of God," he said, "throw yourself down from here. For it is written:" 'He will command his angels concerning you to guard you carefully; they will lift you up in their hands, so that you will not strike your foot against a stone.'" Jesus answered, "It says: 'Do not put the Lord your God to the test.'" When the devil had finished all this tempting, he left him until an opportune time" Luke 4:1-13. No one is exempt from the tests, trials and temptations, it all depends on your integrity and how much you know to be able to stand when the day of trial comes. Jesus gave a promise to us that though in this present world we will have tribulation, that we are to have no fear and be of good cheer and that our peace may remain in us because He has already overcome the world (John 16:33).

The Eighth Example: This leads us to the core of the lesson. We are at the brink of a New World Order and the mark of the beast (666) which is a chip implanted in your skin that will either enable you to buy, sell or trade and without it life will be impossible. This mark entitles you to world citizenship with one ruler, king, master or president. "Then I stood on the sand of the sea. And I saw a beast rising up out of the sea, having seven heads and ten horns, and on his horns ten crowns, and on his heads a blasphemous name. Now the beast which I saw was like a leopard, his feet were like the feet of a bear, and his mouth like the mouth of a lion. The dragon gave him his power, his throne, and great authority. And I saw one of his heads as if it had been mortally wounded, and his deadly wound was healed. And the entire world marveled and followed the beast. So they worshiped the dragon who gave authority to the beast; and they worshiped the beast, saying, "Who is like the beast? Who is able to make war with him?" And he was given a mouth speaking great things and blasphemies, and he was given authority to continue for forty-two months. Then he opened his mouth in blasphemy against God, to blaspheme His name, His tabernacle, and those who dwell in heaven. It was granted to him to make war with the saints and to overcome them. And authority was given him over every tribe, tongue, and nation. All who dwell on the earth will worship him, whose names have not been written in the Book of Life of the Lamb slain from the foundation of the world. If anyone has an ear, let him hear. He who leads into captivity shall go into captivity; he who kills with the sword must be killed with the sword. Here is the patience and the faith of the saints" Revelation 13:1-10.

"Then I saw another beast coming up out of the earth, and he had two horns like a lamb and spoke like a dragon. And he exercises all the authority of the first beast in his presence, and causes the earth and those who dwell in it to worship the first beast, who's deadly wound was healed. He performs great signs, so that he even makes fire come down from heaven on the earth in the sight of men. And he deceives those who dwell on the earth by those signs which he was granted to do in the sight of the beast, telling those who dwell on the earth to make an image to the beast who was wounded by the sword and lived. He was granted power to give breath to the image of the beast, that the image of the beast should both speak and cause as many as would not worship the image of the beast to be killed. He causes all, both small and great, rich and poor, free and slave, to receive a mark on their right hand or on their foreheads, and that no one may buy or sell except one who has the mark or the name of the beast, or the number of his name. Here is wisdom. Let him who has understanding calculate the number of the beast, for it is the number of a man: His number is 666" Revelation 13:11-18. The formation of the New World Order is in effect and the chip which has this number is in circulation as we speak. For the people who dwell in big cities are most vulnerable because technology advances faster in those areas, but it's spreading and one day it will be a necessity in order to survive to have this chip implanted in your skin.

"Then I saw another angel flying in the midst of heaven, having the everlasting gospel to preach to those who dwell on the earth—to every nation, tribe, tongue, and people—saying with a loud voice, "Fear God and give glory to Him, for the hour of His judgment has come; and worship Him who made heaven and earth, the sea and springs of water." And another angel followed, saying, "Babylon is fallen, is fallen, that great city, because she has made all nations drink of the wine of the wrath of her fornication." Then a third angel followed them, saying with a loud voice, "If anyone worships the beast and his image, and receives his mark on his forehead or on his hand, he himself shall also drink of the wine of the wrath of God, which is poured out full strength into the cup of His indignation. He shall be tormented with fire and brimstone in the presence of the holy angels and in the presence of the Lamb. And the smoke of their torment ascends forever and ever; and they have no rest day or night, who worship the beast and his image, and whoever receives the mark of his name." Here is the patience of the saints; here are those who keep the commandments of God and the faith of Jesus. Then I heard a voice from heaven saying to me, "Write: 'Blessed are the dead who die in the Lord from now on.'" "Yes," says the Spirit, "that they may rest from their labors, and their works follow them" Revelation 14:6-13.

I would call this the Example book: All these examples exemplify one thing, GOD is sovereign and His Word does not return to HIM void but accomplishes that which HE sent it to. If HE has commanded then obey to the letter though the letter killeth, Christ came and didn't abolish the law. HE brought hope to a disobedient world.

In closing, this is my message to you "Has the LORD as great delight in burnt offerings and sacrifices, as in obeying the voice of the LORD? Behold, to obey is better than sacrifice, and to hearken than the fat of rams" 1 Samuel 15:22. "What are your multiplied sacrifices to Me?" Says the LORD. "I have had enough of burnt offerings of rams And the fat of fed cattle; And I take no pleasure in the blood of bulls, lambs or goats" Isaiah 1:11. "For I did not speak to your fathers, or command them in the day that I brought them out of the land of Egypt, concerning burnt offerings and sacrifices. But this is what I commanded them, saying, 'Obey My voice, and I will be your God, and you will be My people; and you will walk in all the way which I command you, that it may be well with you.'" Jeremiah 7:22-23. "For I delight in loyalty rather than sacrifice, And in the knowledge of God rather than burnt offerings" Hosea 6:6 "AND TO LOVE HIM WITH ALL THE HEART AND WITH ALL THE UNDERSTANDING AND WITH ALL THE STRENGTH, AND TO LOVE ONE'S NEIGHBOR AS HIMSELF, is much more than all burnt offerings and sacrifices" Mark 12:33.

I hope with all my heart that you'll be found true, when tempted, tested, and tried!

CHAPTER 5

Pain Purpose Power

"But we have this treasure in earthen vessels," (made of clay; a vulnerable substance/matter susceptible to wear and tear) ". . . so that the surpassing greatness of the power will be of God and not from ourselves;" II Corinthians 4:7.

We've all heard that phrase . . . 'no pain no gain'. . . but so often we miss its true meaning. Jesus said "these things I have spoken to you, that in me you might have peace. In the world you shall have tribulation: but be of good cheer; I have overcome the world" John 16:33. ". . . In everything commending ourselves as servants of God, in much endurance, in afflictions, in hardships, in distresses, in stripes, in imprisonments, in tumults, in labors, in sleeplessness, in fastings; by purity, by knowledge, by longsuffering, by kindness, by the Holy Spirit, by sincere love, by the word of truth, by the power of God, by the armor of righteousness on the right hand and on the left, by honor and dishonor, by evil report and good report; as deceivers, and yet true; as unknown, and yet well known; as dying, and behold we live; as chastened, and yet not killed; as sorrowful, yet always rejoicing; as poor, yet making many rich; as having nothing, and yet possessing all things" II Corinthians 6:4-10. "But thanks be to God, who always leads us in triumph in Christ, and manifests through us the sweet aroma of the knowledge of Him in every place" II Corinthians 2:4. And "in all these things we overwhelmingly conquer through Him who loved us" Romans 8:37. "If the world hates you, you know that it has hated Me before it hated you" John 15:18.

On laying the foundation for this topic I'll start by saying that "It is impossible but that offenses will come: but woe to him, through whom they come!" Luke 17:1. These are words spoken by Jesus Himself. Our part Christians is not to dwell on the people causing us pain, because they are already judged, channel that pain purposefully to produce power. As hard as it is to release the hurt and pain that comes from life as a whole, at some point carrying all that jargon can be fatal, toxic and burdensome. "For this reason I say to you, do not be worried about your life, as to what you will eat or what you will drink; nor for your body, as to what you will put on. Is not life more than food and the body more than clothing?" Matthew 6:25. "Cast all your anxiety on him because he cares for you" 1 Peter 5:7. "Cast your burden upon the LORD and He will sustain you; He will never allow the righteous to be shaken" Psalm 55:22. That's one way to succumb those feelings of defeat and failure knowing that in Christ you are more than a conqueror.

Pain without a purpose leads to more pain, insanity. Purpose gives meaning to our pain enabling us to produce the power from the pain that's needed to take us to where we were born to be. "In whom also we have obtained an inheritance, being predestinated according to the purpose of him who worketh all things after the counsel of his own will:" Ephesians 1:11. Before we were born, we were ordained to be on earth with a purpose and a destiny. Jeremiah 1 God was speaking to the prophet Jeremiah about his calling and purpose on earth and Jeremiah didn't have the courage, knowledge nor experience to take on a task he was appointed for, but God assured him that he was meant to be who he was meant to be and that was his purpose in life, to become a prophet to the nations. His excuses as to what he thought he was at the time when he was being sent didn't stop God from using him, nor did the trials and tribulations that he endured in his calling prevent him from pursuing his purpose on earth. Channeling our pain to our advantage produces the power required to finish the job and not go to waste. "for the gifts and the calling of God are irrevocable" Romans 11:29.

This process includes acquiring knowledge. It takes patience and perseverance to keep the way and stay in the path. Focusing on the goal that we might receive our crown should be our motivation. There are many obstacles and stepping stones that we might face but shouldn't be the ticket to quit. Surrounding ourselves with people who have been on the path already and are concerned about our good should be the strategy we should use. Not everyone is happy with our success/es as seen in the book of Nehemiah. When Nehemiah was trying to rebuild the walls of Jerusalem he faced alot of opposition and in spite of the opposition, he completed the task. Some of the opposition can be threatening, overwhelming and beyond us and may require us to have wisdom and humility in order to tackle and overcome those opposing our progress. "Do you not know that those who run in a race all run, but only one receives the prize? Run in such a way that you may win" 1 Corinthians 9:24. Fight the good fight of faith But at the end of it there is a crown, a reward. "This charge I commit to you, son Timothy, according to the prophecies previously made concerning you, that by them you may wage the good warfare, having faith and a good conscience, which some having rejected, concerning the faith have suffered shipwreck," I Timothy 1:18-19. "Who at any time serves as a soldier at his own expense? Who plants a vineyard and does not eat the fruit of it? Or who tends a flock and does not use the milk of the flock?" 1 Corinthians 9:7.

"Therefore do not be ashamed of the testimony of our Lord or of me His prisoner, but join with me in suffering for the gospel according to the power of God," II Timothy 1:8. This is for those called to share the good news of Jesus Christ which includes all of us Christians. ". . . therefore endure hardness, as a good soldier of Jesus Christ" II Timothy 2:3. "I therefore so run, not as uncertainly; so fight I, not as one that beats the air:" 1 Corinthians 9:26 but "I press toward the mark for the prize of the high calling of God in Christ Jesus" Philippians 3:14 "who has saved us and called us with a holy calling, not according to our works, but according to His own purpose and grace which was granted us in Christ Jesus from all eternity," II Timothy 1:9.

After acquiring that knowledge, it's time to apply what we've learned to gain experience and use our experience to produce more fruit (desired results). It takes tenacity. Keep on going even when the going gets tough. Pain is a necessary motivator that enhances us to accomplish what we started. If we had it easy, we would take for granted the good things in life but pain makes us appreciate our journey and value our success/es. We learn from the pain not to repeat the patterns and take the paths that brought us the pain in the first place. Pain is as a fuel that keeps us going because of the understanding we acquire from our pain. "He gave you manna to eat in the desert, something your fathers had never known, to humble and to test you so that in the end it might go well with you" Deuteronomy 8:16. "You shall remember all the way which the LORD your God has led you in the wilderness these forty years, that He might humble you, testing you, to know what was in your heart, whether you would keep His commandments or not" Deuteronomy 8:2.

Pain sometimes is imposed that we may learn to abound in scarcity or in abundance . . . "I rejoiced in the Lord greatly that now at last your care for me has flourished again; though you surely did care, but you lacked opportunity. Not that I speak in regard to need, for I have learned in whatever state I am, to be content: I know how to be abased, and I know how to abound.

Everywhere and in all things I have learned both to be full and to be hungry, both to abound and to suffer need. I can do all things through Christ who strengthens me: (this should be our attitude when pursuing power through/from our pain). Nevertheless you have done well that you shared in my distress. Now you Philippians know also that in the beginning of the gospel, when I departed from Macedonia, no church shared with me concerning giving and receiving but you only. For even in Thessalonica you sent aid once and again for my necessities. Not that I seek the gift, but I seek the fruit that abounds to your account" Philippians 4:10-17.

"Knowing this, that the trying of your faith worketh patience" James 1:3, "so that the proof of your faith, being more precious than gold which is perishable, even though tested by fire, may be found to result in praise and glory and honor at the revelation of Jesus Christ;" 1 Peter 1:7, "so that you will not be sluggish, but imitators of those who through faith and patience inherit the promises" Hebrews 6:12. "By your endurance you will gain your lives" Luke 21:19. "You shall remember the Lord your God, for it is He that gives you power (derived from our pain) to get wealth" Deuteronomy 8:18, "an inheritance may be gotten hastily at the beginning; but the end thereof shall not be blessed" Proverbs 20:21.

"Wealth gotten by vanity shall be diminished: but he that gathered by labour shall increase" Proverbs 13:11.

The children of Israel had to endure pain in order to inherit their promised land (Exodus). Moses had to endure the painful life as a fugitive before becoming the greatest leader ever known. The bible records him being the most humble person on the face of the earth that even the devil disputed over his body after his death. David had to undergo struggles (pain) himself. He lived as a fugitive before he became the king who is; his kingdom became an everlasting kingdom (books of Samuel). Israel as a chosen people have undergone persecution since the time of Abraham. Many times as the Bible records and history tells Israel have been associated with pain as a people and have endured some disheartening atrocious and dehumanizing events but it's the price they pay for being chosen of GOD and Satan hates them as proven in Revelation 12 and all those who believe on HIS name.

"Ye have not chosen me, but I have chosen you, and ordained you, that ye should go and bring forth fruit, and that your fruit should remain: that whatsoever ye shall ask of the Father in my name, he may give it you" John 15:16 . . . "Behold, I have refined you, but not with silver; I have chosen you in the furnace of affliction" Isaiah 48:10 . . ."(for they are Your people and Your inheritance which You have brought forth from Egypt, from the midst of the iron furnace)" 1 Kings 8:51. "But the LORD has taken you and brought you out of the iron furnace, from Egypt, to be a people for His own possession, as today" Deuteronomy 4:20. I have never heard of any preacher certain about Job's tenure of pain even though some scholars have come up with 9 months. I compare it to the time a woman conceives and to the time of giving birth. The beginning and the end are usually the most uncomfortable and especially when she is about to deliver. The news of conception are often received with joy depending on the circumstances, the journey, not so great and then when it's time to push, the pain is most excruciating but after the baby is born there is great joy.

After the events that shook Job to the core as recorded in Job 1, his three friends could not imagine the outcome of events; they happened one after the other, ". . . they sat down on the ground with him for seven days and seven nights with no one speaking a word to him, for they saw that his pain was very great" Job 2:13 and "he lived 140 years after his suffering" according to Job 42:16. "Although affliction comes not forth of the dust, neither does trouble spring out of the ground; Yet man is born to trouble, as the sparks fly upward" Job 5:6-7, and "Man, who is born of woman, Is short-lived and full of turmoil" Job 14:1.

"Now there arose a new king over Egypt, who did not know Joseph, (who was second in command in Egypt during the time of famine in Egypt). And he said to his people, 'Look, the people of the children of Israel are more and mightier than we; come, let us deal shrewdly with them, lest they multiply, and it happen, in the event of war, that they also join our enemies and fight against us, and so go up out of the land.' Therefore they set taskmasters over them to afflict them with their burdens. And they built for Pharaoh supply cities, Pithom and Ramses. But the more they afflicted them, the more they multiplied and grew. And they were in dread of the children of Israel" Exodus 1:8-12. This is what I love about pain and affliction. Often if the affliction is derived from envy and jealousy from our adversaries, God always has a way of magnifying and glorifying us in their presence. "He prepares a table before you in the presence of your enemies: (He always makes our enemies envious of us, it's called being blessed), He anoints your head with oil until your cup runs over" Psalm 23:5. Just like the Israelites in their days in Egypt, ". . . the more they were afflicted, the more they increased," Exodus 1:12. Fear not when afflictions arise, there's always a way out, and tables to be prepared in their presence.

Pain on Purpose Produces Power.

CHAPTER 6

Missing Your Moment:

It requires in-depth sensitivity in the spirit to be able to recognize our moment, day or hour of visitation. Often that moment doesn't come announced and it comes in ways unexpected but "to everything there is a season, and a time to every purpose under the heaven:" Ecclesiastes 3:1, and ". . . there is a proper time and procedure for every delight, though a man's trouble is heavy upon him" Ecclesiastes 8:6. So how do we recognize these moments that only come once in a lifetime? Missing these precious moments means going through another season of disaster and trouble until the season comes full circle again and that can take time, time that should have been used to cease the moment of our visitation. We don't get to hear alot of Christians today talking of angels bringing them tidings. The world has become so wicked and such visitations are reserved for the chosen few, and for the dispensation of the Holy Spirit has enabled Christians to rely on **GOD HIMSELF** by **THIS SPIRIT** as opposed to an angel. But for those who rely and walk by faith and not by sight, who don't sit around waiting for a sign to fall from the sky as this is "that generation that seeketh after a sign" as seen in Matthew 16:4, Mark 8:12 and Luke 11:29, what? when? where? how? who? are very important questions that need to be addressed and learned.

How do we recognize "our time?" There are so many examples I could use in the past and my favorite isn't a biblical character but one we see on a daily basis. It took faith for him to recognize that this was his moment to become president of the United States and this I know for sure for him to 'step outside the box' in spite of his "short comings of his physical appearances that could have sold him short" in a society already programmed, processed and used to see things done a certain way.

According to Judges 4-5 and Hebrews 11:32, "God has chosen the foolish things of the world to put to shame the wise, and God has chosen the weak things of the world to put to shame the things which are mighty; and the base things of the world and the things which are despised God has chosen, and the things which are not, to bring to nothing the things that are, that no flesh should glory in His presence . . ." 1 Corinthians 1:27-29. Talk about taking the bull by its horns. It took years of preparation for him to arrive at his moment, turn his pain to power and made history. For generations to come he will be remembered because he recognized his moment but if he hadn't taken advantage of his deep sight (insight and revelation) we would remember him as the man that gave that famous speech of his father being a goat herdsman, the man who never tried enough and failed to recognize his moment.

"O Jerusalem, Jerusalem, you that kill the prophets, and stone them which are sent to you, how often I would have gathered your children together, even as a hen gathers her chickens under her wings, and you would not!" Matthew 23:37 and because of failure to recognize the moment and hour of visitation "behold, your house is left to you desolate; and I say to you, you will not see Me until the time comes when you say, 'BLESSED IS HE WHO COMES IN THE NAME OF THE LORD!'" Luke 13:35. Israel brought disaster upon herself when she failed to recognize her moment. They were looking for a King in royal garment and not a baby born in a manger and wrapped in swaddling clothes. Just like in John the Baptist's case "as these men were going away, Jesus began to speak to the crowds about John, "what did you go out into the wilderness to see? A reed shaken by the wind? But what went ye out to see? A man clothed in soft raiment? Behold, they that wear soft raiment are in king's houses. But what did you go out to see? A prophet? Yes, I tell you, and one who is more than a prophet" Matthew 11:7-9. What we often expect to see is often not what we're prepared to see. The man John the Baptist came to prepare the way for the Messiah but he wasn't acceptable so they missed their moment of visitation. It will and it has taken some years, some thousands of years before the hour of visitation comes full circle again. In between we've seen the Jews tortured and killed; disaster upon disaster and persecution to unimaginable proportions all because they failed to cease their moment.

"And Jesus answered and spoke to them again by parables and said: "The kingdom of heaven is like a certain king who arranged a marriage for his son, and sent out his servants to call those who were invited to the wedding; and they were not willing to come. Again, he sent out other servants, saying, 'Tell those who are invited, "See, I have prepared my dinner; my oxen and fatted cattle are killed, and all things are ready. Come to the wedding." But they made light of it and went their ways, one to his own farm, and another to his business. And the rest seized his servants, treated them spitefully, and killed them. But when the king heard about it, he was furious. And he sent out his armies, destroyed those murderers, and burned up their city. Then he said to his servants, 'The wedding is ready, but those who were invited were not worthy.

Therefore go into the highways, and as many as you find, invite to the wedding.' So those servants went out into the highways and gathered together all whom they found, both bad and good. And the wedding hall was filled with guests. "But when the king came in to see the guests, he saw a man there who did not have on a wedding garment. So he said to him, 'Friend, how did you come in here without a wedding garment?' And he was speechless. Then the king said to the servants, 'Bind him hand and foot, take him away, and cast him into outer darkness; there will be weeping and gnashing of teeth.' "For many are called, but few are chosen." Matthew 22:1-14

Preparation and determination isn't enough. There are some whose season has come full circle and weren't exactly prepared for it but had what it took to and took the baton to the next level. Overcoming those hurdles life throws at us is a lot harder if caught unprepared. For those with good advisers, coaches or mentors the race can be completed. "Where no counsel is, the people fall: but in the multitude of counselors there is safety" Proverbs 11:14, and "without consultation, plans are frustrated, But with many counselors they succeed' Proverbs 15:22. "Prepare plans by consultation, and make war by wise guidance" Proverbs 20:18 "for by wise guidance you will wage war, and in abundance of counselors there is victory" Proverbs 24:6.

Order has to follow. Proper planning is essential and gathering of information; can't beat that in any given day. Knowing what to do, when the time comes is necessary, knowledge is power. The children of Israel knew of a messiah that was to come by the mouth of His servants the prophets but their minds were programmed a certain way and that's why they did not accept Jesus Christ. They had the knowledge of the messiah, but their method had gotten old and God was doing a new thing, and for the sake of the gentiles Israel missed their moment and the gentiles were grafted in.

GOD had a plan to save the whole world so the Jews rejected HIM and the Gentiles received HIM and were saved. His ways are not our ways neither are His thoughts ours (Isaiah 55:8-9) and that's why we need His guidance in matters far too great for our comprehension. God said in scripture that "behold, I will do a new thing; now it shall spring forth; shall you not know it? I will even make a way in the wilderness and rivers in the desert" Isaiah 43:19. Always be prepared for the moment because when it arrives, it'll more often than not come in ways that we do not expect. Our answer to prayer doesn't flow with our way of thinking because God is Sovereign. ". . . when the fullness of the time was come, God sent forth his Son, made of a woman, made under the law, to redeem them that were under the law, that we might receive the adoption of sons" Galatians 4:4,5. And for you who are sons by adoption, ". . . God has sent forth the Spirit of his Son into your hearts, crying, Abba, Father" Galatians 4:6 and "for all who are being led by the Spirit of God, these are sons of God. For you have not received the spirit of bondage again to fear; but you have received the Spirit of adoption, whereby we cry, Abba, Father. The Spirit Himself testifies with our spirit that we are children of God," Romans 8:14-16. "For you are all sons of God through faith in Christ Jesus" Galatians 3:26. This is all the time we have under the son.

Time and time and again you have heard the story of Christ's birth, life, death, burial and resurrection and there are people who will not receive their invitation to life and the sad part is there are no second chances once death happens without Christ. "Therefore, as the Holy Spirit says: Today, if you will hear His voice, do not harden your hearts as in the rebellion, In the day of trial in the wilderness, where your fathers tested Me, tried Me, and saw My works forty years. Therefore I was angry with that generation, and said, 'They always go astray in their heart, and they have not known My ways.' So I swore in My wrath, they shall not enter My rest" Hebrews 3:7-11. This is the ultimate price we pay for not ceasing our moment. God gets upset, gives another the opportunity designed for us and/or until we end up paying the consequences for missing your hour of visitation for there to be another moment.

Take Heed Therefore and Watch

CHAPTER 7

Babel Reborn (N.W.O)

"And Cush begat Nimrod: he began to be a mighty one in the earth. He was a mighty hunter before the LORD: wherefore it is said, Even as Nimrod the mighty hunter before the LORD. And the beginning of his kingdom was Babel," (meaning confusion) Genesis 18:8-10. "And *the whole earth was of one language, and of one speech.* And it came to pass, as they journeyed from the east, that they found a plain in the land of Shinar; and they dwelt there. And they said one to another, Go to, let us make brick, and burn them thoroughly. And they had brick for stone, and slime had they for mortar. And they said, Go to, *let us build us a city and a tower, whose top may reach unto heaven; and let us make us a name, lest we be scattered abroad upon the face of the whole earth.* And the LORD came down to see the city and the tower, which the children of men builded. And the LORD said, *Behold, the people is one, and they have all one language; and this they begin to do: and now nothing will be restrained from them, which they have imagined to do.* Go to, let us go down, and there confound their language, that they may not understand one another's speech. So the LORD scattered them abroad from thence upon the face of all the earth: and they left off to build the city. Therefore is the name of it called Babel; because the LORD did there confound the language of all the earth: and from thence did the LORD scatter them abroad upon the face of all the earth" Genesis 11:1-9.

Gold is gold, a dollar bill's a dollar bill. No matter the shape, form or size it doesn't its value doesn't change. Metamorphosis may occur due to decay, or reprocessing for a repeat and a reuse but the composition and its matter remains the same regardless of how much damage or destruction you bring upon it to mar its image the value and content remain same neither can time change its matter. My thoughts about this discussion is "That which has been *is* what will be, that which *is* done is what will be done, and *there is* nothing new under the sun. Is there anything of which it may be said, "See, this *is* new?" It has already been in ancient times before us" Ecclesiates 1:9-10. It has been the will of God for brethren to dwell together in unity (Psalm 133:1) and brotherly love to continue (Hebrews 13:1) all in the name of Jesus Christ because . . . there is none other name under heaven given among men, whereby we must be saved, neither is there salvation in any other (Acts 4:12). Dwelling together in the unity of Jesus Christ is His will but when we take Him out of the equation disaster is always eminent, guaranteed. As we see in the Tower of Babel, there was nothing wrong with the building of the tower but their motive was not to return the admiration of their abilities and wisdom and their expertise but turned inward; their god became themselves, glorifying the works of their hands and their leader became a god.

As we've learned through history that repetition comes full circle more often than not as is the way of the world; as it was in the time of Nimrod, so shall it be in days coming. We are at a very pivotal moment in history where Daniel's prophesy is unfolding as seen here. "After this I saw in the night visions, and behold a fourth beast, dreadful and terrible, and strong exceedingly; and it had great iron teeth: it devoured and brake in pieces, and stamped the residue with the feet of it: and it was diverse from all the beasts that were before it; *and it had ten horns*" Daniel 7:7. There are ten (horns or kings) from ten nations already in place and have already formed this end time coalition that is The New World Order. We are in the age of the fourth empire with ten horns or the ten toes in Nebucahdnezzar's dream. Daniel 2:41 describes the fourth empire which was depicted as having 10 toes. The feet and toes were composed partly of iron and partly of clay and deals with a later phase or outgrowth of this fourth empire, symbolized by the feet and ten toes—made up of iron and earthenware, a fragile base for the huge monument. The text clearly implies that this final phase will be marked by some sort of federation rather than by a powerful single realm. Ref: "And the fourth kingdom shall be strong as iron: forasmuch as iron breaketh in pieces and subdueth all things: and as iron that breaketh all these, shall it break in pieces and bruise. And whereas thou sawest the feet and toes, part of potters' clay, and part of iron, the kingdom shall be divided; but there shall be in it of the strength of the iron, forasmuch as thou sawest the iron mixed with miry clay. And as the toes of the feet were part of iron, and part of clay, so the kingdom shall be partly strong, and partly broken. And whereas thou sawest iron mixed with miry clay, they shall mingle themselves with the seed of men: but they shall not cleave one to another, even as iron is not mixed with clay" Daniel 2:40-43.

Then after this Kingdom is coming a Kingdom that God Himself will establish to destroy the fourth kingdom made of iron and clay and this Kingdom established by God will last forever and ever. It is the Kingdom of Our Lord Jesus Christ as seen here ". . . in the days of these kings shall the God of heaven set up a kingdom, which shall never be destroyed: and the kingdom shall not be left to other people, but it shall break in pieces and consume all these kingdoms, and it shall stand for ever" Daniel 2:44. Uniting for a common goal or course and cause is encouraged but as we have seen throughout the Bible, there can only be two Kingdoms and you're either in one or the other. God has always wanted for His people to come together and ". . . dwell together according to knowledge . . ." (1 Peter 3:7) as would a husband a wife without the emotional and physical responsible linked to a husband and a wife. Unity is so important, pleasant as recorded in Psalm 133, ". . . for brethren to dwell together in unity! It is like the precious ointment upon the head, which ran down upon the beard, even Aaron's beard: that went down to the skirts of his garments; as the dew of Hermon, and as the dew that descended upon the mountains of Zion: for there the LORD commanded the blessing, even *life for evermore*" Psalm 133:1-3.

"Then one of the seven angels who had the seven bowls came and talked with me, saying to me . . . So he carried me away in the Spirit into the wilderness. And I saw a woman sitting on a scarlet beast *which was* full of names of blasphemy, having seven heads and ten horns. The woman was arrayed in purple and scarlet, and adorned with gold and precious stones and pearls," Revelation 17:1-4. The image of this woman was symbolizing money and wealth, a society that will entice the world and use the current poor economic conditions to lure to become one with it/ her. But the problem is this, she'll be "having in her hand a golden cup full of abominations and the filthiness of her fornication. And on her forehead a name *was* written: MYSTERY, BABYLON THE GREAT, THE MOTHER OF HARLOTS AND OF THE ABOMINATIONS OF THE EARTH. I saw the woman, drunk with the blood of the saints and with the blood of the martyrs of Jesus. And when I saw her, I marveled with great amazement." Revelation 17:4-6. This is the picture of the 21st Century Society. How to escape; "Wherefore come out from among them, and be ye separate, saith the Lord, and touch not the unclean thing; and I will receive you" II Corinthians 6:17. Depart, depart, go out from there, Touch nothing unclean; Go out of the midst of her, purify yourselves, You who carry the vessels of the LORD" Isaiah 52:11. "I heard another voice from heaven, saying, "Come out of her, my people, so that you will not participate in her sins and receive of her plagues;" Revelation 18:4.

"So the angel said to me, "Why did you marvel? I will tell you the mystery of the woman and of the beast that carries her, which has the seven heads and the ten horns. The beast that you saw was, and is not, and will ascend out of the bottomless pit and go to perdition. And those who dwell on the earth will marvel, whose names are not written in the Book of Life from the foundation of the world, when they see the beast that was, and is not, and yet is. "Here *is* the mind which has wisdom: The seven heads are seven mountains on which the woman sits. There are also seven kings. Five have fallen, one is, *and* the other has not yet come. And when he comes, he must continue a short time. *The beast that was, and is not, is himself also the eighth*, and *is of the seven, and is going to perdition.* "*The ten horns which you saw are ten kings who have received no kingdom as yet*, but they receive authority for one hour (allegoric) as kings with the beast. *These are of one mind*, and they will give their power and authority to the beast" Revelation 7:7-13

A one world system of government is essential if and when Jesus Christ is the center of it. But if the motives are purely motivated by the economical and monetary gain, control and power of a pseudo god/man as it is unfolding and becoming, then the world is inevitably in for an implosion. Man in his wisdom has never been able to hold down power, not for long, there's always a regeneration, revolution or an overturning by a greater vision, people or power in the form of monarchy and government. This is the age of the New World Order which will become the last empire/kingdom before Christ's eternal Kingdom and as this New World Order comes to an end. "And I saw, and behold a white horse: and he that sat on him had a bow; and a crown was given to him: and he went forth conquering, and to conquer" Rev 6:2. The threat of inflation and poverty is at an all time high, people are becoming more and more desperate for a 'savior' to rescue them from their economical plagues and more likely to fall prey to a 'redeemer'. This economical catastrophe we are experiencing is a set up for the coming one world system of government. It's not if it will happen but when. The signs of the times recorded in the bible text have and are becoming a reality.

The stage has been set with changes in the economic system and the dependence on government becoming an essential part of living. Without government, this system implies, hardship is inevitable. And in order for hardship to be eliminated, dependence on government is encouraged. One man (the man of sin) and great influence that's captured the hearts of many by his eloquence of speech and intelligence in governance or policy whose admiration spans global spheres is set to emerge deceiving many to worship his vain glory. Stars are falling, pestilences and tribulations across the globe is taking place and even though the worst hasn't yet been seen e.g. the darkening of the sun from the super volcano and the mega earthquake or the moon turning red which is soon to come in the next couple of months, the stage has been set for his reign. This is the next major event in these end time formations.

Nimrod is reborn!

CHAPTER 8

The Journey of Salvation:

"Jesus answered and said to him, truly, truly, I say to you, except a man be born again, he cannot see the kingdom of God" John 3:3. God by His Spirit has to bring about a conviction. He has to call you after hearing the Word of God because ". . . faith comes by hearing, and hearing by the Word of God" Romans 10:17. "There is no salvation by anyone else, for there is no other name under heaven given among people by which we must be saved" Acts 4:12. "For whoever shall call on the name of the Lord shall be saved" Romans 10:13. Salvation is a journey, a process but it happens instantly. Once you feel the conviction of the Holy Spirit tagging in your heart to change for Him, that's where the journey begins. It takes a change of heart, mind, will and emotions to change the direction of your soul, body and spirit. Your eternal destiny is wholly dependent and governed by this decision of asking Jesus into your heart and trusting Him to be the Lord of your life. "Then Jesus spoke to them again, saying, 'I am the light of the world. He who follows Me shall not walk in darkness, but have the light of life.'" John 8:12. "In him (Jesus Christ) was life; and the life was the light of men and the light shines in darkness; and the darkness comprehended it not" John 1:4-5. "The same came for a witness, to bear witness of the Light that all men through him might believe" John 1:7. "That was the true Light, which lighteth every man that cometh into the world" John 1:9. "The entrance of thy words giveth light; it giveth understanding unto the simple" Psalm 119:130.

⅄ *Acknowledging and Admitting that you are a sinner.*

"For the wages of sin is death, but the gift of God is eternal life through Christ Jesus our Lord" Romans 6:23. "If You, LORD, should mark iniquities, O Lord, who could stand? But there is forgiveness with You, that You may be feared." Psalm 130:3-4. "For there is not a just man upon earth, that doeth good, and sinneth not" Ecclesiastes 7:20. "Who can say, "I have cleansed my heart, I am pure from my sin?" Proverbs 20:9. "*There is none* who understands, *there is none* who seeks God; *they are all gone out of the way*, they are together become unprofitable; *there is none that doeth good, no, not one*" Romans 3:11-12. "For all have sinned and fall short of the glory of God," Romans 3:23. ". . . we are all as an unclean thing, and all our righteousness are as filthy rags; and we all do fade as a leaf; and our iniquities, like the wind, have taken us away" Isaiah 64:6. "Who can say, "I have cleansed my heart, I am pure from my sin"? Proverbs 20:9.

"If they sin against you, (for there is no man that sins not,) and you be angry with them, and deliver them to the enemy, so that they carry them away captives to the land of the enemy, far or near; Yet if they shall bethink themselves in the land where they were carried captives, and repent, and make supplication to you in the land of them that carried them captives, saying, We have sinned, and have done perversely, we have committed wickedness; if they return unto thee with all their heart and with all their soul in the land of their enemies, who carried them captive, and pray unto thee toward their land, which thou gavest unto their fathers, the city which thou hast chosen, and the house which I have built for thy name: then hear thou their prayer and their supplication in heaven thy dwelling-place, and maintain their cause; and forgive Your people who have sinned against You and all their transgressions which they have transgressed against You, and make them objects of compassion before those who have taken them captive, that they may have compassion on them" I Kings 8:46-50.

"And you were dead in your trespasses and sins," Ephesians 2:1. "But God, who is rich in mercy, for his great love with which he loved us, even when we were dead in sins, has quickened us together with Christ, (by grace you are saved;) For by grace are you saved through faith; and that not of yourselves: it is the gift of God:" Ephesians 2:4-5, 8. "In Him (Jesus Christ) we have redemption through His blood, the forgiveness of our trespasses, according to the riches of His grace" Ephesians 1:7. "For the grace of God that brings salvation has appeared to all men," Titus 2:11 "who desires all men to be saved and to come to the knowledge of the truth" I Timothy 2:4.

ᛉ *Believing (it takes faith): t*hat,

(i) *Jesus is the Son of God,*

"For God so loved the world, that He gave His only begotten Son, that whoever believes in Him shall not perish, but have eternal life" John 3:16. How can you say to the one whom the Father has consecrated and sent into the world, 'You are blaspheming,' because I said, 'I am the Son of God'?" John 10:36. "Jesus heard that they had put him out (the blind man whom Jesus healed), and finding him, He said, "Do you believe in the Son of Man? He answered and said, Who is he, Lord, that I might believe on him? And Jesus said to him, You have both seen him, and it is he that talks with you. And he said, Lord, I believe. And he worshiped him." John 9:35-38.

(ii) was sinless,

"For we have not an high priest which cannot be touched with the feeling of our infirmities; but was in all points tempted like as we are, yet without sin" Hebrews 4:15. "For he has made him to be sin for us, who knew no sin; that we might be made the righteousness of God in him" II Corinthians 5:21. "For it was fitting for us to have such a high priest, holy, innocent, undefiled, separated from sinners and exalted above the heavens;" Hebrews 7:26. "You know that He appeared in order to take away sins; and in Him there is no sin" I John 3:5. "WHO COMMITTED NO SIN, NOR WAS ANY DECEIT FOUND IN HIS MOUTH;" I Peter 2:22.

(iii) shed His blood and died on the cross for you,

"For the life of the flesh is in the blood: and I have given it to you on the altar to make an atonement for your souls: for it is the blood that makes an atonement for the soul." Leviticus 17:11. "Greater love has no one than this, that one lay down his life for his friends" John 15:13. "For what the Law could not do, weak as it was through the flesh, God did: sending His own Son in the likeness of sinful flesh and as an offering for sin, He condemned sin in the flesh," Romans 8:3. "Christ redeemed us from the curse of the Law, having become a curse for us—for it is written, "CURSED IS EVERYONE WHO HANGS ON A TREE "—Galatians 3:13. ". . . and the blood of Jesus His Son cleanses us from all sin" I John 1:7 "but put to death the Prince of life, the one whom God raised from the dead, a fact to which we are witnesses" Acts 3:15.

(iv) and rose from the dead.

"But we believe that we are saved through the grace of the Lord Jesus, in the same way as they also are" Acts 15:11. "That if you shall confess with your mouth the Lord Jesus, and shall believe in your heart that God has raised him from the dead, you shall be saved. For with the heart man believes to righteousness; and with the mouth confession is made to salvation." Romans 10:9-10. "He who was delivered over because of our transgressions, and was raised because of our justification" Romans 4:25. "And if Christ be not raised, your faith is vain; you are yet in your sins" I Corinthians 15:17. ". . . saying that the Son of Man must be delivered into the hands of sinful men, and be crucified, and the third day rise again" Luke 24:7. "and he said unto them, Thus it is written, that the Christ should suffer, and rise again from the dead the third day;" Luke 24:46. ""This Jesus God raised up again, to which we are all witnesses" Acts 2:32.

". . . Believe on the Lord Jesus Christ, and you shall be saved, and your house" Acts 16:31. "He who has believed and has been baptized shall be saved; but he who has disbelieved shall be condemned" Mark 16:16. ". . . and he will speak words to you by which you will be saved, you and your entire household" Acts 11:14.

"God sent not his Son into the world to condemn the world; but that the world through him might be saved." John 3:17. "Now the just shall live by faith: but if any man draw back, my soul shall have no pleasure in him" Hebrews 10:38. "Jesus said to him, "Because you have seen Me, have you believed? Blessed are they who did not see, and yet believed" John 20:29 . . . "and though you have not seen Him, you love Him, and though you do not see Him now, but believe in Him, you greatly rejoice with joy inexpressible and full of glory, obtaining as the outcome of your faith the salvation of your souls" I Peter 1:8-9.

"But as many as received him, to them gave he power to become the sons of God, even to them that believe on his name:" John 1:12. "Whoever believes that Jesus is the Christ is born of God, and everyone who loves Him who begot also loves him who is begotten of Him" I John 5:1. "He who believes in the Son of God has the witness in himself; he who does not believe God has made Him a liar, because he has not believed the testimony that God has given of His Son" I John 5:10. "These things I have written to you who believe in the name of the Son of God, that you may know that you have eternal life, and that you may *continue to* believe in the name of the Son of God" I john 5:13.

⚘ *Confession*:

"If we confess our sins, He is faithful and righteous to forgive us our sins and to cleanse us from all unrighteousness" I John 1:9. This is what God requires of us as people who've missed Him and gone ahead of the Spirit, and sinned "Come now, and let us reason together," Says the LORD, "Though your sins are as scarlet, They will be as white as snow; Though they are red like crimson, They will be like wool" Isaiah 1:18. "Have I covered my transgressions like Adam, By hiding my iniquity in my bosom," Job 31:33. We know now that the blood of Jesus was shed and can cleanse us from all sin. Ask Him to "Purge me (you) with hyssop, and I shall be clean: wash me, and I shall be whiter than snow" Psalm 51:7. "I though and considered my ways And turned my feet to Your testimonies" Psalm 119:59. "When I kept silence, my bones waxed old through my roaring all the day long. For day and night your hand was heavy on me: my moisture is turned into the drought of summer. So I acknowledge my sin to you, and my iniquity have I not hid. I said, I will confess my transgressions to the LORD; and you forgave the iniquity of my sin" Psalm 32:3-5. "He that covers his sins shall not prosper: but whoever confesses and forsakes them shall have mercy" Proverbs 28:13.

"If they shall confess their iniquity, and the iniquity of their fathers, with their trespass which they trespassed against me, and that also they have walked contrary to me; And that I also have walked contrary to them, and have brought them into the land of their enemies; if then their uncircumcised hearts be humbled, and they then accept of the punishment of their iniquity: Then will I remember my covenant with Jacob, and also my covenant with Isaac, and also my covenant with Abraham will I remember; and I will remember the land" Leviticus 26:40-42. "And said, Truly I say to you, Except you be converted, and become as little children, you shall not enter into the kingdom of heaven" Matthew 18:3. "I tell you, No: but, except you repent, you shall all likewise perish" Luke 13:3. "And that repentance and remission of sins should be preached in his name among all nations, beginning at Jerusalem" Luke 24:47.

"*Repent you therefore, and be converted*, that your sins may be blotted out, when the times of refreshing shall come from the presence of the Lord" Acts 3:19. "Peter said to them, "*Repent, and each of you be baptized in the name of Jesus Christ for the forgiveness of your sins; and you will receive the gift of the Holy Spirit*" Acts 2:38. "but kept declaring both to those of Damascus first, and also at Jerusalem and then throughout all the region of Judea, and even to the Gentiles, *that they should repent and turn to God, performing deeds appropriate to repentance*" Acts 26:20. "And many that believed came, and confessed, and showed their deeds" Acts 19:18. "For whoever shall call on the name of the Lord shall be saved" Romans 10:13, Acts 2:21. Again, "If we confess our sins, he is faithful and just to forgive us our sins, and to cleanse us from all unrighteousness" I John 1:9. "If anyone sees his brother sinning a sin *which does* not *lead* to death, he will ask, and He will give him life for those who commit sin not *leading* to death" I John 5:16. ". . . The time is fulfilled, and the kingdom of God is at hand; repent and believe in the gospel" Mark 1:15.

⅄ *Water Baptism:*

"He who believes and is baptized will be saved; but he who does not believe will be condemned" Mark 16:16. Jesus as our role model gave a commission before He departed to His Heavenly Father, "And Jesus came and spoke to them, saying, "All authority has been given to Me in heaven and on earth. Go therefore and make disciples of all the nations, baptizing them in the name of the Father and of the Son and of the Holy Spirit" Matthew 28:18-19. Jesus Himself had to be baptized so that He could model show us the pathway to eternal life. He was the example and all who believe in Him should emulate His example. "In those days Jesus came from Nazareth in Galilee and was baptized by John in the Jordan" Mark 1:9. "The next day John saw Jesus coming toward him, and said, "Behold! The Lamb of God who takes away the sin of the world! This is He of whom I said, 'after me comes a Man who is preferred before me, for He was before me.' I did not know Him; but that He should be revealed to Israel, therefore I came baptizing with water.' And John bore witness, saying, "I saw the Spirit descending from heaven like a dove, and He remained upon Him (after Jesus got baptized) I did not know Him, but He who sent me to baptize with water said to me, 'Upon whom you see the Spirit descending, and remaining on Him, this is He who baptizes with the Holy Spirit.' And I have seen and testified that this is the Son of God." John 1:29-34.

"This is He who came by water and blood—Jesus Christ; not only by water, but by water and blood. And it is the Spirit who bears witness, because the Spirit is truth. For there are three that bear witness in heaven: the Father, the Word, and the Holy Spirit; and these three are one. For there are three that bear witness *in earth:* *the Spirit, and the water, and the blood:* and these three agree in one. If we receive the testimony of men, the testimony of God is greater; for the testimony of God is this, that He has testified concerning His Son" I John 5:6-9. "I indeed baptize you with water unto repentance. but he that cometh after me is mightier than I, whose shoes I am not worthy to bear: he shall baptize you with the Holy Ghost, and with fire:" Matthew 3:11, Mark 1:8. "John the Baptist appeared in the wilderness preaching a baptism of repentance for the forgiveness of sins. And there went out to him all the land of Judea, and they of Jerusalem, and were all baptized of him in the river of Jordan, confessing their sins." mark 1:4-5. "And all the people that heard him, and the publicans, justified God, being baptized with the baptism of John" Luke 7:29. "As they went along the road they came to some water; and the eunuch said, "Look! Water! What prevents me from being baptized?" Acts 8:36. "But when they believed Philip preaching the good news about the kingdom of God and the name of Jesus Christ, they were being baptized, men and women alike" Acts 8:12. "Then Peter said to them, Repent, and be baptized every one of you in the name of Jesus Christ for the remission of sins, and you shall receive the gift of the Holy Ghost" Acts 2:38. "Can any man forbid water, that these should not be baptized, which have received the Holy Ghost as well as we?" Acts 10:47.

"When they heard this, they were baptized in the name of the Lord Jesus" Acts 19:5. "Know you not, that so many of us as were baptized into Jesus Christ were baptized into his death? Therefore we are buried with him by baptism into death: that like as Christ was raised up from the dead by the glory of the Father, even so we also should walk in newness of life" Romans 6:3-4. "For all of you who were baptized into Christ have clothed yourselves with Christ" Galatians 3:27. "For by one Spirit are we all baptized into one body, whether we be Jews or Gentiles, whether we be bond or free; and have been all made to drink into one Spirit" I Corinthians 12:13. There is "One Lord, one faith, one baptism" Ephesians 4:5. "Baptism, which is like that water, now saves you. Baptism doesn't save by removing dirt from the body. Rather, baptism is a request to God for a clear conscience. It saves you through Jesus Christ, who came back from death to life" I Peter 3:21. ""Then I will sprinkle clean water on you, and you will be clean; I will cleanse you from all your filthiness and from all your idols" Ezekiel 36:25, symbolizing old testament cleansing that hadn't anything to do with the death burial and resurrection of Christ yet, but "Let us draw near with a true heart in full assurance of faith, having our hearts sprinkled from an evil conscience, and our bodies washed with pure water" Hebrews 10:22.

⋏ *Baptism in The Holy Spirit:*

"But I tell you the truth, it is to your advantage that I go away; for if I do not go away, the Helper will not come to you; but if I go, I will send Him to you" John 16:7. "But this He spoke of the Spirit, whom those who believed in Him were to receive; for the Spirit was not yet given, because Jesus was not yet glorified" John 7:39. "If you love me, keep my commandments. And I will pray the Father, and he shall give you another Comforter that he may abide with you for ever; even the Spirit of truth; whom the world cannot receive, because it sees him not, neither knows him: but you know him; for he dwells with you, and shall be in you. But I will not leave you comfortless: I will come to you." John 14:15-18. "But a natural man does not accept the things of the Spirit of God, for they are foolishness to him; and he cannot understand them, because they are spiritually appraised" I Corinthians 2:14. "But the Helper, the Holy Spirit, whom the Father will send in My name, He will teach you all things, and bring to your remembrance all that I said to you" John 14:26. "When the Helper comes, whom I will send to you from the Father, that is the Spirit of truth who proceeds from the Father, He will testify about Me," John 15:26. "In the same way the Spirit also helps our weakness; for we do not know how to pray as we should, but the Spirit Himself intercedes for us with groaning that cannot be uttered;" Romans 8:26.

"He said to them, "Did you receive the Holy Spirit when you believed?" And they said to him, "No, we have not even heard whether there is a Holy Spirit. And he said to them, To what then were you baptized? And they said to John's baptism. Then said Paul, John truly baptized with the baptism of repentance, saying to the people, that they should believe on him which should come after him, that is, on Christ Jesus. When they heard this, they were baptized in the name of the Lord Jesus. And when Paul had laid his hands on them, the Holy Ghost came on them; and they spoke with tongues, and prophesied" Acts 19:2-6. Sometimes baptism of The Holy Spirit with the evidence of speaking in 'other tongues' comes before baptism as seen in here "Can any man forbid water, that these should not be baptized, which have received the Holy Ghost as well as we?" Acts 10:47. There are times after praying the sinner's prayer (conversion) the Holy Spirit decides to fill your Spirit with His fullness. So there isn't a particular order, but you have to receive Jesus Christ as the savior and Lord of your life. "I (John the Baptist) indeed baptize you with water to repentance. but he that comes after me is mightier than I, whose shoes I am not worthy to bear. he shall baptize you with the Holy Ghost, and with fire" Matthew 3:11, "for John baptized with water, but you will be baptized with the Holy Spirit not many days from now" Acts 1:5. "but He who sent me to baptize in water said to me, 'He upon whom you see the Spirit descending and remaining upon Him, this is the One who baptizes in the Holy Spirit" John 1:33. "I baptized you with water; but He will baptize you with the Holy Spirit" Mark 1:4.

". . . when the day of Pentecost was fully come, they were all with one accord in one place . . . . suddenly there came a sound from heaven as of a rushing mighty wind, and it filled the entire house where they were sitting. And there appeared to them cloven tongues like as of fire, and it sat on each of them. And they were all filled with the Holy Spirit and began to speak with other tongues, as the Spirit was giving them utterance." Acts 2:1-4. "For he who speaks in a tongue does not speak to men but to God, for no one understands *him;* however, in the spirit he speaks mysteries. But he who prophesies speaks edification and exhortation and comfort to men. 4 He who speaks in a tongue edifies himself, but he who prophesies edifies the church" I Corinthians 14:2-4. "And when they had prayed, the place where they had gathered together was shaken, and they were all filled with the Holy Spirit and began to speak the word of God with boldness" Acts 4:31. "But you will receive power when the Holy Spirit has come upon you; and you shall be My witnesses both in Jerusalem, and in all Judea and Samaria, and even to the remotest part of the earth" Acts 1:8. ". . . Who, when they were come down, prayed for them, that they might receive the Holy Ghost: (For as yet he was fallen on none of them: only they were baptized in the name of the Lord Jesus.). Then they began laying their hands on them, and they were receiving the Holy Spirit." Acts 8:15-17. "And I remembered the word of the Lord, how He used to say, 'John baptized with water, but you will be baptized with the Holy Spirit" Acts 11:16. "And God, which knows the hearts, bore them witness, giving them the Holy Ghost, even as he did to us; And put no difference/distinction between us and them, purifying their hearts by faith" Acts 15:8. "For the kingdom of God is not in word but in power" I Corinthians 4:20. Even in the wilderness "they were all baptized unto Moses in the cloud (fire) and in the sea (water)" I Corinthians 10:2. "How God anointed Jesus of Nazareth with the Holy Ghost and with power: who went about doing good, and healing all that were oppressed of the devil; for God was with him" Acts 10:38.

⅄ *Spiritual Growth:*

"Whom will he teach knowledge? And whom will he make to understand the message? Those *just* weaned from milk? Those *just* drawn from the breasts? For precept *must be* upon precept, precept upon precept, Line upon line, line upon line, Here a little, there a little. For with stammering lips and another tongue He will speak to this people, to whom He said, 'This *is* the rest *with which* You may cause the weary to rest,' And, 'This *is* the refreshing';" Isaiah 28:9-12.

". . . for you have been born again not of seed which is perishable but imperishable, that is, through the living and enduring word of God" I Peter 1:23. "As newborn babes, desire the sincere milk of the word, that you may grow thereby:" I Peter 2:2, "For the word of God is quick, and powerful, and sharper than any two edged sword, piercing even to the dividing asunder of soul and spirit, and of the joints and marrow, and is a discerner of the thoughts and intents of the heart" Hebrews 4:12. ""Is not My word like fire?" declares the LORD, "and like a hammer which shatters a rock?" Jeremiah 23:29. ""He who rejects Me and does not receive My sayings, has one who judges him; the word I spoke is what will judge him at the last day" John 12:48. "For this reason we also constantly thank God that when you received the word of God which you heard from us, you accepted it not as the word of men, but for what it really is, the word of God, which also performs its work in you who believe" I Thessalonians 2:13 "and have tasted the good word of God and the powers of the age to come," Hebrews 6:5.

"But we are bound to give thanks always to God for you, brothers beloved of the Lord, because God has from the beginning chosen you to salvation through sanctification of the Spirit and belief of the truth:" II Thessalonians 2:13. "He has made My mouth like a sharp sword, In the shadow of His hand He has concealed Me; And He has also made Me a select arrow, He has hidden Me in His quiver" Isaiah 49:2. "He put on righteousness like a breastplate, And a helmet of salvation on His head; And He put on garments of vengeance for clothing And wrapped Himself with zeal as a mantle" Isaiah 59:17, "And take the helmet of salvation, and the sword of the Spirit, which is the word of God:" Ephesians 6:17, "so that He might sanctify her, having cleansed her by the washing of water with the word," Ephesians 5:26. "Grace and peace be multiplied to you in the knowledge of God and of Jesus our Lord;" II Peter 1:2. "But grow in grace, and in the knowledge of our Lord and Savior Jesus Christ. To him be glory both now and for ever. Amen" II Peter 3:18.

⚔ *Pray:*

"Watch you therefore, and pray always, that you may be accounted worthy to escape all these things that shall come to pass, and to stand before the Son of man" Luke 21:36. "And it came to pass, that, as he was praying in a certain place, when he ceased, one of his disciples said unto him, Lord, teach us to pray, as John also taught his disciples. And he said unto them, when ye pray, say, Our Father which art in heaven, Hallowed be thy name. Thy kingdom come. Thy will be done, as in heaven, so in earth. Give us day by day our daily bread. And forgive us our sins; for we also forgive every one that is indebted to us. And lead us not into temptation; but deliver us from evil" Luke 11:1-4. "And I say unto you, Ask, and it shall be given you; seek, and ye shall find; knock, and it shall be opened unto you. For every one that asketh receiveth; and he that seeketh findeth; and to him that knocketh it shall be opened. If a son shall ask bread of any of you that is a father, will he give him a stone? or if he ask a fish, will he for a fish give him a serpent? Or if he shall ask an egg, will he offer him a scorpion? If ye then, being evil, know how to give good gifts unto your children: how much more shall your heavenly Father give the Holy Spirit to them that ask him?" Luke 1:9-13.

"Whenever you stand praying, forgive, if you have anything against anyone, so that your Father who is in heaven will also forgive you your transgressions" Mark 11:25. "And when you pray, you shall not be as the hypocrites are: for they love to pray standing in the synagogues and in the corners of the streets, that they may be seen of men. Truly I say to you, they have their reward" Matthew 6:5. ""Whenever you fast, do not put on a gloomy face as the hypocrites do, for they neglect their appearance so that they will be noticed by men when they are fasting. Truly I say to you, they have their reward in full" Matthew 6:16.

"Pray without ceasing" I Thessalonians 5:17. "With all prayer and petition pray at all times in the Spirit, and with this in view, be on the alert with all perseverance and petition for all the saints, And for me, that utterance may be given to me, that I may open my mouth boldly, to make known the mystery of the gospel," I Thessalonians 6:18-19. "praying at the same time for us as well, that God will open up to us a door for the word, so that we may speak forth the mystery of Christ, for which I have also been imprisoned;" Colossians 4:3. "Pray for us, for we are sure that we have a good conscience, desiring to conduct ourselves honorably in all things" Hebrews 13:18. "Brothers, pray for us" I Thessalonians 5:25. "Finally, brethren, pray for us that the word of the Lord will spread rapidly and be glorified, just as it did also with you;" II Thessalonians 3:1. "Though I speak with the tongues of men and of angels, but have not love, I have become sounding brass or a clanging cymbal" I Corinthians 12:1.

"Praying always with all prayer and supplication in the Spirit, and watching thereunto with all perseverance and supplication for all saints;" Ephesians 6:18. "Devote yourselves to prayer, keeping alert in it with an attitude of thanksgiving;" Colossians 4:2. "First of all, then, I urge that entreaties and prayers, petitions and thanksgivings, be made on behalf of all men" I timothy 2:1. "Be anxious for nothing, but in everything by prayer and supplication with thanksgiving let your requests be made known to God"

Philippians 4:6. "In the same way the Spirit also helps our weakness; for we do not know how to pray as we should, but the Spirit Himself intercedes for us with groaning that cannot be uttered;" Romans 8:26. "These all with one mind were continually devoting themselves to prayer, along with the women, and Mary the mother of Jesus, and with His brothers" Acts 1:14. "For he who speaks in a tongue does not speak to men but to God, for no one understands *him;* however, in the spirit he speaks mysteries. But he who prophesies speaks edification and exhortation and comfort to men. He who speaks in a tongue edifies himself, but he who prophesies edifies the church" I Corinthians 14:2-4.

This is the reason why we pray . . . Watch and pray, that ye enter not into temptation: the spirit indeed is willing, but the flesh is weak" Matthew 26:41.

⚓ *Do good works in His name:*

"How God anointed Jesus of Nazareth with the Holy Ghost and with power: *who went about doing good*, and healing all that were oppressed of the devil; for God was with him" Acts 10:38. It's easy to be good and do good but to represent Him in a society that hates the gospel and the idea that someone died for their sin can be a challenge. ""You will be hated by all because of My name, but it is the one who has endured to the end who will be saved" Matthew 10:22. Jesus said that "these things I have spoken to you, that in me you might have peace. In the world you shall have tribulation: but be of good cheer; I have overcome the world" John 16:33. The fact that someone overcame the world means that it is possible to bear His cross and follow him, emulating His good works in spite of the opposition. I'm not talking about working miracles and healing the sick and raising the dead, even though these come in the package depending on your faith, the power that HE had has been given unto you but ". . . let us not be weary *in well doing*: for in due season we shall reap, *if we faint not*" Galatians 6:9.

In one of His sermons, Jesus spoke and said "I am the true vine, and my Father is the husbandman. Every branch in me that beareth not fruit he taketh away: and every branch that beareth fruit, he purgeth it, that it may bring forth more fruit. Now ye are clean through the word which I have spoken unto you. Abide in me, and I in you. As the branch cannot bear fruit of itself, except it abide in the vine; no more can ye, except ye abide in me. I am the vine, ye are the branches: He that abides in me, and I in him, the same brings forth much fruit: for without me ye can do nothing" John 15:1-5. In order to bear good fruit you have to be engrafted and rooted and grounded in Him and His word to produce the kind of fruit He desires. "Herein is my Father glorified, that ye bear much fruit; so shall ye be my disciples" John 15:8. But "If a man abide not in me, he is cast forth as a branch, and is withered; and men gather them, and cast them into the fire, and they are burned" John 15:6. God does not need or want people that do nothing. We are His workmanship; He went to work and created the heavens and the earth, and everything in it. He expects production. Laziness produces poverty, and poverty is not of God even though there are poor people in this world because of the fallen state of man. The plan of redemption was to restore man to the glory that he lost when man disobeyed God.

"Pure religion and undefiled before God and the Father is this, to visit the fatherless and widows in their affliction, and to keep himself unspotted from the world" James 1:27. If we claim to be who we are without the works, the fruits, then our work becomes futile, in vain and without value. We are commanded to "learn to do good; Seek justice, Reprove the ruthless, Defend the orphan, Plead for the widow" Isaiah 1:17 because "the LORD protects the strangers; He supports the fatherless and the widow, But He thwarts the way of the wicked" Psalm 146:9. Since ". . . the poor shall never cease out of the land: therefore I command you, saying, You shall open your hand wide to your brother, to your poor, and to your needy, in your land" Deut 15:11. "When you cut down your harvest in your field, and have forgotten a sheaf in the field, you shall not go again to fetch it: it shall be for the stranger, for the fatherless, and for the widow: that the LORD your God may bless you in all the work of your hands" Deut 24:19. "And when ye reap the harvest of your land, thou shalt not wholly reap the corners of thy field, neither shalt thou gather the gleanings of thy harvest. And you shall not glean your vineyard, neither shall you gather every grape of your vineyard; you shall leave them for the poor and stranger: I am the LORD your God" Leviticus 19:9-10.

In addition to helping those in need because of circumstances beyond their control, Jesus gave a commission in ". . . All authority in heaven and on earth has been given to me. Therefore *go and make disciples of all nations, *baptizing them in the name of the Father and of the Son and of the Holy Spirit, and *teaching them to obey everything I have commanded you. And surely I am with you always, to the very end of the age" Matthew 28:18. "For it is precept upon precept, precept upon precept, line upon line, line upon line, here a little, there a little" Isaiah 28:8. "Every good Christian is known for his ability to duplicate himself; Reproduction, It's a numbers game as some sales people would put it. "The fruit of the righteous is a tree of life; and he that wins souls is wise" Proverbs 11:30. Growth and stability is evident in the fruit/s one is able to bear. No matter where we start, or how small the beginning may seem, being consistent is what will bring us the results we so desire. Not forgetting that there is a reward at the end, "if we faint not." This is the consequence of laying down our lives for others but the work must go on: "You/we will be hated by all because of My name, but it is the one who has endured to the end who will be saved" Matthew 10:22. "For consider Him who has endured such hostility by sinners against Himself, so that you/we will not grow weary and lose heart" Hebrews 12:3. For His name sake we know that we will suffer rejection and hatred but God has promised a reward. "Therefore, since we have this ministry, as we received mercy, we do not lose heart," II Corinthians 4:1. "Therefore, my beloved brethren, be steadfast, immovable, always abounding in the work of the Lord, knowing that your toil is not in vain in the Lord" 1 Corinthians 15:58. ". . . being patient, brethren, until the coming of the Lord, the farmer waits for the precious produce of the soil, being patient about it, until it gets the early and late rains" James 5:7, "each man's work will become evident; for the day will show it because it is to be revealed with fire, and the fire itself will test the quality of each man's work" I Corinthians 3:13.

⋏ *Gathering Together as One:*

Finding and committing you to a bible believing church is very essential. We are one body, one Lord even our savior Jesus Christ and it is His will that we "not forsaking the assembling of ourselves together, as the manner of some is; but exhorting one another: and so much the more, as you see the day approaching, assemble ourselves together" Hebrews 10:25, "but encourage one another day after day, as long as it is still called "Today," so that none of you will be hardened by the deceitfulness of sin" Hebrews 3:13. As in the days of the apostles, "they were continually devoting themselves to the apostles' teaching and to fellowship, to the breaking of bread and to prayer. And awe came upon every soul, and many wonders and signs were being done through the apostles. And all who believed were together and had all things in common. And they were selling their possessions and belongings and distributing the proceeds to all, as any had need. And day by day, attending the temple together and breaking bread in their homes, they received their food with glad and generous hearts, praising God and having favor with all the people. And the Lord added to their number day by day those who were being saved" Acts 2:42-47.

"Behold, how good and how pleasant *it is* for brethren to dwell together in unity! *It is* like the precious oil upon the head, running down on the beard, the beard of Aaron, running down on the edge of his garments. *It is* like the dew of Hermon, descending upon the mountains of Zion; for there the LORD commanded the blessing— Life forevermore" Psalm 133:1-3. There is a blessing that God commands over the church when we gather together that you can only obtain in a Christian gathering. An empowering; an anointing that can only come from the unification of the body of Christ. "Let brotherly love continue" Hebrews 13:1. "Be devoted to one another in brotherly love; give preference to one another in honor;" Romans 12:10. "Since you have in obedience to the truth purified your souls for a sincere love of the brethren, fervently love one another from the heart," I Peter 1:22. "Now as to the love of the brethren, you have no need for anyone to write to you, for you yourselves are taught by God to love one another;" I Thessalonians 4:9.

⅄ *The Lord's Table: (Holy Communion):*

This is a very essential part of fellowshipping with the family of God. We partake in the remembrance of Jesus Christ's suffering, death, burial and resurrection and we are commanded/requested to partake of the Lord's Table as often as possible. "I speak as to wise men; judge for you what I say. The cup of blessing which we bless, is it not the communion of the blood of Christ? The bread which we break, is it not the communion of the body of Christ? For we, *though* many, are one bread *and* one body; for we all partake of that one bread" 1 Corinthians 10:15-17. The only criteria required to partake of this communion is Jesus Christ. Once you have accepted Jesus Christ it is required that you be a partaker of His body. As the scripture says "You (we) cannot drink the cup of the Lord and the cup of demons; you cannot partake of the Lord's Table and of the table of demons. Or do we provoke the Lord to jealousy? Are we stronger than He?" 1 Corinthians 10:21-22. Only and only when you have wholly and completely given your heart to Jesus and surrendered your life and will and accepted Him as your Lord and savior, can you be eligible to participate, but otherwise don't you dare.

"Therefore whoever eats this bread or drinks *this* cup of the Lord in an unworthy manner will be guilty of the body and blood of the Lord. But let a man examine himself, and so let him eat of the bread and drink of the cup. For he who eats and drinks in an unworthy manner eats and drinks judgment to himself, not discerning the Lord's body. For this reason many *are* weak and sick among you, and many sleep. For if we would judge ourselves, we would not be judged. But when we are judged, we are chastened by the Lord, that we may not be condemned with the world. Therefore, my brethren, when you come together to eat, wait for one another. But if anyone is hungry, let him eat at home, lest you come together for judgment. And the rest I will set in order when I come." 1 Corinthians 11:27-34.

"For I received from the Lord that which I also delivered to you: that the Lord Jesus on the *same* night in which He was betrayed took bread; and when He had given thanks, He broke *it* and said,

"Take, eat; this is My body which is broken for you; do this in remembrance of Me." In the same manner *He* also *took* the cup after supper, saying, "This cup is the new covenant in My blood. This do as often as you drink *it,* in remembrance of Me." For as often as you eat this bread and drink this cup, you proclaim the Lord's death till He comes." 1 Corinthians 11:23-26. It is a privilege and an honor to participate and partake of His body because as often as we partake of His body, we do it in remembrance of Him, until He returns. Be a partaker.

"And I say also to you, that you are Peter, and on this rock I will build my church; and the gates of hell shall not prevail against it" Matthew 16:18.

CHAPTER 8

Crossroads: The Valley of Decision

"I will gather all the nations and bring them down to the valley of Jehoshaphat. Then I will enter into judgment with them there on behalf of My people and My inheritance, Israel, Whom they have scattered among the nations; and they have divided up My land" Joel 3:2. "The LORD utters His voice before His army; surely His camp is very great, for strong is he who carries out His word. The day of the LORD is indeed great and very awesome, and who can endure it? Let the nations be aroused and come up to the valley of Jehoshaphat, for there I will sit to judge all the surrounding nations. Put ye in the sickle, for the harvest is ripe: come, get you down; for the press is full, the fats overflow; for their wickedness is great. Multitudes, multitudes in the valley of decision: for the day of the LORD is near in the valley of decision." Joel 3:11-14. The word Jehoshaphat literally means "The Lord judges." The importance significance of this story parallels itself to what's happening today with Israel and the surrounding nations. And I strongly believe, whatever happens to Israel directly affects those connected to her by virtue of the covenant (Jesus Christ).

The Valley of Jehoshaphat is where the final conflict occurs. We see all these surrounding nations gathered against her (Israel) to annihilate her and take what was promised to her: Jerusalem and where the temple ought to be . . . 'the place of worship.' What's so fascinating is that when all this is happening and war breaks forth, God shows up to rescue her. "Then upon Jahaziel the son of Zechariah, the son of Benaiah, the son of Jeiel, the son of Mattaniah, a Levite of the sons of Asaph, came the Spirit of the Lord in the midst of the congregation; And he said, Hearken ye, all

Judah, and ye inhabitants of Jerusalem, and thou king Jehoshaphat, Thus saith the Lord unto you, Be not afraid nor dismayed by reason of this great multitude; for the battle is not yours, but God's" II Chronicles 20:14-15. After King Jehoshaphat sought the Lord with prayer and fasting and sanctified a fast concerning the heathen nations, God promises victory. "It came to pass after this also, that the children of Moab, and the children of Ammon, and with them other beside the Ammonites, came against Jehoshaphat to battle. Then there came some that told Jehoshaphat, saying, There cometh a great multitude against thee from beyond the sea on this side Syria; and, behold, they be in Hazazon-tamar, which is Engedi. And Jehoshaphat feared, and set himself to seek the Lord, and proclaimed a fast throughout all Judah. And Judah gathered themselves together, to ask help of the Lord: even out of all the cities of Judah they came to seek the Lord . . ." II Chronicles 20:1-13. Israel was threatened as an inheritance and as a nation.

After King Jehoshaphat's honest and sincere prayer for intervention, God delivered Israel out of the hand of its enemies round about. It wasn't one nation but a multitude of nations that were gathered around. God promised Israel the Promised Land and the promise stands to this day. "And Jehoshaphat bowed his head with his face to the ground: and all Judah and the inhabitants of Jerusalem fell before the Lord, worshipping the Lord. And the Levites, of the children of the Kohathites, and of the children of the Korhites, stood up to praise the Lord God of Israel with a loud voice on high. And they rose early in the morning, and went forth into the wilderness of Tekoa: and as they went forth, Jehoshaphat stood and said, Hear me, O Judah, and ye inhabitants of Jerusalem; Believe in the LORD your God, so shall ye be established; believe his prophets, so shall ye prosper" II Chronicles 20:18-20.

The same scene is unfolding today. Nations are conspiring together against Israel and it couldn't happen at a better time. Timing here playing a major role, when all these surrounding nations finished conspiring, 'in the fullness of time' they will make an attempt to 'wipe Israel off the map' but God is not nor has He ever been a man that He should lie, He will come through for Israel because the battle is not there's and prophesy must be fulfilled. This battle has a direct significance and impact in our lives as believers.

Evil has increased and the sin of the land is great and grievance. This is where the road divided, the sheep from the goats; evil against those called by His name. There will be eventually an eternal separation between evil and good and we have come to that point. The great cleansing is at hand and it's my prayer that you clean up your act, get it together and get with the program. We have come full circle, big band is lurking because it's time, but those who love the Lord and called according to His purpose (Romans 8:28) will be preserved.

"But it is not as though the word of God has failed For they are not all Israel who are descended from Israel; nor are they all children because they are Abraham's descendants, but: "THROUGH ISAAC YOUR DESCENDANTS WILL BE NAMED." That is, it is not the children of the flesh who are children of God, but the children of the promise are regarded as descendants" Romans 9"6-8. This is so related! Remember Abraham and his many sons found in Genesis 25:1-17, {from his wife Sarah-(Gen 21:1-3), Hagar, Sarah's maid-(Gen 25:12) and Keturah, Abraham's second wife after Sarah died-(Gen 25:1)}. God promised a blessing over Ishmael and I believe that He blessed Abraham's "other children" but the one that carried the covenant/ promise was Isaac who came from his wife Sarah the free woman. "And Abraham gave all that he had unto Isaac, but unto the sons of the concubines, which Abraham had, Abraham gave gifts, and sent them away from Isaac his son, while he yet lived, eastward, unto the east country." Genesis 25:5, 6. The surrounding nations of Israel were descendants of Abraham as well and from the lineage of Abraham. Abraham sent them away before his death and separated his 'other' sons from his promised son and Promised Land. The Arab (Muslim) nations are all descendants of Abraham. Even though God has blessed them with tremendous wealth, His promise and covenant is with Isaac. At the beginning I mentioned Christians who've made a covenant with Israel through Jesus Christ. Jesus was of the lineage of Isaac and not Ishmael or Abraham's other sons. So these nations that are round about Israel are nations belonging to Abraham by virtue of blood/lineage but the enemies of Jehovah seek to destroy the covenant child and descendant by covenant and God has promised Israel eternal protection. "THOUGH

THE NUMBER OF THE SONS OF ISRAEL BE LIKE THE SAND OF THE SEA, IT IS THE REMNANT THAT WILL BE SAVED;" Romans 9:27.

There will be a great transfer of wealth; the wealth of the sinner has been laid up for the just!! "A good man leaveth an inheritance to his children's children: and the wealth of the sinner is laid up for the just" Proverbs 13:22, and Just as in the days of King ". . . Jehoshaphat and his people came to take away the spoil of them, they found among them in abundance both riches with the dead bodies, and precious jewels, which they stripped off for themselves, more than they could carry away: and they were three days in gathering of the spoil, it was so much. And on the fourth day they assembled themselves in the valley of Berachah; for there they blessed the Lord: therefore the name of the same place was called, the valley of Berachah, unto this day. Then they returned, every man of Judah and Jerusalem, and Jehoshaphat in the forefront of them, to go again to Jerusalem with joy; for the Lord had made them to rejoice over their enemies. And they came to Jerusalem with psalteries and harps and trumpets unto the house of the Lord. And the fear of God was on all the kingdoms of those countries, when they had heard that the Lord fought against the enemies of Israel. So the realm of Jehoshaphat was quiet: for his God gave him rest round about" II Chronicles 20:25-30.

"BEHOLD, I LAY IN ZION A STONE OF STUMBLING AND A ROCK OF OFFENSE, AND HE WHO BELIEVES IN HIM WILL NOT BE DISAPPOINTED" Romans 9:33.

. . . So be not afraid, the battle is not yours but the Lord's . . .

CHAPTER 9

The Fruit of Redemption and Restoration: Living the WORD!!

"Pure religion and undefiled before God and the Father is this, to visit the fatherless and widows in their affliction, and to keep himself unspotted from the world" James 1:27. If we claim to be who we are without the works, the fruits, then our work becomes futile, in vain and without value. We are commanded to "learn to do good; Seek justice, Reprove the ruthless, Defend the orphan, Plead for the widow" Isaiah 1:17 because "the LORD protects the strangers; He supports the fatherless and the widow, But He thwarts the way of the wicked" Psalm 146:9. Since ". . . the poor shall never cease out of the land: therefore I command you, saying, you shall open your hand wide to your brother, to your poor, and to your needy, in your land" Deut 15:11. "When you cut down your harvest in your field, and have forgotten a sheaf in the field, you shall not go again to fetch it: it shall be for the stranger, for the fatherless, and for the widow: that the LORD your God may bless you in all the work of your hands" Deut 24:19. "And when ye reap the harvest of your land, thou shalt not wholly reap the corners of thy field; neither shalt thou gather the gleanings of thy harvest. And you shall not glean your vineyard, neither shall you gather every grape of your vineyard; you shall leave them for the poor and stranger: I am the LORD your God" Leviticus 19:9-10.

The Purpose of giving a tenth part of your income (the tithe) in support of The Work of God has always been to have the Levite taken care of because they "have no inheritance" among the Israelites, the tithe was given to them "for an inheritance, for their service which they serve, even the service of the tabernacle of the congregation." (Num. 18:21, 31). "And if a stranger (alien/refugee/immigrant) dwells with you in your land, you shall not mistreat him. The stranger (alien/refugee/immigrant) who dwells among you shall be to you as one born among you, and you shall love him as yourself; for you were strangers (aliens/refugees/immigrants) in the land of Egypt: I am the LORD your God" Leviticus 19:33-34. He is "a Father of the fatherless and a judge for the widows, Is God in His holy habitation" Psalm 68:5. Therefore "You shall not afflict any widow or orphan. If thou afflict them in any wise, and they cry at all unto me, I will surely hear their cry; and my wrath shall wax hot, and I will kill you with the sword; and your wives shall be widows, and your children fatherless." Exodus 22:22-24. This is God's attitude toward the widow. Even though not often practiced today due to the "evolution of the mind," modern culture and civilization. "If brethren dwell together, and one of them die, and have no child, the wife of the dead shall not marry without unto a stranger: her husband's brother shall go in unto her (gross), and take her to him to wife, and perform the duty of a husband's brother unto her.

And it shall be that the firstborn which she beareth shall succeed in the name of his brother which is dead, that his name be not put out of Israel. And if the man like not to take his brother's wife, then let his brother's wife go up to the gate unto the elders, and say, My husband's brother refuseth to raise up unto his brother a name in Israel, he will not perform the duty of my husband's brother. Then the elders of his city shall call him, and speak unto him: and if he stand to it, and say, I like not to take her; Then shall his brother's wife come unto him in the presence of the elders, and loose his shoe from off his foot, and spit in his face, and shall answer and say, So shall it be done unto that man that will not build up his brother's house. And his name shall be called in Israel, The house of him that hath his shoe loosed" Deuteronomy 25:5-10.

"When you have finished laying aside all the tithe of your increase in the third year—the year of tithing—and have given it to the Levite, the stranger, the fatherless, and the widow, so that they may eat within your gates and be filled, then you shall say before the LORD your God: 'I have removed the holy tithe from my house, and also have given them to the Levite, the stranger, the fatherless, and the widow, according to all Your commandments which You have commanded me; I have not transgressed Your commandments, nor have I forgotten them. I have not eaten any of it when in neither mourning, nor have I removed any of it for an unclean use, nor given any of it for the dead. I have obeyed the voice of the LORD my God, and have done according to all that You have commanded me. Look down from Your holy habitation, from heaven, and bless Your people Israel and the land which You have given us, just as You swore to our fathers, "a land flowing with milk and honey" Deuteronomy 26:12-15.

"For who hath despised the day of small things? For they shall rejoice, and shall see the plummet in the hand of Zerubbabel with those seven; they are the eyes of the LORD, which run to and fro through the whole earth" Zechariah 4:10. "Though your beginning was small, yet your latter end should greatly increase" Job 8:7. Rebuilding and restoring is inevitable. At some point in our Christian walk there will be a rebuilding process, repairing of the breach and restoring the old waste places, in order to make the place habitable. One of the reasons why this nation has been so blessed is because of the care she has projected to the needy, the poor or disadvantaged. Modeling what the Word of God says and with all our might and living the scripture. Joshua 1:8 commands "This book of the law shall not depart out of thy mouth; but thou shalt meditate therein day and night, that thou mayest observe to do according to all that is written therein: for then thou shalt make thy way prosperous, and *then thou shalt have good success*." Bring relief to those in need both here and abroad. Suffering is eminent and when defenseless children become victims it is the responsibility of those who are able to relieve the oppressed and defend the cause of the stranger, the orphan and the widow. This should be your greatest motivation.

In addition to helping those in need because of circumstances beyond their control, Jesus gave a commission in ". . . All authority in heaven and on earth has been given to me. Therefore *go and make disciples of all nations, *baptizing them in the name of the Father and of the Son and of the Holy Spirit, and *teaching them to obey everything I have commanded you. And surely I am with you always, to the very end of the age" Matthew 28:18. "For it is precept upon precept, precept upon precept, line upon line, line upon line, here a little, there a little" Isaiah 28:8. "Every good Christian is known for his ability to duplicate himself; Reproduction, It's a numbers game as some sales people would put it. "The fruit of the righteous is a tree of life; and he that wins souls is wise" Proverbs 11:30. Growth and stability is evident in the fruit/s one is able to bear. No matter where we start, or how small the beginning may seem, being consistent is what will bring us the results we so desire. Not forgetting that there is a reward at the end, "if we faint not." This is the consequence of laying down our lives for others but the work must go on: "You/we will be hated by all because of My name, but it is the one who has endured to the end who will be saved" Matthew 10:22. "For consider Him who has endured such hostility by sinners against Himself, so that you/we will not grow weary and lose heart" Hebrews 12:3. For His name sake we know that we will suffer rejection and hatred but God has promised a reward.

"Therefore, since we have this ministry, as we received mercy, we do not lose heart," II Corinthians 4:1. "Therefore, my beloved brethren, be steadfast, immovable, always abounding in the work of the Lord, knowing that your toil is not in vain in the Lord" 1 Corinthians 15:58. ". . . being patient, brethren, until the coming of the Lord, the farmer waits for the precious produce of the soil, being patient about it, until it gets the early and late rains" James 5:7. ". . . let us not be weary in well doing: for in due season we shall reap, if we faint not" Galatians 6:9.

. . . and the God of Heaven will restore abundant life to us . . .

CHAPTER 10

The Controversy

Hosea . . . explains in detail why God's was angry at the people of that generation. Knowledge had increased (as in these last days) but they seemed to have acquired and accumulated knowledge about everything else accept the knowledge of Him. The controversy, contention, dispute, debate, discussion, or agitation of contrary opinions is also seen here; "Hear the word of the LORD, you children of Israel, for the LORD brings a charge (controversy) against the inhabitants of the land: There is no truth or mercy or knowledge of God in the land" Hosea 4:1. "My people are destroyed for lack of knowledge. Because you have rejected knowledge, I also will reject you from being priest for Me; Because you have forgotten the law of your God, I also will forget your children. The more they increased, the more they sinned against Me" Hosea 4:6-7. Micah records similar contentions and controversy God had against His people.

"Hear ye now what the LORD saith; Arise, contend thou before the mountains, and let the hills hear thy voice. Hear ye, O mountains, the LORD's controversy, and ye strong foundations of the earth: for the LORD hath a controversy with his people, and he will plead with Israel. O my people, what have I done unto thee? And wherein have I wearied thee? Testify against me. For I brought thee up out of the land of Egypt, and redeemed thee out of the house of servants; and I sent before thee Moses, Aaron, and Miriam. O my people, remember now what Balak king of Moab consulted, and what Balaam the son of Beor answered him from Shittim unto Gilgal; that ye may know the righteousness of the LORD. Wherewith shall I come before the LORD, and bow myself before the high God? Shall I come before him with burnt offerings, with calves of a year old? Will the LORD be pleased with thousands of rams, or with ten thousands of rivers of oil? Shall I give my firstborn for my transgression, the fruit of my body for the sin of my soul? He hath shewed thee, O man, what is good; and what doth the LORD require of thee, but to do justly, and to love mercy, and to walk humbly with thy God" Micah 6:1-8.

We have had the tendency to have compassion the disadvantaged and seen "good" people come to the rescue of the down trodden. There are organizations that tackle worldwide/ global problems related to poverty and disease but where is God in all of that. We have pushed God aside and not needed Him in our schools, governments and yes even churches. "Wherefore the Lord said, Forasmuch as this people draw near me with their mouth, and with their lips do honor me, but have removed their heart far from me, and their fear toward me is taught by the precept of men:" Isaiah 29:13. The love of God is taught by the precepts of men and not according to God's precepts. "They come to you as people come, and sit before you as My people and hear your words, but they do not do them, for they do the lustful desires expressed by their mouth, and their heart goes after their gain" Isaiah 33:31. We have become lukewarm neither hot nor cold, "having a form of godliness and denying the power thereof, from such turn away" II Timothy 3:5. There can be no manifestation of God's wonders if there is no knowledge of Him. The earth groans and has been groaning for the manifestations of the sons of God. "For the earnest expectation of the creature waiteth for the manifestation of the sons of God" Romans 8:19.

We are that generation. We have gathered and increased knowledge just like the bible said we would in the lat days according to Daniel, "But thou, O Daniel, shut up the words, and seal the book, even to the time of the end: many shall run to and fro, and knowledge shall be increased" Daniel 12:4. "Ever learning, and never able to come to the knowledge of the truth" II Timothy 3:7. Everything has become permissible and acceptable from the pulpit to the pews, from the judicial governments to the local courts to the society at large and we've rejected the one thing that will bring us health and wealth and that is the knowledge of God. Paul said this in one of his letters. Even though all things are permissible, based on our freewill, not everything is beneficial. "All things are lawful for me, but all things are not expedient: all things are lawful for me, but all things edify not" I Corinthians 10:23. "All things are lawful for me, but not all things are profitable. All things are lawful for me, but I will not be mastered by anything" I Corinthians 6:12. "So then we pursue the things which make for peace and the building up of one another" Romans 14:19. He doesn't require a lot from us but as written in Micah 6:8, and "that's to do justly, and to love mercy, and to walk humbly with thy God" Micah 6:8, "For I desired mercy, and not sacrifice; and the knowledge of God more than burnt offerings" Hosea 6:6.

"Come, and let us return unto the LORD: for he hath torn, and he will heal us; he hath smitten, and he will bind us up" Hosea 6:1. Yep, ". . . turn thou to thy God: keep mercy and judgment and wait on thy God continually" Hosea 12:6; "*Now* we command you, brethren, in the name of our Lord Jesus Christ, that you keep away from every brother who leads an unruly life and not according to the tradition which you received from us" II Thessalonians 3:6; and ". . . have nothing to do with worldly fables fit only for old women (who had sayings that had nothing to do with the Testament back in the olden days). On the other hand, discipline yourself for the purpose of godliness" I Timothy 4:7. "O Israel, return unto the LORD thy God; for thou hast fallen by thine iniquity. *Take with you words*, and turn to the LORD: *say unto him, take away all iniquity, and receive us graciously:* so will we render the calves of our lips" Hosea 14:1-2. "*I will heal their backsliding, I will love them freely:*" Hosea 14:4. "Who is wise, and he shall understand these things? Prudent and he shall know them? For the ways of the LORD are right, and the just shall walk in them: but the transgressors shall fall therein" Hosea 14:9. ". . . It is written, Man shall not live by bread alone (whatever it is that you do respectfully, respectably to put food on the table), but *by every word that proceedeth out of the mouth of God*" Deut 8:3, Matthew 4:4.

"With gentleness correct(ing) those who are in opposition, if perhaps God may grant them repentance leading to the knowledge of the truth," II Timothy 2:25. "For God did not send the Son into the world to judge the world, but that the world might be saved through Him" John 3:17. "Who will have all men to be saved *and to come to the knowledge of the truth*" 1 Timothy 2:4. "Do I have any pleasure in the death of the wicked," declares the Lord GOD, "rather than that he should turn from his ways and live?" Ezekiel 18:23. "For I have no pleasure in the death of anyone who dies," declares the Lord GOD. "Therefore, repent and live." Ezekiel 18:32. "Sow with a view to righteousness, reap in accordance with kindness; break up your fallow ground, for it is time to seek the LORD until He comes to rain righteousness on you" Hosea 10:12. "But as for me, I will watch expectantly for the LORD; I will wait for the God of my salvation. My God will hear me" Micah 7:7 . . .

. . . and remove this controversy from us . . .

CHAPTER 11

Hew yourselves Broken Cisterns that Hold Water

" "For My people have committed two evils: They have forsaken Me, the fountain of living waters, and *hewn themselves cisterns*—broken cisterns *that can hold no water*" Jeremiah 2:13. As a body, it is essential for the sake of humility for one to remain broken if they can but able to hold water. The water we're talking about is directly linked to the Holy Spirit and His functions through us, the fruits that we bear because of His presence in our lives. Without Him the Fountain of living waters, we cannot operate as we should. ". . . If any man thirst, let him come unto me, and drink. Whoever believes in/on Me, out of his/her belly shall flow rivers of living water" John 7:37-38 and ". . . if you knew the gift of God, and who it is that says to you 'give me a drink,' you would have asked Him and He would give you living water" John 4:10. The inability to hold water is a sign of weakness that derives from lack of God's Word in your life. Just like Mary pondered the Words of Promise from God in her heart in Luke 2:19;Like 2:51, God's word we should be hidden in our heart, that we might not sin against you, Psalm 119:11 and the law of our God should be in our hearts; that our steps do not slip, Psalm 37:31.

"Listen! Behold, a sower went out to sow and it happened, as he sowed, that some seed fell by the wayside; and the birds of the air came and devoured it. Some fell on stony ground, where it did not have much earth; and immediately it sprang up because it had no depth of earth. But when the sun was up it was scorched, and because it had no root it withered away. And some seed fell among thorns; and the thorns grew up and choked it, and it yielded no crop. But other seed fell on good ground and yielded a crop that sprang up, increased and produced: some thirtyfold, some sixty and some a hundred." And He said to them, "He who has ears to hear, let him hear!" Mark 4:1-9.

He further explains the purpose of the Parable:

". . . when He was alone, those around Him with the twelve asked Him about the parable. And He said to them, "**To you** it has been given to know the mystery of the kingdom of God; **but to those who are outside**, all things come in parables, so that seeing they may see and not perceive, and hearing they may hear and not understand; Lest they should turn, and their sins be forgiven them'" Mark 4:10-12.

The Parable of the Sower Explained:

". . . He said to them, "Do you not understand this parable? How then will you understand all the parables? The sewer sows the word. And these are the ones by the wayside where the word is sown. When they hear, Satan comes immediately and takes away the word that was sown in their hearts. These likewise are the ones sown on stony ground who, when they hear the word, immediately receive it with gladness; and they have no root in themselves, and so endure only for a time. Afterward, when tribulation or persecution arises for the word's sake, immediately they stumble. Now these are the ones sown among thorns; they are the ones who hear the word, and the cares of this world, the deceitfulness of riches, and the desires for other things entering in choke the word, and it becomes unfruitful. But these are the ones sown on good ground, those who hear the word, accept it, and bear fruit: some thirty-fold, some sixty, and some a hundred" Mark 4:13-20, Matthew 13:1-23 and Luke 8:1-15.

The inability to bear fruit either from the Word of God based on Mark 4:11 or from Galatians 5:22-23 which include "love, joy, peace, patience, kindness, goodness, faithfulness, gentleness and self-control. Against such things there is no law," bears negative fruits that derive from the flesh. Example: "Now the deeds of the flesh are evident, which are: immorality, impurity, sensuality . . . jealousy, outbursts of anger . . . those who practice such things shall not inherit the kingdom of God" Gals. 5:19, 20, 21. "A continual dropping in a very rainy day and a contentious woman are alike. Whoever hides her hides the wind, and the ointment of his right hand, which denudes itself. "Proverbs 27:15-16. I have met afew contentious people; that's not to say that in this day and age there aren't contentious men. But my point is if the Word is not evidently present then the Spirit cannot abide either. The Word and the Water go hand in hand.

"This is he that came by water and blood, even Jesus Christ; not by water only, but by water and blood. And it is the Spirit that bears witness, because the Spirit is truth" 1 John 5:6. This is how I see it in addition to John 19:34 when He hang on the cross. The Water in this teaching symbolizes the Spirit of God and the Blood, the blood that was from the hymen because she (Mary) was untouched and the usual shedding during and after labor. Mary shed blood, the blood of the baby was not from Joseph as in all babies, so there was no sin of the father passed down to the son, but of God Himself! . . . and the Water from the Holy Sprit, who overshadowed her in order for her to conceive, "Then Mary said to the angel, "How can this be, since I do not know a man?" And the angel answered and said to her, "The Holy Spirit will come upon you, and the power of the Highest will overshadow you; therefore, also, that Holy One who is to be born will be called the Son of God" Luke 1:34-35, and at the cross ". . . one of the soldiers pierced His side with a spear, and immediately blood and water came out" John 19:34. These two passages of scripture illustrate that Water and blood, even Jesus Christ who is the Word go together. "In the beginning was the Word, and the Word was with God, and the Word was God. He (the Word) was in the beginning with God" John 1:1, 2. "And the Word became flesh and dwelt among us, and we have seen his glory, glory as of the only Son from the Father, full of grace and truth" John 1:14.

It is by and through Jesus Christ that the Water (symbol of The Holy Spirit also called Counselor) is given. "Nevertheless I tell you the truth; It is expedient for you that I (Jesus Christ) go away: for if I go not away, the Comforter (The Holy Spirit) will not come to you; but if I depart, I will send him to you" John 16:7 "But the Helper, the Holy Spirit, whom the Father will send in My name, He will teach you all things, and bring to your remembrance all that I said to you" John 14:26; "I will ask the Father, and He will give you another Helper, that He may be with you forever;" John 14:16. "If a man abides not in me, he is cast forth as a branch, and is withered; and men gather them, and cast them into the fire, and they are burned. If you abide in me, and my words abide in you, you shall ask what you will, and it shall be done to you" John 15:6, 7. "Every branch in Me that does not bear fruit, He takes away; and every branch that bears fruit, He prunes it so that it may bear more fruit" John 15:2. The inability to bear good fruit is directly linked to the inability to hold Water. God was complaining in Jeremiah 2:13 that the people have made themselves cisterns according to their own understanding, according to the flesh and not the Holy Spirit, that cannot hold, keep or contain the Water. They crack and give way, and are faulty because of the cares of this world. They leak under the pressures that come with the lack of God's Word in someone's life, hence the lack of good fruit. These are the ones that are ultimately annihilated if they are not or cannot be corrected so that the earth can continue to bear good fruit and the bad fruit that is sown in the flesh ceases to exist.

The Holy Spirit has to bring about the atmosphere for change and answer to prayer. "You send forth your spirit, they are created: and you renew the face of the earth" Psalm 104:30. "Then He said to me, "Prophesy to the breath, prophesy, son of man, and say to the breath, 'Thus says the Lord GOD, "Come from the four winds, O breath, and breathe on these slain, that they come to life" Ezekiel 37:9. Only when the Spirit of God is present can there be change/answer to prayer. ". . . the earth was without form, and void; and darkness was on the face of the deep. And the Spirit of God moved on the face of the waters, then God said, Let there be light: and there was light" Gen 1:2-3. He (The Spirit) brought about the atmosphere by moving over the face of the waters.

Empty vessels make most noise. "The words of a wise man's mouth *are* gracious, but the lips of a fool shall swallow him up; The words of his mouth begin with foolishness, and the end of his talk *is* raving madness. A fool also is full of words: a man cannot tell what shall be; and what shall be after him, who can tell him?" Ecclesiastes 10:12-14 but "the tongue of the wise makes knowledge acceptable, But the mouth of fools spouts folly" Proverbs 15:2. "For the dream comes through much effort and the voice of a fool through many words" Ecclesiastes 5:3. "In the multitude of words there wants not sin (sin is inevitable): but he that refrains his lips is wise" Proverbs 10:19 but "he who restrains his words has knowledge, and he who has a cool spirit is a man of understanding" Proverbs 17:27. Emptiness as a result of inability to hold water brings about a lack of productivity. In Jeremiah 2:13 God complains of making ourselves cisterns according to our own understanding after the flesh that can't hold Water. These are the people that God ultimately annihilates so that those that remain can continue to bring forth good fruit upon the earth. It is the bad, fleshy fruits sown that breed destruction and death. God honors brokenness, He is near the broken hearted, people susceptible to His way and His Word. "The sacrifices of God are a broken spirit: a broken and a contrite heart, O God, you will not despise" Psalm 51:17 and "The LORD is near to the brokenhearted and saves those who are crushed in spirit" Psalm 34:18, because it is the broken that will adhere to and keep His Word and Way.

"The law of the LORD is perfect, converting the soul: the testimony of the LORD is sure, making wise the simple: "The statutes of the LORD are right, rejoicing the heart: the commandment of the LORD is pure, enlightening the eyes" psalm 19:7,8. "The works of His hands are truth and justice; All His precepts are sure" Psalm 111:7. "So He humbled you, allowed you to hunger, and fed you with manna which you did not know nor did your fathers know, that He might make you know that man shall not live by bread alone; but man lives by every word that proceeds from the mouth of the LORD" Deut 8:3. Peter talked about a people whose wells/cisterns ". . . *are wells without water*, clouds that are carried with a tempest; to whom the mist of darkness is reserved for ever" II Peter 2:17. "For when they speak great swelling words of vanity, they allure through the lusts of the flesh, through much wantonness, those that were clean escaped from them who live in error. While they promise them liberty, they themselves are the servants of corruption: for of whom a man is overcome, of the same is he brought in bondage. For if after they have escaped the pollutions of the world through the knowledge of the Lord and Savior Jesus Christ, they are again entangled therein, and overcome, the latter end is worse with them than the beginning" II Peter 2:18-20.

Keep His Word, and He'll fill you up till your cup runs over

CHAPTER 12

Lamech 777

The number 7 has always been significant to wrath and mercy. Wrath and mercy go hand in hand, where the righteous obtain favor through mercy in the time of judgment or wrath. ". . . in wrath remember mercy" Habakkuk 3:2. God has always shown mercy to His people, even when His wrath is directed towards His people, mercy was eminent and He turned judgment to favor and had mercy on his people.

It has been a little over 6,000 years since creation and we have entered the 7,000th which is supposed to be a time of rest from the trials and tribulations. Psalm 90:4 reads "For a thousand years in Your sight Are like yesterday when it passes by, Or as a watch in the night." another portion of scripture that proves this theory "But, beloved, be not ignorant of this one thing, that one day is with the Lord as a thousand years, and a thousand years as one day" II Peter 3:8. I have argued that God actually took six thousand years to complete creation, and rested for the thousand years and what we've been doing the past six thousand is recreating and replenishing the earth as HE did for six thousand years and are about to enter the next thousand which will be a blessed time with the Lord and a glorious time of rest. Whether I'm right or wrong, one thing I know for sure is we're entering His rest!

The Rest of The Seventh Year

"And the LORD spoke to Moses on Mount Sinai, saying, "Speak to the children of Israel, and say to them: 'When you come into the land which I give you, then the land shall keep a Sabbath to the LORD. Six years you shall sow your field, and six years you shall prune your vineyard, and gather its fruit; but in the seventh year there shall be a Sabbath of solemn rest for the land, a Sabbath to the LORD. You shall neither sow your field nor prune your vineyard. What grows of its own accord of your harvest you shall not reap, nor gather the grapes of your untended vine, for it is a year of rest for the land. And the Sabbath produce of the land shall be food for you: for you, you're male and female servants, your hired man, and the stranger who dwells with you, for your livestock and the beasts that are in your land—all its produce shall be for food. And you shall count seven Sabbaths of years for yourself, seven times seven years; and the time of the seven Sabbaths of years shall be to you forty-nine years" Leviticus 25:1-8. Even for the Hebrew servant that served in the camp of the Israelites God commanded rest. "Now these are the judgments which you shall set before them: If you buy a Hebrew servant, he shall serve six years; and in the seventh he shall go out free and pay nothing" Exodus 21:1,2

"Death and life are in the power of the tongue: and they that love it shall eat the fruit thereof" Prov 18:21. Power of prophesy is so evident in the case of Seth's Lamech. Adam had two descendants named Lamech, one came from the righteous lineage through Seth and the other from the unrighteous murderous lineage of Cain. Cain's Lamech who had two wives and he (Lamech) confessed to killing a man for wounding him, a young man for injuring him (Gen 4:23). And what follows next is astounding. He speaking of his consequence spoke and said "If Cain shall be avenged sevenfold, truly Lamech seventy and sevenfold" Gen 4:24. They understood the number 7 was associated with the fullness and completion, wrath and mercy. He wanted to pay double for what he had done and that was 7 times and 7.

The famous story of Jacob also brings to light the meaning of the number 7. He worked for his uncle for seven years in order to marry Laban's younger daughter Rachael, but since Jacob had deceived his father and stole the birth right from his brother Esau, he had to reap what he had sown so at the end of the 7 years of labor, Laban deceived him and gave him Leah instead. Even though he had paid the price for a bride, she wasn't the bride of his choice. After the first 7 years God made him pay for the deceit and was a time of wrath but the next 7 years he obtained mercy from God and God rewarded him for his labor and gave him what was he was meant to have.

Back to Seth's Lamech! "When Lamech had lived 182 years, he had a son. He named him Noah and said, 'He will comfort us in the labor and painful toil of our hands caused by the ground the LORD has cursed.' After Noah was born, Lamech lived 595 years and had other sons and daughters. Altogether, Lamech lived 777 years, and then he died" Gen 5:28-31. He prophesied over his son's destiny saying that his son Noah would comfort that generation because of the curse! A very simple yet powerful word/prophesy over his son and what's even more powerful is that the prophesy came true. There had to be a cleansing for the earth had become evil and polluted. "Now it came to pass, when men began to multiply on the face of the earth, and daughters were born to them, that the sons of God saw the daughters of men, that they were beautiful; and they took wives for themselves of all whom they chose. And the LORD said, 'My Spirit shall not strive[a] with man forever, for he is indeed flesh; yet his days shall be one hundred and twenty years.' There were giants on the earth in those days, and also afterward, when the sons of God came in to the daughters of men and they bore children to them. Those were the mighty men who were of old, men of renown. Then the LORD saw that the wickedness of man was great in the earth, and that every intent of the thoughts of his heart was only evil continually. And the LORD was sorry that He had made man on the earth, and He was grieved in His heart. So the LORD said, 'I will destroy man whom I have created from the face of the earth, man and beast, creeping thing and birds of the air, for I am sorry that I have made them.' But Noah found grace in the eyes of the LORD" Gen 6:1-8

"This is the genealogy of Noah. Noah was a just man, perfect in his generations. Noah walked with God. And Noah begot three sons: Shem, Ham, and Japheth. The earth also was corrupt before God, and the earth was filled with violence. So God looked upon the earth, and indeed it was corrupt; for all flesh had corrupted their way on the earth. And God said to Noah, 'The end of all flesh has come before Me, for the earth is filled with violence through them; and behold, I will destroy them with the earth. Make yourself an ark of gopher wood; make rooms in the ark, and cover it inside and outside with pitch. And this is how you shall make it: The length of the ark shall be three hundred cubits, its width fifty cubits, and its height thirty cubits. You shall make a window for the ark, and you shall finish it to a cubit from above; and set the door of the ark in its side. You shall make it with lower, second, and third decks. And behold, I Myself am bringing floodwaters on the earth, to destroy from under heaven all flesh in which is the breath of life; everything that is on the earth shall die. But I will establish My covenant with you; and you shall go into the ark—you, your sons, your wife, and your sons' wives with you. And of every living thing of all flesh you shall bring two of every sort into the ark, to keep them alive with you; they shall be male and female. Of the birds after their kind, of animals after their kind, and of every creeping thing of the earth after its kind, two of every kind will come to you to keep them alive. And you shall take for yourself of all food that is eaten, and you shall gather it to yourself; and it shall be food for you and for them." Thus Noah did; according to all that God commanded him, so he did" Gen 6:9-30. God took comfort in judgment but even in the judgment, mercy was eminent. Noah found grace and mercy was extended to him and his family. And because he found grace in the eyes of God, the animals found grace and obtained mercy and were saved from destruction but it took a righteous Lamech to perceive the time of visitation and in so doing his lineage lives on! He perceived, he prophesied and his household was saved!

"Know therefore and understand, that from the going forth of the command . . . The end of it shall be with a flood," Daniel 25-26. Just as it was in the days of Noah so shall it be in this generation. We are at the brink of judgment mercy! Jesus said "And as were the days of Noah, so shall be the coming of the Son of man" Matt 24:37, Luke 17:26. "For as in the days that were before the flood they were eating and drinking, marrying and giving in marriage, until the day that Noah entered into the ark, and knew not until the flood came, and took them all away; so shall also the coming of the Son of man be" Matt 24:38-39. "Then shall two be in the field; the one shall be taken, and the other left. Two women will be grinding at the mill; one will be taken and one will be left. Watch therefore: for you know not what hour your Lord does come. But know this, that if the good man of the house had known in what watch the thief would come, he would have watched, and would not have suffered his house to be broken up. Therefore be you also ready: for in such an hour as you think not the Son of man comes" Matt 24:40-45.

Forgiveness in the book of Matthew was seventy times seventy times. In biblical language a time meant a year. So if you were to forgive for 7 years that only meant that forgiveness should be extended round the clock. Peter didn't know what he was saying but really very significant. He stretched it upto seven times which meant seven years meaning there should be no end to forgiveness. Leaving no room for wrath or mercy just plain forgiveness all the time every time. "Then Peter came to Him and said, "Lord, how often shall my brother sin against me, and I forgive him? Up to seven times?" Jesus said to him, "I do not say to you, up to seven times, but up to seventy times seven" Matt 18:21-22.

In closing, while the prophet Elijah was interceding with his face between his knees, he sent his servant to check for clouds seven times before a cloud the shape/size of a man's hand appeared. It hadn't rained in Israel for three and a half years according to the Word of the Lord by the mouth of Elijah. "And Elijah went up to the top of Carmel; and he cast himself down upon the earth, and put his face between his knees, and said to his servant, Go up now, look toward the sea. And he went up, and looked, and said, there is nothing. And he said, Go again seven times. And it came to pass at the seventh time, that he said, Behold, there ariseth a little cloud out of the sea, like a man's hand. And he said, Go up, say unto Ahab, Prepare thy chariot, and get thee down that the rain stop thee not. And it came to pass in the meanwhile, that the heaven was black with clouds and wind, and there was a great rain" 1 Kings 18:42-45. God had completed His judgment over Isreal and was going to rain a blessing upon the land.

I haven't exausted the teaching but all this means that time's up! The prophesy has been given and it's been 6 years to God, 6,000 years to us humans. We are entering the 7th year of rest to God and 7,000th year to us humans. We have accomplished our work of recreating and repaying the damage done by Adam, and God has called for a Sabbath and blessed the sabbath. Call it heresy, call it what you want you want. You don't have to believe me the proof has been in the pudding. Search the scriptures, the signs are all up in the scriptures. "The words of the LORD are pure words; As silver tried in a furnace on the earth, refined seven times" Psalm 12:6.

History repeats itself when lessons aren't learned: This lesson of forgiveness and sowing and reaping. "While the earth remaineth, seedtime and harvest, and cold and heat, and summer and winter, and day and night shall not cease." Genesis 8:22

"God is not mocked. Whatsoever a man soweth so shall he reap" Galatians 6:7

"In the first year of Darius the son of Ahasuerus, of the lineage of the Med . . . es, . . . in the first year of his reign I, Daniel, understood by the books the number of the years specified by the word of the LORD, given through Jeremiah the prophet, that He would accomplish seventy years in the desolations of Jerusalem." Daniel 9:1-2

The Parable of the Unmerciful Servant

"Then Peter came to Jesus and asked, "Lord, how many times shall I forgive my brother or sister who sins against me? Up to seven times?" Jesus answered, "I tell you, not seven times, but seventy-seven times.[a] "Therefore, the kingdom of heaven is like a king who wanted to settle accounts with his servants." Matt 18:21-23

My biggest concern: sowing seeds of unforgiveness as opposed to following the laws of forgiveness i.e. 70 times (years) in Daniel 9:1-2 and infamous 16th century transatlantic incident 70x7=490 times. There were and are two races of people in the world that have been in contention with each other. The good race and the bad race. Sin was conceived and God spoke curses into the ground. From the very beginning if you read closely to the Pentateuch the moral of the story has been about obedience and blessings, disobedience and cursings. Cain brough that which was cursed "out of the ground"(Genesis 3:17). Cursed was the ground for man's sake. Atonement hadn't been made yet. Abel not that he was more favorable but that he brought forth that which was acceptable. God had to shed blood to atone. Abel shed bleed to atone. Not the kind of atonement you think. It's wrong to kill. Animal sacrifices in the Old Testament were initiated by GOD Himself to atone for sin.

The first human sacrifice was performed by Cain when he slew his brother. Cain needed to "make good" not that he was any worse than his brother. His and motives were right and heart was in the right place and GOD even told him in Genesis 4:7 after his countenance had fallen over the matter that "If thou doest well, shalt thou not be accepted? and if thou doest not well, sin lieth at the door. And unto thee shall be his desire, and thou shalt rule over him." GOD gave Cain a promise that IF you do well, and he did but it wasn't acceptable because he brought that which was cursed! GOD loved Cain even after he killed his own brother, GOD still had compassion on him. He deserved to die but GOD had mercy on him. GOD made Cain ruler over him.

Cain reinforced the "bad race" in that anyone coming through him would have the stain of his actions and would be liable to some extent for his actions, having absolutely nothing to with his actions. Cain's bloodline as we see later through Lamech brought forth a race of rebels! Vengence was to be taken for anyone who slew Cain seven fold according to Genesis 4:15. God put a curse on him and cursed was the ground again because of Abel's innocent blood that received his life. We begin to see a shift in profession. Cain's decendants went from being farmers to contractors, herdsment and musicians.

I'm most interested in Zilla's TubalCain. The generation of Masons was born here as it reads. Cain's grandson Lamech had two wives and Zilla brought forth a son who became "an instructor of every artificer in brass and iron" Genesis 4:22. I believe in my heart this is where Masonry was born. The Masons are concentrated on following a set of instructions. They have their own set of rules and regulations, laws and requirements and to be one you have to be initiated and educated according to their teachings and completion of these teachings qualifies you to promotions. The have 33 ranks the highest of the ranks are the 33rd Degree Masons.

In Christ "there is neither Jew nor Greek, there is neither bond nor free, there is neither male nor female: for ye are all one in Christ Jesus." Romans 3:28. In Christ the hidden mysteries are hidden IN GOD and GOD and HE reveals these hidden mysteries as it clearly states that "what I tell you in darkness, that speak ye in light; and what ye hear (whispered) in the ear, that preach ye upon the rooftops. "He revealeth the deep and secret things: he knoweth what is in the darkness, and the light dwelleth with him." Daniel 2:22. The Book of Daniel 2:29-30 continues to read that "as for thee, O king, thy thoughts came into thy mind upon thy bed, what should come to pass hereafter: and he that revealeth secrets maketh known to thee what shall come to pass." ". . . But there is a God in heaven that revealeth secrets" Daniel 2:28.

"But as for me, this secret is not revealed to me for any wisdom that I have more than any living, ***but for their sakes*** that shall make known the interpretation to the king, and that thou mightest know the thoughts of thy heart." Daniel 2:30. **This is where the Mason err**. They're teachings are shrouded in mysteries and secrecy! GOD reveals secrets to mankind ***for the sake of the people***!! GOD so loveth the world, enough to reveal HIS plan of redemption right from the Book of Genesis when Adam and Eve sinned. He told Satan himself, didn't need to hide it that her seed shall bruise his head, and Satan shalt bruise his heel. The Mason and other secret societies are NOT of GOD! These are Satan's tools of deception to lure mankind to Gehena (Hell).

If you read the whole book of Daniel chapter 2 you will understand that GOD reveals, not conceals. We have an adversary and HE wants you to know. "Daniel answered and said, Blessed be the name of God for ever and ever: for wisdom and might are his: And he changeth the times and the seasons: he removeth kings, and setteth up kings: he giveth wisdom unto the wise, and knowledge to them that know understanding: He revealeth the deep and secret things: he knoweth what is in the darkness, and the light dwelleth with him. I thank thee, and praise thee, O thou God of my fathers, who hast given me wisdom and might, and hast made known unto me now what we desired of thee: for thou hast now made known unto us the king's matter." Daniel 2:20-23.

In conclusion of this chapter, we've been through the 400 and something years since the unraveling of the seed of unforgiveness began. Innocent people that had absolutely nothing to do with hateful actions and practices get caught up in the consequences by decent and the circle isn't quite yet complete. There's still an imbalance until HIS GLORIOUS APPEARING when the circle closes in for eternity and eternal rest attained. Let's not repeat the cycle of reaping the seeds of unforgiveness whose price is too high. God has been merciful.

Whatever You Do, Do Not Be Left Behind!

CHAPTER 13

Refiner's Fire

When I think of fire I think of gold and the process it takes to get impurities out. Gold is refined by/in fire. It has to go through several processes in order to get impurities out. That's why there are different classifications of gold. It all depends on the purification stages it goes through. Example 10K is the least pure. 14K gold is not as pure as 18K, and 24K is the purest of gold that you'll find in the market. It's lustre is richer, shinier and most attractive.

Gold is a dense "precious" metal, meaning it has the component parts closely compacted together permitting little if any light to pass through all because of its denseness, example: dense smoke"; "heavy fog"; "impenetrable gloom." This reminds me of God's Glory: "And it came to pass, when the priests came out of the holy place, that the cloud filled the house of the Lord, *so that the priests could not continue ministering because of the cloud; for the glory of the Lord filled the house of the Lord*" 1 Kings 8:10-11. Then the cloud covered the tabernacle of meeting, and the glory of the Lord filled the tabernacle. *And Moses was not able to enter the tabernacle of meeting, because the cloud rested above it, and the glory of the Lord filled the tabernacle*" Exodus 40:34-35. This quality exemplifies the God that lives in us. He doesn't come alone but His glory resides in us, and just as the precious metal is dense, so are we as Spirit filled Christians.

Gold is also a soft "precious" metal which means it gives way easily under pressure, as a feather pillow or moist clay; easily cut, marked, shaped, or worn away, as pine wood or pure gold. It is also yielding readily to pressure or weight. "This is the word that came to Jeremiah from the LORD: 'Go down to the potter's house, and there I will give you my message.' So I went down to the potter's house, and I saw him working at the wheel. But the pot he was shaping from the clay was marred in his hands;* so the potter formed it into another pot, shaping it as seemed best to him*. Then the word of the LORD came to me: "O house of Israel, can I not do with you as this potter does?" declares the LORD. "*Like clay in the hand of the potter, so are you in my hand, O house of Israel*" Jeremiah 18:1-6. God desires that we be as soft as clay so that it's easy for Him to mold us. And when we harden ourselves He breaks us and continues with His molding work so that we can be worthy, precious people that He wants us to be.

Gold is shiny meaning glistening, glossy, lustrous, sheeny, shiny, shining, and radiant. Reflecting light; filled with light. "You are the *light of the world. A city on a hill cannot be hidden. Neither do people light a lamp and put it under a bowl. Instead they put it on its stand, and it gives light to everyone in the house. In the same way, let your light shine before men, that they may see your good deeds and praise your Father in heaven," Matt 5:14-16. As God's precious children, because of His glory and reflection of His glory that resides in us, we cannot hide His glory, it shines forth!

The following characteristic of gold is reflected in this scripture: "We are pressed but not crushed, persecuted not abandoned, struck down but not destroyed" 2 Corinthians 4:8-9. Gold is malleable and ductile. Malleable meaning it is capable of being shaped or formed, as by hammering or pressure, it is easily controlled or influenced; tractable, and able to adjust to changing circumstances; adaptable: And ductile which means that it can be stretched, drawn, or hammered thin *without breaking; not brittle. Just as Christians ought to be soft as clay, the malleability and ductility of a Christian enables the work of God in you bring you to perfection. This is a quality that God desires in us. He doesn't want His people to be stiff necked, ridged people who wouldn't adhere to His commands. God almost destroyed His people that He brought out of the land of Egypt to take them to His promised land. They had quickly turned away from Him and started worshipping an image of a calf. "And the LORD said to Moses, 'Go, get down! For your people whom you brought out of the land of Egypt have corrupted themselves.

They have turned aside quickly out of the way which I commanded them. They have made themselves a molded calf, and worshiped it and sacrificed to it, and said, 'This is your god, O Israel that brought you out of the land of Egypt!'" And the LORD said to Moses, 'I have seen this people, and* indeed it is a stiff-necked people! Now therefore, let Me alone, that My wrath may burn hot against them and I may consume them and I will make of you a great nation'" Exodus 32:7-10.

In addition to those qualities, gold is also difficult to counterfeit! Either you're a true Christian or not. "Either make the tree good and its fruit good, or make the tree bad and its fruit bad; for the tree is known by its fruit" Matt 12:33. "For each tree is known by its own fruit. For men do not gather figs from thorns, nor do they pick grapes from a briar bush" Luke 6:(44. "Can a fig tree, my brethren, produce olives, or a vine produce figs? Nor can salt water produce fresh" James 3:12. "You shall know them by their fruits. Do men gather grapes of thorns, or figs of thistles?" Matt 7:16.

All gold is exactly alike regardless of where it is mined. Regardless of where you live or what part of the world you come from, "there is neither Jew nor Greek, there is neither slave nor free man, there is neither male nor female; for you are all one in Christ Jesus" Galatians 3:28. "For in Christ Jesus neither circumcision nor uncircumcision means anything, but faith working through love" Galatians 5:6. We are all one in Christ therefore all look alike by the fruit we bear. There is One Spirit, One Lord. "There is one body and one Spirit, just as you were called in one hope of your calling; one Lord, one faith, one baptism; one God and Father of all, who is above all, and through all, and in you all" Ephesians 4:4-6 "For you are all the children of God by faith in Christ Jesus" Galatians 3:26.

Gold is found, sought out. It is mined and you have to find the mines! "You whom I have taken from the ends of the earth, and called you from the chief men thereof, and said to you, You are my servant; I have chosen you, and not cast you away" Isaiah 41:9. "For the LORD's portion is his people; Jacob is the lot of his inheritance. *He found him in a desert land, and in the waste howling wilderness; he led him about, he instructed him, he kept him as the apple of his eye" Deuteronomy 32:9-10. "But now listen, O Jacob, My servant, And Israel, whom I have chosen:" Isaiah 44:1.

"For you are a holy people to the LORD your God, and the LORD has chosen you to be a people for His own possession out of all the peoples who are on the face of the earth" Deuteronomy 14:2. "You have not choose Me, but I chose you and appointed you that you should go and bear fruit, and that your fruit should remain, that whatever you ask the Father in My name He may give you" John 15:16.

Gold is rare, uncommon, infrequently occurring and costly meaning it is marked by wide separation of component particles. "For you are bought with a price: therefore glorify God in your body, and in your spirit, which are God's" 1 Corinthians 6:20. "You were bought with a price; do not become slaves of men" 1 Corinthians 7:23. "For as much as you know that you were not redeemed with corruptible things, as silver and gold, from your vain conversation received by tradition from your fathers; but with the precious blood of Christ, as of a lamb without blemish and without spot:" 1 Peter 1:18-19. We are not cheap; someone paid a hefty price that we may be redeemed!! We are uncommon. No other religion teaches about redemption by blood. "Hereby perceive we the love of God, because he laid down his life for us: and we ought to lay down our lives for the brothers" 1 John 3:16. "Greater love has no man than this that a man lay down his life for his friends" John 15:13. We know that He loves us and that are valuable because of the cost, the price He paid for us.

No change in its shape or form affects its value. It doesn't matter what hardships, trials and temptations we face, we do not lose our value. "For I am persuaded, that neither death, nor life, nor angels, nor principalities, nor powers, nor things present, nor things to come, nor height, nor depth, nor any other creature, shall be able to separate us from the love of God, which is in Christ Jesus our Lord" Romans 8:38-39. "Blessed be the God and Father of our Lord Jesus Christ, which according to his abundant mercy hath begotten us again unto a lively hope by the resurrection of Jesus Christ from the dead, to an inheritance incorruptible, and undefiled, and that fadeth not away, reserved in heaven for you, who are kept by the power of God through faith unto salvation ready to be revealed in the last time. Wherein ye greatly rejoice, though now for a season, if need be, ye are in heaviness through manifold temptations: That the trial of your faith, *being much more precious than of gold that perisheth, though it be tried with fire, might be found unto praise and honor and glory at the appearing of Jesus Christ:" 1 Peter 3:3-7.

Gold is a good conductor of heat meaning it is a material which permits a flow of energy. A material which allows the flow of charged particles is an electrical conductor. ""All authority in heaven and on earth has been given to me. Go therefore and make disciples of all nations, baptizing them in the name of the Father and of the Son and of the Holy Spirit, and teaching them to obey everything that I have commanded you. And remember, I am with you always, to the end of the age" Matthew 28:18-20). "So we are ambassadors for Christ, since God is making his appeal through us" II Cor. 5:20. "As you go, proclaim the good news" Matt. 10:7. "This is now, beloved, the second letter I am writing to you in which I am stirring up your sincere mind by way of reminder, that you should remember the words spoken beforehand by the holy prophets and the commandment of the Lord and Savior spoken by your apostles" II Peter 3:1-2. As a body our main objective is to reproduce ourselves and make disciples. We are responsible for every lost soul that hasn't heard the good news of the gospel. "But if the watchman see the sword come, and blow not the trumpet, and the people be not warned; if the sword come, and take any person from among them, he is taken away in his iniquity; but his blood will I require at the watchman's hand" Ezekiel 33:6. "When I say to the wicked, 'You will surely die,' and you do not warn him or speak out to warn the wicked from his wicked way that he may live, that wicked man shall die in his iniquity, but his blood I will require at your hand" Ezekiel 3:18. "Again, when a righteous man turns away from his righteousness and commits iniquity, and I place an obstacle before him, he will die; since you have not warned him, he shall die in his sin, and his righteous deeds which he has done shall not be remembered; but his blood I will require at your hand" Ezekiel 3:20. We should be infecting and affecting this society whether they'll hear or not (Ezekiel 2:7), with the message of Jesus Christ and the love of God. What happens after that is up to them but we still ought to warn them of impending judgment whether they'll be counted worthy or not. "But if you on your part warn a wicked man to turn from his way and he does not turn from his way, he will die in his iniquity, but you have delivered your life" Ezekiel 33:9.

Gold is in not only found and extracted from the earthly mines and sold in stores and other markets in this world but Gold is also Heaven and decks the streets of Heaven! "The construction of its wall was of jasper; and the city was pure gold, like clear glass. The foundations of the wall of the city were adorned with all kinds of precious stones: the first foundation was jasper, the second sapphire, the third chalcedony, the fourth emerald, the fifth sardonyx, the sixth sardius, the seventh chrysolite, the eighth beryl, the ninth topaz, the tenth chrysoprase, the eleventh jacinth, and the twelfth amethyst. The twelve gates were twelve pearls: each individual gate was of one pearl. And the street of the city was pure gold, like transparent glass" Revelation 21:18-21. Jesus told His disciples and followers that "In my Father's house are many mansions: if it were not so, I would have told you. I go to prepare a place for you" John 14:2. "Precious in the sight of the LORD is the death of his saints" Psalms 116:15. "He shall spare the poor and needy, and shall save the souls of the needy. He will rescue their life from oppression and violence, and their blood will be precious in his sight; And he shall live, and to him shall be given of the gold of Sheba: prayer also shall be made for him continually; and daily shall he be praised" Psalms 72:13-15.

"According to the grace of God which is given unto me, as a wise masterbuilder, I have laid the foundation, and another buildeth thereon. But let every man take heed how he buildeth thereupon. For other foundation can no man lay than that is laid, which is Jesus Christ. Now if any man build upon this foundation gold, silver, precious stones, wood, hay, stubble; Every man's work shall be made manifest: for the day shall declare it, *because it shall be revealed by fire; and the fire shall try every man's work of what sort it is. If any man's work abides which he hath built thereupon, he shall receive a reward. If any man's work shall be burned, he shall suffer loss: but he himself shall be saved; yet so as by fire" 1 Corinthians 3:10-15.

Therefore "I counsel thee to buy of me gold tried in the fire, that thou mayest be rich; and white raiment, that thou mayest be clothed, and that the shame of thy nakedness do not appear; and anoint thine eyes with eye salve, that thou mayest see. As many as I love, I rebuke and chasten: be zealous therefore, and repent. Behold, I stand at the door, and knock: if any man hear my voice, and open the door, I will come in to him, and will sup with him, and he with me" Revelation 3:17-20. "The fear of the LORD is clean, enduring forever: the judgments of the LORD are true and righteous altogether. More to be desired are they than gold, yea, than much fine gold: sweeter also than honey and the honeycomb" Psalm 19:9-10. "The words of the LORD are pure words; As silver tried in a furnace on the earth, refined seven times" Psalm 12:6

Be Refined in The Fire of His Spirit and be More Precious Than Gold.

CHAPTER 14

Raising the Standard

"So shall they fear the name of the LORD from the west, and his glory from the rising of the sun. When the enemy shall come in like a flood, the Spirit of the LORD shall lift up a standard against him" Isaiah 59:19. "The thief comes not, but for to steal, and to kill, and to destroy: I am come that they might have life, and that they might have it more abundantly" John 10:10. "Righteousness exalts a nation: but sin is a reproach to any people" Proverbs 14:34. "When the righteous are in authority, the people rejoice: but when the wicked bears rule, the people mourn" Proverbs 29:2. "Set up the standard toward Zion: retire, stay not: for I will bring evil from the north, and a great destruction" Jeremiah 4:6

There cannot be a standard without the Standard Setter; there cannot be a standard without righteousness. It won't be long that "Now is the judgment of this world: now shall the prince of this world be cast out" John 12:31. Before the fall of man the earth was perfect as we all know, there was no sorrow, no sickness, no disease, no wars, no hatred, everything was in perfect balance and the standard of living was as God designed it to be until the destroyer came into the picture. "The LORD God took the man and put him in the Garden of Eden to work it and take care of it. And the LORD God commanded the man, saying, of every tree of the garden you may freely eat: But of the tree of the knowledge of good and evil, you shall not eat of it: for in the day that you eat thereof you shall surely die" Gen 2:15-17. Rule of thumb, touch no unclean thing, in other words, God gave a command and warned the man of violating that command. Man refused to heed the command and judgment entered into the world.

After the man ate the fruit, their eyes were opened; they became aware and realized that they had no clothes on. Jesus (reincarnate) automatically knew that there had been a shift, a change in the Spiritual atmosphere in His Holy Place. Pollution had permeated His garden just like in the case with the woman with the issue of blood where He felt virtue leaving him because the unclean woman had made Him unclean according to Jewish law. "The LORD said to Moses and Aaron, 'Speak to the Israelites and say to them: 'When any man has a bodily discharge, the discharge is unclean. Whether it continues flowing from his body or is blocked, it will make him unclean. This is how his discharge will bring about uncleanness: Any bed the man with a discharge lies on will be unclean, and anything he sits on will be unclean. Anyone who touches his bed must wash his clothes and bathe with water, and he will be unclean till evening. Whoever sits on anything that the man with a discharge sat on must wash his clothes and bathe with water, and he will be unclean till evening. Whoever touches the man who has a discharge must wash his clothes and bathe with water, and he will be unclean till evening. If the man with the discharge spits on someone who is clean, that person must wash his clothes and bathe with water, and he will be unclean till evening. Everything the man sits on when riding will be unclean, and whoever touches any of the things that were under him will be unclean till evening; whoever picks up those things must wash his clothes and bathe with water, and he will be unclean till evening. Anyone the man with a discharge touches without rinsing his hands with water must wash his clothes and bathe with water, and he will be unclean till evening" Leviticus 15:1-15.

Adam and Eve lost their home, security, comfort and their standard of living went from heaven to hell. They had to be evicted and cast out because they had participated and meddled with an unclean spirit making them unclean in the process. The garden of God became unclean. Jesus knew this when HE came looking for Adam and Eve, that virtue had left the garden and the glory had departed! Much like what has been happening to this generation. It is not the will of God for people to live in shame and discomfort. Jesus Himself said during one of His meetings while He was here on earth. ""I will not speak much more with you, for the ruler of the world is coming, and he has nothing in Me" John 14:30. What follows astounds me because if Adam had done what Jesus did in the passage following and ignored or got away from Satan as he was having a conversation with his wife, they and we'd still have our perfect home. "But that the world may know that I love the Father; and as the Father gave me commandment, even so I do. Arise, let us go hence" John 14:31. Unlike Jesus he entertained, contemplated and executed the idea. "There is a way which seems right to a man, but its end is the way of death" Proverbs 16:25' 14:12.

Righteousness and right standing with God is the key to obtain and maintain the standard that God has set for us. Only and only when we have lived up to His expectations then will change come. "And the LORD said to Moses, I will do this thing also that you have spoken: for you have found grace in my sight, and I know you by name" Ex 33:17. "For I know the plans I have for you," declares the LORD, "plans to prosper you and not to harm you, plans to give you hope and a future" Jeremiah 29:11. His plan for us is to prosper and not harm for the sake of the future. But we have often traded the Standard of life for a cheaper and easier way out and it has cost humanity, generations and because we exchange our trust in the one true God for the destroyer!

"The Mighty One, God the LORD, has spoken and called the earth from the rising of the sun to its going down. Out of Zion, the perfection of beauty, God will shine forth" Psalm 50:1-2. "He shall call to the heavens from above, and to the earth, that He may judge His people: Gather My saints together to Me, those who have made a covenant with Me by sacrifice. Let the heavens declare His righteousness, for God Himself is Judge. Selah. Hear, O My people, and I will speak O Israel, and I will testify against you; I am God, your God! I will not rebuke you for your sacrifices or your burnt offerings, which are continually before Me. I will not take a bull from your house, or goats out of your folds. For every beast of the forest is Mine, and the cattle on a thousand hills. I know all the birds of the mountains, and the wild beasts of the field are Mine. If I were hungry, I would not tell you; for the world is Mine, and all its fullness. Will I eat the flesh of bulls, or drink the blood of goats? Offer to God thanksgiving, and pay your vows to the Most High, call upon Me in the day of trouble; I will deliver you, and you shall glorify Me." Psalm 50:4-15

"But to the wicked God says, what right have you to declare My statutes, Or take My covenant in your mouth? Seeing you hate instruction, and cast My words behind you? When you saw a thief, you consented with him, and have been a partaker with adulterers. You give your mouth to evil, and your tongue frames deceit. You sit and speak against your brother; you slander your own mother's son. These things you have done and I kept silent; you thought that I was altogether like you; but I will rebuke you, and set them in order before your eyes" Psalm 50:16-21. "Now consider this, you who forget God, lest I tear you in pieces, and there be none to deliver: whoever offers praise glorifies Me; And to him who orders his conduct aright, I will show the salvation of God." Psalm 50:22—the end!

"The silver is mine, and the gold is mine, said the LORD of hosts" Haggai 2:4!, "With him is strength and wisdom: the deceived and the deceiver are His" Job 12:16

Bless the LORD, O my soul. O LORD my God, thou art very great; thou art clothed with honor and majesty. Who covers yourself with light as with a garment: who stretches out the heavens like a curtain: Who lays the beams of his chambers in the waters: who makes the clouds his chariot: who walks upon the wings of the wind: Who makes his angels spirits; his ministers a flaming fire: Who laid the foundations of the earth, that it should not be removed forever. You cover it with the deep as with a garment: the waters stood above the mountains. At your rebuke they fled; at the voice of your thunder they hasted away. They go up by the mountains; they go down by the valleys unto the place which you have founded for them. You hast set a bound that they may not pass over; that they turn not again to cover the earth. He sends the springs into the valleys, which run among the hills. They give drink to every beast of the field: the wild asses quench their thirst. By them shall the fowls of the heaven have their habitation which sing among the branches. He waters the hills from his chambers: the earth is satisfied with the fruit of your works. He causes the grass to grow for the cattle, and herb for the service of man: that he may bring forth food out of the earth; and wine that makes glad the heart of man, and oil to make his face to shine, and bread which strengthens man's heart. The trees of the LORD are full of sap; the cedars of Lebanon, which he hath planted; where the birds make their nests: as for the stork, the fir trees are her house. The high hills are a refuge for the wild goats; and the rocks for the conies. He appointed the moon for seasons: the sun knows his going down. You make darkness, and it is night: wherein all the beasts of the forest do creep forth. The young lions roar after their prey, and seek their meat from God. The sun rises, they gather themselves together, and lay them down in their dens. Man goes forth unto his work and to his labor until the evening." Psalm 104:1-23

"O LORD, how manifold are your works! In wisdom have you made them all: the earth is full of your riches. So is this great and wide sea, wherein are things creeping innumerable, both small and great beasts. There go the ships: there is that leviathan, which you have made to play therein. These wait all upon thee; that thou may give them their meat in due season. That you give them they gather: you open your hand, they are filled with good. You hide thy face, they are troubled: You take away their breath; they die, and return to their dust. You send forth your spirit, they are created: and you renew the face of the earth. The glory of the LORD shall endure for ever: the LORD shall rejoice in his works. He looks on the earth, and it trembles: he touches the hills, and they smoke. I will sing unto the LORD as long as I live: I will sing praise to my God while I have my being. My meditation of him shall be sweet: I will be glad in the LORD. Let the sinners be consumed out of the earth, and let the wicked be no more. Bless thou the LORD, O my soul. Praise ye the LORD" Psalm 104: 24-35.

His Will will be done! "Declaring the end from the beginning, and from ancient times the things that are not yet done, saying, My counsel shall stand, and I will do all my pleasure" Isaiah 46:10, because HE knows the end from the beginning! "The LORD of hosts has sworn saying, 'Surely, just as I have intended so it has happened, and just as I have planned so it will stand" Isaiah 14:24. What we have done for generations has infected and affected the generations to come. It started with Adam and will go on until the coming of the Lord Jesus Christ. Those who take heed not trade the Most High for a counterfeit are assured of safety, but woe unto them that defiantly disregard their maker. "Her priests have done violence to My law and have profaned My holy things; they have made no distinction between the holy and the profane, and they have not taught the difference between the unclean and the clean; and they hide their eyes from My Sabbaths, and I am profaned among them" Ezekiel 22:26.

"And the word of the LORD came to me, saying, "Son of man, these men have set up their idols in their hearts, and put before them that which causes them to stumble into iniquity. Should I let Myself be inquired of at all by them? Therefore speak to them, and say to them, 'Thus says the Lord GOD: Every one of the house of Israel who sets up his idols in his heart, and puts before him what causes him to stumble into iniquity, and then comes to the prophet, I the LORD will answer him who comes, according to the multitude of his idols, that I may seize the house of Israel by their heart, because they are all estranged from Me by their idols. Therefore say to the house of Israel, 'Thus says the Lord GOD: "Repent, turn away from your idols, and turn your faces away from all your abominations. For anyone of the house of Israel, or of the strangers who dwell in Israel, who separates himself from Me and sets up his idols in his heart and puts before him what causes him to stumble into iniquity, then comes to a prophet to inquire of him concerning Me, I the LORD will answer him by Myself. I will set My face against that man and make him a sign and a proverb and I will cut him off from the midst of My people. Then you shall know that I am the LORD.

"The way of a fool is right in his own eyes, But a wise man is he who listens to counsel" Proverbs 12:15. "Therefore what benefit were you then deriving from the things of which you are now ashamed? For the outcome of those things is death" Romans 6:21. A separation/distinction between the Holy and the profane, unclean and the unclean has to be taught. For some discerning between both is easier than others . . . "Moreover, they shall teach My people the difference between the holy and the profane, and cause them to discern between the unclean and the clean" Ezekiel 44:23. "Have you not done this to yourself by your forsaking the LORD your God When He led you in the way?" Jeremiah 2:17. "Your ways and your deeds have brought these things to you. This is your evil. How bitter! How it has touched your heart!" Jeremiah 4:18. "Your iniquities have turned away these things, and your sins have withheld good things from you" Jeremiah 5:25. "Acquaint now yourself with him, and be at peace: thereby good shall come to you" Job 22:21."

"Lets Get Back to Eden and Get On Top of the "World""

CHAPTER 15

Arriving at the Place Called Grace

"**B**ut Jesus went to the Mount of Olives. Now early in the morning He came again into the temple, and all the people came to Him; and He sat down and taught them. Then the scribes and Pharisees brought to Him a woman caught in adultery. And when they had set her in the midst, they said to Him, 'Teacher, this woman was caught in adultery, in the very act. Now Moses, in the law, commanded us that such should be stoned. But what do You say?' This they said, testing Him, that they might have something of which to accuse Him. But Jesus stooped down and wrote on the ground with His finger, as though He did not hear. So when they continued asking Him, He raised Himself up and said to them, 'He who is without sin among you, let him cast the first stone at her.' And again He stooped down and wrote on the ground. Then those who heard it, being convicted by their conscience, went out one by one, beginning with the oldest even to the last. And Jesus was left alone, and the woman standing in the midst. When Jesus had raised Himself up and saw no one but the woman, He said to her, 'Woman, where are those accusers of yours? Has no one condemned you?' She said, 'No one, Lord.' And Jesus said to her, 'Neither do I condemn you; go and sin no more'" Matt 8:1-11.

There was judgment and condemnation before Grace. The Law condemns to damnation but Grace intervenes. "Christ is become of no effect unto you, whosoever of you are justified by the law; ye are fallen from grace" Gal 5:4. If you turn your back on grace, the law will judge and condemn you. We know that Jesus came to fulfill the law and not do away with it is written in Matt 5:17-20. ; "Do not think that I have come to abolish the Law or the Prophets;

I have not come to abolish them but to fulfill them. I tell you the truth, until heaven and earth disappear, not the smallest letter, not the least stroke of a pen will by any means disappear from the Law until everything is accomplished. Anyone who breaks one of the least of these commandments and teaches others to do the same will be called least in the kingdom of heaven, but whoever practices and teaches these commands will be called great in the kingdom of heaven. For I tell you that unless your righteousness surpasses that of the Pharisees and the teachers of the law, you will certainly not enter the kingdom of heaven." This He said so that His people would not be slack, lazy or complacent in the things of God as seen in the verses before that.

Unpardonable Sin:

Before Jesus Christ appeared, the Hebrew people were under the law/Torah. There were consequences of sin and rewards for obedience as it is today. What's different today is the dispensation of Grace. ". . . For the law killeth, but the Spirit (Grace) brings life . . ." II Corinthians 3:6. There are sins that could be pardoned and unpardonable sins. "Wherefore I say unto you, all manner of sin and blasphemy shall be forgiven unto men: but the blasphemy [against] the [Holy] Ghost shall not be forgiven unto men. And whosoever speaketh a word against the Son of man, it shall be forgiven him: but whosoever speaketh against the Holy Ghost, it shall not be forgiven him, neither in this world, neither in the [world] to come. Either make the tree good (grace), and his fruit good; or else make the tree corrupt (law), and his fruit corrupt: for the tree is known by [his] fruit" Matt 12:31-33. Blasphemy against the Holy Ghost is the highway to hell with no way of turning around. Also seen in Luke 12:10 "And whosoever shall speak a word against the Son of man, it shall be forgiven him: but unto him that blasphemeth against the Holy Ghost it shall not be forgiven." Mark 3:27-29 "No man can enter into a strong man's house, and spoil his goods, except he will first bind the strong man; and then he will spoil his house. Verily I say unto you, All sins shall be forgiven unto the sons of men, and blasphemies wherewith so ever they shall blaspheme: But he that shall blaspheme against the Holy Ghost hath never forgiveness, but is in danger of eternal damnation: Because they said, He hath an unclean spirit."

"But I say to you, that you resist not evil: but whoever shall smite you on your right cheek, turn to him the other also" Matthew 5:39. "Whoever hits you on the cheek, offer him the other also; and whoever takes away your coat, do not withhold your shirt from him either" Luke 6:29. Grace says turn the other cheek Vs. avenging yourself. It was and is still written in the Law "Your eye shall not pity. It shall be life for life, eye for eye, tooth for tooth, hand for hand, foot for foot" Deuteronomy 19:21, Exodus 21:24 "fracture for fracture, eye for eye, tooth for tooth; whatever injury he has given a person shall be given to him" Lev 24:20, but Grace says forgive seventy times seven, "Then Peter came to Jesus and asked, 'Lord, how many times shall I forgive my brother when he sins against me? Up to seven times?' Jesus answered, 'I tell you, not seven times, but seventy-seven times" Matthew 18:21-22. "You have heard that it has been said, an eye for an eye, and a tooth for a tooth: But I say to you, that you resist not evil: but whoever shall smite you on your right cheek, turn to him the other also. And if any man will sue you at the law, and take away your coat, let him have your cloak also. Whoever forces you to go one mile, go with him two" Matthew 5:38-41.

"You have heard that it was said to the people long ago, 'Do not murder, and anyone who murders will be subject to judgment.' But I tell you that anyone who is angry with his brother will be subject to judgment. Again, anyone who says to his brother, 'Raca,' is answerable to the Sanhedrin. But anyone who says, 'You fool!' will be in danger of the fire of hell" Matt 5:21. "Dearly beloved, avenge not yourselves, but rather give place to wrath: for it is written, Vengeance is mine; I will repay, said the Lord" Romans 12:19. "Therefore, if you are offering your gift at the altar and there remember that your brother has something against you, leave there your gift before the altar, and go your way; first be reconciled to your brother, and then come and offer your gift" Matthew 5:23-24. "Settle matters quickly with your adversary who is taking you to court. Do it while you are still with him on the way, or he may hand you over to the judge, and the judge may hand you over to the officer, and you may be thrown into prison. I tell you the truth; you will not get out until you have paid the last penny" Matthew 5:25. "You have heard that it was said, 'Love your neighbor[a] and hate your enemy.' But I tell you: Love your enemies and pray for those who persecute you, that you may be sons of your Father in heaven. He causes his sun to rise on the evil and the good, and sends rain on the righteous and the unrighteous. If you love those who love you, what reward will you get? Are not even the tax collectors doing that? And if you greet only your brothers, what are you doing more than others? Do not even pagans do that? Be perfect, therefore, as your heavenly Father is perfect." Matthew 5:43-48.

"Cursed is the man who does not uphold the words of this law by carrying them out." Then all the people shall say, "Amen!" Deuteronomy 27:26. "For as many as are of the works of the law are under the curse: for it is written, Cursed is every one that continues not in all things which are written in the book of the law to do them" Galatians 3:10. Clearly "But that no man is justified by the law in the sight of God, it is evident: for, the just shall live by faith." Since the fall of man it is impossible to adhere and to and obey all the laws of God, otherwise this whole generation would be under the curse totally dismissing the work Christ did on Calvary Grace came so that we could have pardon for our iniquities and weaknesses and have a chance to have the slate wiped clean. The letter killeth and those who are under the law are judged by it but Grace intervenes and enables you to have chances. The blood of Jesus Christ cleanses us from all sin making it possible to live free and clear without a guilty conscience because of grace. Our righteousness is as filthy rags! We cannot be cleansed accept through Jesus Christ, therefore we need to embrace and put on His righteousness so that we are able to stand in His presence sinless. There is no man that sinneth not and that's what Christ came to do. To do away with the sin that so easily beset us and give us the grace that we need to enter the Kingdom of Heaven cleansed and washed by His word, blood and power.

"Christ has redeemed us from the curse of the law, being made a curse for us: for it is written, Cursed is every one that hangs on a tree:" Galatians 3:13. Christ took the curse from us and pinned it in Himself. He became the accursed thing that we might have grace and pardon. Grace is the unearned, underserved privilege that delivers you from the unpleasant dooming circumstances. It is the unmerited favor and blessing that catapults you to a place of rest, peace, love, prosperity and every blessing imaginable. Grace opens doors of opportunity and advancement/success, the law opens doors to condemnation and judgment. Grace goes hand in hand with love; Law goes hand in hand with hate and unforgiveness. Grace produces the fruit of forgiveness and is a result of forgiveness, Law produces the fruit of unforgiveness and is a result of unforgiveness.

Therefore Give Grace Not Law.

CHAPTER 16

Guarding the Entrances
to Your Soul, Body And Spirit.

Let's talk about these entrances that could either lead you to destruction or detour you. The whole being is a component of Soul and Spirit concealed by a Body. God was the model to which humans were created. God is made up of Father, Son and Holy Spirit. He is a Triune Being, therefore humans are a reflection of this Being. The Father is the Mind, the Body is Christ and The Spirit of course is the Holy Ghost (My interpretation). Ref: "In the beginning God" Gen 1:1. God (in His creative ability created from the mind), created the heavens and the earth. God here is projecting and seen as one person but in Gen 1:26, He is seen as several people in One. John 1:1, speaks of God being three people as One as well. "In the beginning was the Word, {(. . . the Word became flesh and dwelt among us John 1:14) Which is The Body}, and the Word was with God, and the Word was God. He was in the beginning with God (The Father/MasterMind). All things were made through Him, and without Him nothing was made that was made. In Him was life (breathe of life/ the Holy Spirit), and the life (Zoe), was the light of men. And the light shines in the darkness, and the darkness did not comprehend it." John 1:1. We all know that Jesus did not begin His ministry until the Holy Ghost decended on Him. He even instructed his followers to remain in Jerusalem until The Holy Spirit was sent to them, then continued with His ministry.

So God used this intricate model of His to design and create the human race. Ref:

Then God said, "Let Us make man in Our image, according to Our likeness; . . . So God created man in His own image; in the image of God He created him; male and female He created them." Gen 1:26-27. So Adam's Anatomy is compiled of:

1. <u>The soul; in it was/is the mind, emotions and will.</u>

- The mind is the processor (intellect) of bodily functions: what is seen, heard, felt, tasted and smelled
- The emotions are the outcome of bodily functions, and able to express feelings based on what is processed by these bodily functions spontaneously (physiological changes). Out of it comes or spring the issues of life and is often called the heart because the emotions are tied to the heart.
- The will is the ability to deliberately decide based on the above factors (i.e. the intellect vs. emotions). The will is the mover/shaker. The will makes deliberate decisions based on all of these factors described above to suite oneself. You create or destroy a life based on this thing called will. You obey or disobey God or the powers that be, which are ordained by God by the way, (Rom 13:1).

2. <u>The spirit; is the force or breathe of the Almighty:</u>

(. . . and breathed into his nostrils the breath of life. Genesis 2:7). It can be polluted. It is like an empty vessel that can be filled with the breath of Life (God) or another. It is the driving force of what you believe and cannot be felt, (. . . and man became a living being, Genesis 2:7). I have heard people say that they feel spirits and that's not it. You can sense a spirit and know when there's a presence with you or around you but cannot feel a spirit like an emotion. When you die, the spirit goes back to its maker but the soul goes wherever, either with your spirit to heaven or hell. There is a separation between your soul and spirit if you go to hell. Because God breathed into your Spirit, nothing can or ever will be able to fill the spirit person but God . . . I have heard people say after all they've done in their lives, the still feel empty. That's because your spirit man is your connector/channel to the spiritual realm and the mind is always the processor of what is in your spirit, depending on what you feed and fill your spirit with. God takes back His spirit, when you die because His breath of life is not in it anymore, but your soul goes up or down. You either become eternally one with the spirit or eternally separated from your spirit! The devil is not or ever has or ever been the Giver of Life!! ONLY GOD IS!

3. <u>The Body;</u>

. . . was formed out of the dust of the ground by God, (Gen 2:7). The way dust comes in different colors so do humans. That's where race derives from, along with the geographical location and how it relates to the regions, beliefs and myths of a particular race. A belief/myth and a behavioral pattern becomes norm, hence culture of a people is born. Getting back to the body, it houses and covers the mind and spirit. Brain for instance is the physical component of the mind and will. The heart is the physical manifestation of the emotions. With the eyes we see, with the ears we hear, with the nose we smell, with the tongue we taste and with our fingers and other physical parts we are able to feel and all of these functions are processed by the mind. It is written that the life is in the blood. I would say that the blood is a natural/physical component that symbolizes the unseen life of the spirit. This is all a compilation of my thoughts and ideas. Like Paul said it is I that speak and not the Lord, I say the same as well. God promised his covenant keeping people that they are covered, literally. The physically body and the spiritual body (Body of Christ) covers the soul and spirit both physically and spiritually!!!

Entrance 1: The Mouth/WORDS

"It is not what enters into the mouth that defiles the man, but what proceeds out of the mouth, this defiles the man" Matt 15:11, and ". . . the things that proceed out of the mouth come from the heart, and those defile the man," Matt 15:18 "for out of the abundance of the heart the mouth speaks" Matt 12:34. "For by your words you shall be justified, and by your words you shall be condemned" Matt 12:27 and ". . . every careless word that people speak, they shall give an accounting for it in the day of judgment" Matt 12:36. "And the tongue is a fire, a world of iniquity: so is the tongue among our members, that it defiles the whole body, and sets on fire the course of nature; and it is set on fire of hell" James 3:6.

Solution: {tame the tongue (James 3:1-12)}

"Jesus answered, 'It is written: Man does not live on bread alone, but by every word that proceeds from the mouth of God'" Matt/ Luke 4:4, "avoid/shun profane and vain babblings (Godless, worldly and empty) chatter for they will increase to more ungodliness" II Timothy 2:16 "let your speech always be with grace, as though seasoned with salt, so that you will know how you should respond to each person" Col 4:6. "If anyone does not stumble in word, he is a perfect man, able also to bridle the whole body" James 3:1. "Better is the poor that walks in his integrity, than he that is perverse in his lips, and is a fool" Proverbs 19:1

Entrance 2: The Eyes

"Your eye is the lamp of your body. When your eyes are good, your whole body also is full of light. But when they are bad, your body also is full of darkness" Luke 11:34-36; Matt 6:22-23. What you see is what you get. If you allow your eyes to see evil, then the darkness of the evil will fill your body, and if you allow yourself to see good, light will fill your body. "Woe to you, blind guides, who say, 'Whoever swears by the temple, that is nothing; but whoever swears by the gold of the temple is obligated." Matt 23:16 "You blind guides, who strain out a gnat and swallow a camel!" Matt 23:24. Unless there's light in the way no one can see the path.

Solution:

Saturate your lives with the light of the gospel by reading, and exposing our eyes to that which is Holy. "Leave those blind guides alone (for there is no light in their eyes). If a blind man leads a blind man, both will fall into a pit" Matt 15:14. "For the commandment is a lamp and the teaching is light; and reproofs for discipline are the way of life" Prov 6:23. "Thy word is a lamp unto my feet, and a light unto my path" Psalm 119:105 got to get the Light through the eyes.

Entrance 3: The Ears

"This is the only thing I want to find out from you: did you receive the Spirit by the works of the Law, or by hearing with faith?" Gal 3:2. "So then, does He who provides you with the Spirit and works miracles among you, do it by the works of the Law, or by hearing with faith?" Gal 3:5. Do not be like these categories of people . . . "and in them is fulfilled the prophecy of Isaiah, which said, By hearing you shall hear, and shall not understand; and seeing you shall see, and shall not perceive" Matt 13:14. ". . . If you do not obey the voice of the LORD, but rebel against the commandment of the LORD, then the hand of the LORD will be against you, as it was against your fathers" 1 Sam 12:14-15

Solution:

". . . Faith comes by hearing, hearing by the word of God" Rom 10:17. "However, they did not all heed the good news; for Isaiah says, "LORD, WHO HAS BELIEVED OUR REPORT?" Romans 10:16: Heeding good news. It is life to those who hearken. Expose yourself to the Word of God. "If you fear the LORD and serve Him and obey His voice, and do not rebel against the commandment of the LORD, then both you and the king who reigns over you will continue following the LORD your God" 1 Sam 12:14-14. "Only if you carefully obey the voice of the LORD your God, to observe with care all these commandments which I command you today" Deuteronomy 15:5, "and all these blessings shall come upon you and overtake you, because you obey the voice of the LORD your God:" Deuteronomy 28:2.

Entrance 4: Taste

Eating of foods forbidden to man has the potential of destroying the temple by causing terminal illnesses that cannot be cured by modern medicine. The children of Israel were given instructions on what to eat, what not to eat, what to touch and what not to touch. "Now the LORD spoke to Moses and Aaron, saying to them, 'Speak to the children of Israel, saying, (i) 'These are the animals which you may eat . . . whatever divides the hoof, having cloven hooves and chewing the cud that you may eat. Nevertheless these you shall not eat among those that chew the cud or those that have cloven hooves: the camel, because it chews the cud but does not have cloven hooves, is unclean to you; the rock hyrax, because it chews the cud but does not have cloven hooves, is unclean to you; the hare, because it chews the cud but does not have cloven hooves, is unclean to you; and the swine, though it divides the hoof, having cloven hooves, yet does not chew the cud, is unclean to you. Their flesh you shall not eat, and their carcasses you shall not touch. They are unclean to you. (ii)These you may eat of all that are in the water: whatever in the water has fins and scales, whether in the seas or in the rivers that you may eat. But all in the seas or in the rivers that do not have fins and scales, all that move in the water or any living thing which is in the water, they are an abomination to you . . . and you shall regard their carcasses as an abomination. Whatever in the water does not have fins or scales that shall be an abomination to you. (iii)And these you shall regard as an abomination among the birds; they shall not be eaten, they are an abomination: the eagle, the vulture, the buzzard, the kite, and the falcon after its kind; every raven after its kind, the ostrich, the short-eared owl, the sea gull, and the hawk after its kind; the little owl, the fisher owl, and the screech owl; the white owl, the jackdaw, and the carrion vulture; the stork, the heron after its kind, the hoopoe, and the bat. (iv)All flying insects that creep on all fours shall be an abomination to you. Yet these you may eat of every flying insect that creeps on all fours: those which have jointed legs above their feet with which to leap on the earth. These you may eat: the locust after its kind, the destroying locust after its kind, the cricket after its kind, and the grasshopper after its kind. But all other flying insects which have four feet shall be an abomination to you." Leviticus 11:1-23. (v) ". . . You shall not boil a young goat in its mother's milk" Deuteronomy 14:21.

Entrance 5: The Eyes

"Do you not know that unrighteousness will not inherit the Kingdom of God? Do not be deceived. Neither fornicators, nor idolaters, nor adulterers, nor homosexuals, nor sodomites . . . will inherit the Kingdom of God" 1 Corinthians 6:9. "No temptation has overtaken you except that which is common to man. But God is faithful who will not allow you to be tempted beyond what you are able, but with the temptation will also make a way of escape, that you may be able to bear it" 1 Corinthians 10:13. "Do you not know that your body is the temple of the Holy Spirit, who is in you, whom you have received from God? You are not your own" 1 Corinthians 6:19. "Meats for the belly and belly for meats: but God will destroy it and them. Now the body is not for fornication, but for the Lord; and the Lord for the body" 1 Corinthians 6:13. "For all that is in the world, the lust of the flesh, the lust of the eyes, and the pride of life, and the pride of life—is not of the Father, but is of the world" 1 John 2:15.

Solution:

"Give no room/place to the devil" Ephesians 4:27, "and submit therefore to God. Resist the devil and he will flee from you" James 4:7. "All things are lawful for me but not all things are expedient/helpful. All things are lawful for me but I will not be brought under the power of any" 1 Corinthians 6:12.

Avoid Fornication! "Flee also youthful lusts; but pursue righteousness, faith, love, peace with those who call on the Lord with a pure heart" II Timothy 2:22. "But fornication and all uncleanness or covetousness, let it not be named among you, as is fitting for saints;" Ephesians 5:3. There is no better way to say it. Staying away is the only way (celibacy), OR pursue the ultimate solution . . . "Marriage is honorable among all and the bed undefiled; but fornicators and adulterers GOD will judge" Hebrews 13:4.

MIND, WILL, and EMOTIONS:

We mentioned earlier that the mind is the processor. It is your responsibility to block or allow what goes in to your mind for processing and out of it as well. 'Cast down imaginations and every high thing that exalts itself against the knowledge of God; bring into captivity every thought to the obedience of Christ' II Corinthians 10:15. ". . . do not be conformed to this world, but be transformed by the renewing of your mind, that you may prove what is that good, and acceptable and the perfect will of God" Rom 12:22. "And that you be renewed in the spirit of your mind" Ephesians 4:23, ". . . try to learn what is pleasing to the Lord" Ephesians 5:10, by reading His Word.

"He who has no rule over his spirit is like a city broken down, and without walls" Proverbs 25:28, "and he who is slow to anger is better than the mighty, and he who rules his spirit than he who captures/takes a city" Proverbs 16:32. "There are many devices in a man's heart; never the less the counsel of God that shall stand" Proverbs 19:21. "Counsel in the heart of a man is like deep water, but a man of understanding will draw it out" Proverbs 20:5. "He taught me also, and said to me, 'let your heart retain my words; keep my commandments and live" Proverbs 4:4 and "above all else GUARD YOUR HEART with all diligence, for out of springs/ comes the issues of life" Proverbs 4:23 "the just man walks in his integrity and his children are blessed after him" Proverbs 20:7.

THE BODY as YOUR TEMPLE:

"You are the children of the Lord you God; you shall not cut yourselves, nor shave the front of your head for the dead!! For you are a Holy people to the Lord your God, and the Lord has chosen you to be a people for Himself, a special treasure above all people who are on the face of the earth" Deuteronomy 14:1-2, "For you were bought with a price, therefore glorify God in your body and in your spirit which are God's" 1 Corinthians 6:20.

". . . Be not deceived: drunkards, shall not inherit the kingdom of God" 1 Corinthians 6:10

"Let us behave properly as in the day, not in carousing and drunkenness, not in sexual promiscuity and sensuality, not in strife and jealousy" Romans 13:13; "Wine is a mocker, strong drink a brawler, And whoever is intoxicated by it is not wise" Proverbs 20:1. "But actually, I wrote to you not to associate with any so-called brother if he is an immoral person, or covetous, or an idolater, or a reviler, or a drunkard, or a swindler—not even to eat with such a one" 1 Corinthians 5:11; and most of all ". . . be not drunk with wine, wherein is excess; but be filled with the Spirit;" Ephesians 5:18. The bible condemns excessive use of wine even though apostle Paul encourages believers to drink a little wine for the benefit of the stomach . . . "Drink no longer water, but use a little wine for your stomach's sake and your often infirmities" 1 Timothy 5:23, and in communion and breaking of bread wine was used. "Woe unto them that rise up early in the morning, that they may follow strong drink; that continue until night, till wine inflames them!" Isaiah 5:11. "Now the works of the flesh are manifest, which are these . . . drunkenness . . ." Galatians 5:19-20.

Laziness (slothfulness) and lack of exercise leads to excess buildup of fat that has the ability to shut bodily functions down. Too much buildup of fat is unhealthy. Scripture says, "by much slothfulness, the building decayeth and through idleness of the hands the house droppeth through" Ecclesiastes 10:18. We're talking about the building that is the temple where the Holy Spirit resides. It has to be taken care of like you would the one you physically live in.

"But you are a chosen generation, a royal priesthood, an holy nation, a peculiar people; that you should show forth the praises of him who has called you out of darkness into his marvelous light;" 1 Peter 2:9. "Now may the God of peace Himself sanctify you completely, and may your whole Spirit, Soul and Body be preserved blameless at the coming of our Lord Jesus Christ" 1 Thessalonians 5:23.

Be on your Guard and Beware . . . You Are royalty!

CHAPTER 17

New Wine Withheld

"Awake, you drunkards, and weep; and howl, all you drinkers of wine, because of the new wine; for it is cut off from your mouth" Joel 1:5. "The grain offering and the drink offering are cut off from the house of the LORD. The priests mourn, the ministers of the LORD, The field is wasted, and the land mourns; for the corn is wasted: the new wine is dried up, the oil languishes" Joel 1:9-10. "Has not the food been cut off before our very eyes—joy and gladness from the house of our God? The seeds are shriveled beneath the clods. The storehouses are in ruins, the granaries have been broken down, for the grain has dried up. How the cattle moan! The herds mill about because they have no pasture; even the flocks of sheep are suffering" Joel 1:16-18. "Yea, truth faileth (and is lacking); and he who departeth from evil maketh himself a prey: and the LORD saw it, and it displeased him that there was no judgment" Isaiah 59:15. Yea this are the last days and ". . . the Spirit speaks expressly, that in the latter times some shall depart from the faith, giving heed to seducing spirits, and doctrines of devils;" I Timothy 4:1.

It has been said from the pulpits and those that have experienced God know that it gets worse before it gets better. For God to establish the new He has to remove the old and in order to get the old out there has to be a disturbance and a shaking. The boat must be rocked in order for change to come. There'll be grievances and offenses to lead you to that change. Like a woman in travail when the baby is about to pop, we're in the birthing room about to give birth to whatever it is we've been carrying as a body as individuals. Here is dilemma; there are those that will give birth to real babies (miracles and a manifestation of their expectations) and those that'll give birth to wing according Is 58. Depending on how your pregnancy has been and how you have handled Spiritual things, there will be a reaping, a birthing.

God has a solution and this is it. "Mourn like a virgin in sackcloth grieving for the husband of her youth." Joel 1:8. "Gird yourselves, and lament, you priests: howl, you ministers of the altar: come, lie all night in sackcloth, you ministers of my God: for the meat offering and the drink offering is withheld from the house of your God" Joel 1:13-14. "Even now,' declares the Lord, 'return to me with all your heart, with fasting and weeping and mourning. Rend your heart, and not your garments, and turn to the LORD your God: for he is gracious and merciful, slow to anger, and of great kindness, and repents him of the evil. Who knows if he will return and repent, and leave a blessing behind him; even a meat offering and a drink offering to the LORD your God?" Joel 2:12-14.

"And Moses said unto Aaron, Take a censer, and put fire therein from off the altar, and put on incense, and go quickly unto the congregation, and make atonement for them: for there is wrath gone out from the LORD; the plague is begun. And Aaron took as Moses commanded, and ran into the midst of the congregation; and, behold, the plague was begun among the people: and he put on incense, and made atonement for the people. And he stood between the dead and the living; and the plague was stayed. Now they that died in the plague were fourteen thousand and seven hundred, beside them that died about the matter of Korah. And Aaron returned unto Moses unto the door of the tabernacle of the congregation: and the plague was stayed" Numb 16:46-50

Until the spirit be poured on us from on high, and the wilderness be a fruitful field, and the fruitful field be counted for a forest. Then judgment shall dwell in the wilderness, and righteousness remains in the fruitful field. Isaiah 32:15-16. "No one tears a patch from a new garment and sews it on an old one. If he does, he will have torn the new garment, and the patch from the new will not match the old. And no one pours new wine into old wineskins. If he does, the new wine will burst the skins, the wine will run out and the wineskins will be ruined. No, new wine must be poured into new wineskins. And no one after drinking old wine wants the new, for he says, 'The old is better.'" Luke 5:36-39

It will take a united effort; this is not a one man's show. One can chase a thousand and two can put ten thousand to flight. It'll take fasting, praying, giving, wisdom for strategy and observing to according to all that is written there in, in order to bring it to pass. In a nut shell get ready to bring forth. Your time has come but you have to work for it. It won't come cheap but you'll get it for free.

Harness The Power!!

CHAPTER **18**

Protecting Promise

Every time God wanted to reveal Himself to someone in a Godless society, He searched, found, called and revealed His plan and purpose coupled with a promise of reward and separated him/her from their familiar surroundings and environment to a secluded place where He could get their undivided attention. It doesn't end there, after a series of tests and trials to test their faithfulness; He fulfills His promise (His covenant) and gives them His rest. An example: "For the LORD's portion is his people; Jacob is the lot of his inheritance. He found him in a desert land, and in the waste howling wilderness; he led him about, he instructed him, he kept him as the apple of his eye. As an eagle stirreth up her nest, fluttereth over her young, spreadeth abroad her wings, taketh them, beareth them on her wings:" Deuteronomy 32:9-11. That has been the case since the beginning of time. Even though He does not change, He does a new thing with the same result of getting them to their final destination.

"The LORD had said to Abram, 'Leave your country, your people and your father's household and go to the land I will show you. I will make you into a great nation and I will bless you; I will make your name great, and you will be a blessing. I will bless those who bless you, and whoever curses you I will curse; and all peoples on earth will be blessed through you" Genesis 12:1-3. After Abram left, Genesis 12:4-6, ". . . the LORD appeared to Abram and said, "To your descendants I will give this land" Genesis 12:7. Abraham had to be separated from his comfort zone and unbelieving family in order to protect the promise of God to him. Not knowing where he was going, showed his faith in the God who led Him, and the bible says in Romans 4:3 that "it was accounted to him for righteousness."

Hearing is not the problem, the greatest challenge is stepping out by faith knowing and believing that "faithful is He that called you and he will do it" I Thessalonians 5:24; Psalms 37:4-5. Trust in God must be shaken in order to be found true. "He will not leave you comfortless," John 14:18 ". . . will not leave you nor forsake you" Deuteronomy 31:8, Josh 1:5; Hebrews 13:6. You are never alone. He'll give you His rod and His staff to protect you. * His rod to correct you and *His staff to shepherd you, But He will bless you and your descendants for obeying and standing on His word and trusting that He will fulfill every promise. Adam lost His promise but Jesus restored it. God is Holy and everything around Him that belongs to Him must be Holy. If there's rebellion in the camp, He will cause you to separate yourself from the wickedness and keep you for Him. He hates sin and in order to get rid of the sin, often the sinner is taken in the process. In order for you to protect the things God has entrusted you like a good steward, there'll be a separation.

"The sons of Abraham were Isaac and Ishmael" I Chronicles 1:28. Abraham (and Sarah) separated Isaac from Ishmael, "Now Sarah saw the son of Hagar the Egyptian, whom she had borne to Abraham, mocking Isaac. Therefore she said to Abraham, 'Drive out this maid and her son, for the son of this maid shall not be an heir with my son Isaac. Abraham became very disturbed because of his son. But God said to Abraham, 'Do not be distressed because of the lad and your maid; whatever Sarah tells you, listen to her, for through Isaac your descendants shall be named. And of the son of the maid I will make a nation also, because he is your descendant.' So Abraham rose early in the morning and took bread and a skin of water and gave them to Hagar, putting them on her shoulder, and gave her the boy, and sent her away. And she departed and wandered about in the wilderness of Beersheba." Genesis 21:9-14.

Abraham separated himself from Lot, "So Abram said to Lot, 'Please let there be no strife between you and me, or between my herdsmen and your herdsmen, for we are brothers. Is not the whole land before you' Please separate from me; if to the left, then I will go to the right; or if to the right, then I will go to the left" Genesis

13:8-9 read the whole of Gen 13. For there to be peace between the two families there had to be a separation and after they separated, then God told Abraham to lift up his eyes and look as far as his eyes could see because God had given Him those lands. But there had to be a separation!

And Jacob began to see the blessings of God after he left his parents when his brother wanted to kill him. His mother told him to leave as we see here "Now therefore, my son, obey my voice, and arise, flee to Haran, to my brother Laban" Genesis 27:43. "So Isaac called for Jacob and blessed him and commanded him: 'Do not marry a Canaanite woman . . . May God Almighty bless you and make you fruitful and increase your numbers until you become a community of peoples. May he give you and your descendants the blessing given to Abraham, so that you may take possession of the land where you now live as an alien, the land God gave to Abraham" Genesis 28:1-4. "Now Esau saw that Isaac had blessed Jacob and sent him away to Paddan-aram to take to himself a wife from there, and that when he blessed him he charged him, saying, 'You shall not take a wife from the daughters of Canaan,' and Jacob obeyed his father and mother and had gone to Paddan Aram." Genesis 28:6-7. From Genesis 29, he found his mother's side of the family, lived with his mother's brother and prospered, but he had to physically separate himself from his brother in order to protect his promise. He worked for his uncle and God blessed him indeed. It took some drama on his part. He deceived his father and Laban his uncle deceived him in return . . . but God blessed him all the same because he separated himself from his familiar surroundings.

"Wherefore Come ye out from among them, and be ye separate, saith the Lord, and touch no unclean thing; And I will receive you," II Corinthians 6:17. There has to be a separation in order to protect your promise. God desires your undivided attention.

Protect Your Promise

CHAPTER **19**

Blamers Of God, It's A Cleansing, A Trial and Yes God's Either In It or Not!!!

To The Redeemed:

From time to time Christians have had the tendency to blame God for their negative circumstances. Job couldn't say it better. He learnt to live with or without as seen in this passage of scripture, "But he said to her, you speak as one of the foolish women speaks. What? Shall we receive good at the hand of God, and shall we not receive evil? In all this did not Job sin with his lips" Job 2:10. He maintained a perfect attitude and was thankful in everything. The Bible speaks of blessings and rewards to those who maintain a positive attitude. "Blessed is a man who perseveres under trial; for once he has been approved, he will receive the crown of life which the Lord has promised to those who love Him" James 1:12.

In Job 1:18-19, "While he was still speaking, another also came and said, 'Your sons and your daughters were eating and drinking wine in their oldest brother's house, when suddenly a mighty wind swept in from the desert and struck the four corners of the house. It collapsed on them and they are dead, and I am the only one who has escaped to tell you!" BUT God was not in it! "Then Job arose and tore his robe and shaved his head, and he fell to the ground and worshiped" Job 1:20.

Elijah is a man that walked with God. And one day "the LORD said, 'go out and stand on the mountain in the presence of the LORD, for the LORD is about to pass by." Then a great and powerful wind tore the mountains apart and shattered the rocks before the LORD, but the LORD was not in the wind. After the wind there was an earthquake, but the LORD was not in the earthquake. And after the earthquake a fire; but the LORD was not in the fire: and after the fire a still small voice" I Kings 19:11-12.

Jesus said that tribulation will come; another passage reads that we as Christians will have to face offensive situations, but woe to the person through whom these offenses come. "And the tempter came and said to Him, "If You are the Son of God, . . ." Matthew 4:3. These situations will arise more times than we can count, and the way to handle situations like these is preparation. That day when evening came, he said to his disciples, "Let us go over to the other side. Leaving the crowd behind, they took him along, just as he was, in the boat. There were also other boats with him. And there arose a great storm of wind, and the waves beat into the ship, so that it was now full. Jesus Himself was in the stern, asleep on the cushion; (God was not in it) and they woke Him and said to Him, "Teacher, do you not care that we are perishing?? And he arose, and rebuked the wind, and said to the sea, Peace, be still. And the wind ceased, and there was a great calm" Mark 4:35-39.

Solution 1: Prophesy to the wind;

"Then said he to me, Prophesy to the wind, prophesy, son of man, and say to the wind" Ezekiel 37:9

Solution 2: Rebuke the wind;

"And he arose, and rebuked the wind, and said unto the sea, Peace, be still. And the wind ceased, and there was a great calm" Mark 4:39.

Solution 3: If all else fails, look to Jesus.

"He who dwells in the secret place of the Most High shall abide under the shadow of the Almighty. I will say of the LORD, 'He is my refuge and my fortress; My God, in Him I will trust.' Surely He shall deliver you from the snare of the fowler and from the perilous pestilence. He shall cover you with His feathers, and under His wings you shall take refuge; His truth shall be your shield and buckler. You shall not be afraid of the terror by night, nor of the arrow that flies by day, nor of the pestilence that walks in darkness, nor of the destruction that lays waste at noonday. A thousand may fall at your side, and ten thousand at your right hand; but it shall not come near you. Only with your eyes shall you look, and see the reward of the wicked. Because you have made the LORD, who is my refuge, even the Most High, your dwelling place, no evil shall befall you, nor shall any plague come near your dwelling; for He shall give His angels charge over you, to keep you in all your ways. In their hands they shall bear you up, lest you dash your foot against a stone. You shall tread upon the lion and the cobra, the young lion and the serpent you shall trample underfoot. Because he has set his love upon Me, therefore I will deliver him; I will set him on high, because he has known My name. He shall call upon Me, and I will answer him; I will be with him in trouble; will deliver him and honor him. With long life I will satisfy him and show him My salvation." Psalms 91:1-16

God has given His people everything they need for this journey that enables us to overcome every problem. God uses these circumstances in the lives of believers' in order to flex our spiritual muscles and to learn to trust Him and if a cleansing occurs the righteous will be purged the wicked eliminated.

But To The Unbeliever:

I say to you it's judgment time. If the hand of God is not on you, God is so in it and the covering of the Almighty isn't on you, leaving you vulnerable and susceptible to doom, danger and destruction. Unlike the redeemed of the Lord, when trouble comes upon you, it comes to consume and destroy. "Therefore, thus says the Lord GOD, 'I will make a violent wind break out in My wrath. There will also be in My anger a flooding rain and hailstones to consume it in wrath" Ezekiel 13:13. "And the LORD shall cause his glorious voice to be heard, and shall show the lighting down of his arm, with the indignation of his anger, and with the flame of a devouring fire, with scattering, and tempest, and hailstones" Is

30:30. God is so in it!! "Behold, a whirlwind of the LORD is gone forth in fury, even a grievous whirlwind: it shall fall grievously on the head of the wicked" Jeremiah 23:19. "Behold, the whirlwind of the LORD goes forth with fury, a continuing whirlwind (sweeping tempest): it shall fall with pain on the head of the wicked" Jeremiah 30:23.

"This is what the LORD says: . . . But I will kindle a fire in the wall of Rabbah, and it shall devour the palaces thereof, with shouting in the day of battle, with a tempest in the day of the whirlwind:" Amos 1:14. "And the temple of God was opened in heaven, and there was seen in his temple the ark of his testament: and there were lightning, and voices, and thunder, and an earthquake, and great hail" Revelation 11:19.

"And there fell on men a great hail out of heaven, every stone about the weight of a talent: and men blasphemed God because of the plague of the hail; for the plague thereof was exceeding great" Revelation 16:21. "So I will pour out my wrath on them and consume them with my fiery anger, bringing down on their own heads all they have done, declares the Sovereign LORD." Ezekiel 22:31.

"From the LORD of hosts you will be punished with thunder and earthquake and loud noise, with whirlwind and tempest and the flame of a consuming fire" Isaiah 29:6. "Also, you son of man, thus said the Lord GOD to the land of Israel; An end, the end is come on the four corners of the land. Now the end is upon you, and I will send My anger against you; I will judge you according to your ways and bring all your abominations upon you. For My eye will have no pity on you, nor will I spare you, but I will bring your ways upon you, and your abominations will be among you; then you will know that I am the LORD! "Thus says the Lord GOD, 'A disaster, unique disaster, behold it is coming!" Ezekiel 7:2-5. I don't like to be the prophet of doom but the message has to be conveyed. Choose Life that you might live. "Say ye to the righteous, that it shall be well with him: for they shall eat the fruit of their doings" Is 3:10. But "woe to the wicked! it shall be ill with him: for the reward of his hands shall be given him," Isaiah 3:11.

The mother of all cleansing:

"And the LORD said, "My Spirit shall not strive with man forever, for he is indeed flesh; yet his days shall be one hundred and twenty years.' There were giants on the earth in those days, and also afterward, when the sons of God came in to the daughters of men and they bore children to them. Those were the mighty men who were of old, men of renown. Then the LORD saw that the wickedness of man was great in the earth, and that every intent of the thoughts of his heart was only evil continually. And the LORD was sorry that He had made man on the earth, and He was grieved in His heart. So the LORD said, 'I will destroy man whom I have created from the face of the earth, man and beast, creeping thing and birds of the air, for I am sorry that I have made them.' But Noah found grace in the eyes of the LORD. This is the genealogy of Noah.

Noah was a just man, perfect in his generations. Noah walked with God. And Noah begot three sons: Shem, Ham, and Japheth. The earth also was corrupt before God, and the earth was filled with violence. So God looked upon the earth, and indeed it was corrupt; for all flesh had corrupted their way on the earth. And God said to Noah, 'The end of all flesh has come before Me, for the earth is filled with violence through them; and behold, I will destroy them with the earth. Make yourself an ark of gopher wood; make rooms in the ark, and cover it inside and outside with pitch. And this is how you shall make it: The length of the ark shall be three hundred cubits, its width fifty cubits, and its height thirty cubits. You shall make a window for the ark, and you shall finish it to a cubit from above; and set the door of the ark in its side. You shall make it with lower, second, and third decks.

And behold, I Myself am bringing floodwaters on the earth, to destroy from under heaven all flesh in which is the breath of life; everything that is on the earth shall die. But I will establish My covenant with you; and you shall go into the ark—you, your sons, your wife, and your sons' wives with you. And of every living thing of all flesh you shall bring two of every sort into the ark, to keep them alive with you; they shall be male and female. Of the birds after their kind, of animals after their kind, and of every creeping thing of the earth after its kind, two of every kind will come to you to keep them alive. And you shall take for yourself of all food that is eaten, and you shall gather it to yourself; and it shall be food for you and for them. Thus Noah did; according to all that God commanded him, so he did" Gen 6:3-22. God is Holy, therefore everything that belongs to Him must be Holy, including the earth and everything it it!

Behold I place before you Life and Death

CHAPTER 20

The Substance Called Faith

Faith in my definition is the commodity of value that the potential of creating, producing, bringing forth, bearing fruit, bringing to existence and making a reality into the natural realm what could only exist as a dream, vision, desire or hope.

"Now faith is the substance of things hoped for, the evidence of things not seen" Hebrews 11:1. We have to have the capability of "calling those things which be not as though they were," Romans 4:7. It is a complex substance acquired and deposited by belief in a Supernatural being, God that enables you to achieve the impossible. It is often bigger that you.

A few of its characteristics include:

1. It is a NOW Commodity:

As recorded above, Hebrews 11:1 clearly states "now faith is . . ." Like new wine on new wineskin in Luke 5:37, 38, as God's mercies are new every morning (Lamentations 3:23-24) and like fresh manna that was only good for the day in Exodus 16:4-21, old faith is stale faith. It doesn't do any good and it is powerless. God is doing a new thing (Isaiah 43:19) and we have to have faith right now and needs to remain a now factor. It operates on present participle mode. We believe God (through faith) right now for miracles, manifestations, signs and wonders, dreams and visions to bud and become a reality which are right now mere dreams, night visions and nonexistent in the natural realm. The ongoing process of believing God and having faith in the present for the future is continuous, thus present participle.

2. Cannot Please God Without It:

"And without faith it is impossible to please God, because anyone who comes to him must believe that he exists and that he rewards those who earnestly seek him" Hebrews 11:6. God complains about children in whom there is no faith in Deuteronomy 32:12 and again in Matthew 17:17 about the faithless and perverse generation and was concerned how long he was going to bear with them. Faith is the heart of Christianity without it you cannot please God nor enter into your rest (place of promise for His covenant keeping children), Psalms 95:9-11, Numbers 14:23, Deuteronomy 1:35, Hebrews 4:3. It's like a man without a heart or brain. Cannot function properly let alone live without faith as a Christian. You might as well be a blasphemous uncircumcised Philistine (Pagan). The bible refers to faithless people as reprobate, resisting the truth according to II Timothy 3:8. God called it "an evil heart of unbelief" in Hebrews 3:12. Fear and doubt are enemies of faith and work against faith so that the outcome of faith doesn't come to fruition. Fear and doubt is a miracle blocker and that's why Jesus didn't perform many miracles if at all in cities and towns where there was unbelief and lack of faith (Matthew 13:58). If manifestations are to take place then faith has to be present. The lack of faith brings a lack of fruition of dreams and visions. It is God who brings them to pass therefore God has to be pleased and we can only please Him through faith. A sad truth is "even after Jesus had done all these miraculous signs in their presence, they still would not believe in him" John 12:37.

3. It comes in Measures:

"In accordance with the measure of faith God has given us . . . we ought to think and act with humility and not more highly than we ought," Romans 12:3. God deposits a certain measure of faith in our spirits depending on how well we know Him and how determined we are in seeing results. For babes he gives little faith and as you get to know Him that faith increases. But there were rare cases like with the story of the Phoenician woman and the crumbs from the masters table in the gospels, she was a gentile and had seen the miracles and wasn't going to take no for an answer. So she pushed for a miracle and Jesus had to give her want she wanted because of her faith. Faith is tied to the knowledge of Him and begins where the will of God is known. Matthew 15:28 records of a woman with great faith and because of her great faith her daughter was healed. Matthew 8:10 and Luke 7:9 records faith, that startled and surprised Jesus to the point where He confessed and commented that "He had not seen such great faith in all of Israel." He replied, because you have so little faith. I tell you the truth, if you have faith as small as a mustard seed, you can say to this mountain, 'Move from here to there' and it will move. Nothing will be impossible for you? Matthew 17:20.? If that is how God clothes the grass of the field, which is here today and tomorrow is thrown into the fire, will he not much more clothe you, O you of little faith?? Matthew 6:30. "He replied, you of little faith, why are you so afraid? Then he got up and rebuked the winds and the waves, and it was completely calm? Matthew 8:26. "Immediately Jesus stretched out His hand and took hold of him, and said to him, "You of little faith, why did you doubt?" Matthew 14:31.

The Solution:

"Let us draw near with a true heart in full assurance of faith, having our hearts sprinkled from an evil conscience, and our bodies washed with pure water" Hebrews 10:22. Have to have faith in complete and full measures for a manifestation of God's promises.

4. Comes by Hearing:

Factual people always dwell on the fact that Peter started to sink because he doubted and pay less attention to the fact that he actually walked on water. Jesus' disciples saw Him walk on water and were terrified and thought it was a ghost, "but immediately Jesus spoke unto them saying 'take courage, it is I: do not be afraid.' And Peter answered Him and said 'Lord if it be you bid me come to you on the water.' And He said 'come!' And Peter got out of the boat walked on water and came toward Jesus" Matthew 14:27-29. "So then faith comes by hearing and hearing by the Word of God"

Romans 10:17; "Man shall not live by bread alone but by every Word that proceeds out of the mouth of God" Matthew 4:4; Luke 4:4. "This only would I learn of you, Received you the Spirit by the works of the law, or by the hearing of faith" Galatians 3:2. "He therefore that ministers to you the Spirit, and works miracles among you, does he it by the works of the law, or by the hearing of faith" Galatians 3:5. "Truly I say to you, whoever says to this mountain, 'Be taken up and cast into the sea,' and does not doubt in his heart, but believes that what he says is going to happen, it will be granted him" Mark 11:23; Matt 21:21.

5. Acts as a Shield:

"Above all, taking the shield of faith, with which you shall be able to quench all the fiery darts of the wicked" Ephesians 6:16. "But let us, who are of the day, be sober, putting on the breastplate of faith and love; and for a helmet, the hope of salvation" I Thessalonians 5:8. Faith is a shield.

6. Should be blind:

"('For we walk by faith, not by sight: ')" II Corinthians 5:7. "But when he saw the wind, he was afraid and, beginning to sink, cried out, 'Lord, save me'! Immediately Jesus stretched out His hand and took hold of him, and said to him, "You of little faith, why did you doubt?" Matthew 14:31. "The disciples went and woke him, saying, "Master, Master, we're going to drown!" He got up and rebuked the wind and the raging waters; the storm subsided, and all was calm" Luke 8:24. This should be the attitude of faith. Not looking at the negative circumstances surrounding us but having faith that all is well. The story of Elisha and the Shunammite woman is a good example of not looking at negative circumstances however hard. "Then he said, 'About this time next year you shall embrace a son.' And she said, 'No, my lord. Man of God, do not lie to your maidservant!' But the woman conceived, and bore a son when the appointed time had come, of which Elisha had told her. And the child grew. Now it happened one day that he went out to his father, to the reapers. And he said to his father, 'My head, my head!' So he said to a servant, 'Carry him to his mother.' When he had taken him and brought him to his mother, he sat on her knees till noon, and then died. And she went up and laid him on the bed of the man of God, shut the door upon him, and went out. Then she called to her husband, and said, 'Please send me one of the young men and one of the donkeys that I may run to the man of God and come back.' So he said, 'Why are you going to him today? It is neither the New Moon nor the Sabbath.' And she said, 'It is well" II Kings 4:16-23.

7.   Should be Strong, Steadfast and Unchanging:

In order for your faith to bring forth, it has to be strong unfailing commanding and unyielding. It's a battle and you have to fight as a Christian. There will be times when your faith will be tested and tried and had better standing the test of time. "Fight the good fight of the faith, take hold of the eternal life to which you were called when you made your good confession in the presence of many witnesses" I Timothy 6:12. "And being not weak in faith, he considered not his own body now dead, when he was about an hundred years old, neither yet the deadness of Sarah's womb" Romans 4:19: "Be on your guard; stand firm in the faith; be men of courage; be strong" I Corinthians 16:13. "Who through faith subdued and conquered kingdoms, worked righteousness, obtained promises, stopped the mouths of lions" Hebrews 11:33. "For whatsoever (whosoever) is born of God overcomes the world: and this is the victory that overcomes the world, even our faith" I John 5:4. My favorite example on faith's strength is found in Romans 4:19, "And being not weak in faith, he considered not his own body now dead, when he was about an hundred years old, neither yet the deadness of Sarah's womb." Do not let your heart grow weak, trust in God! "But let him ask in faith, nothing wavering. For he that wavers is like a wave of the sea driven with the wind and tossed. For let not that man think that he shall receive any thing of the Lord. He is a double-minded man, unstable in all his ways" James 1:6-8. "As a result, we are no longer to be children, tossed here and there by waves and carried about by every wind of doctrine, by the trickery of men, by craftiness in deceitful scheming;" Ephesians 4:14.

8. <u>Works by Love:</u>

"For in Jesus Christ neither circumcision avails anything, nor uncircumcision; but faith which works by love" Galatians 5:6. Love needs to be present in order for faith to become effective. "If I have the gift of prophecy and can fathom all mysteries and all knowledge, and if I have a faith that can move mountains, but have not love, I am nothing" I Corinthians 13:2. "That Christ may dwell in your hearts by faith; that you, being rooted and grounded in love," Ephesians 3:17. Faith alone cannot function without first the Love of God dwelling in our hearts. "There abides these three faith, hope and love, but the greatest of all is love" I Corinthians 13:13. "Constantly bearing in mind your work of faith and labor of love . . ." I Thessalonians 1:3.

9. <u>Have to Work IT:</u>

"We continually remember before our God and Father your work produced by faith . . ." I Thessalonians 1:3. ". . . and fulfill all the good pleasure of his goodness, and the work of faith with power:" II Thessalonians 1:11. "What does it profit, my brothers, though a man say he has faith, and have not works" can faith save him??" James 2:14. "Even so faith, if it has not works, is dead, being alone. Yes, a man may say, you have faith, and I have works: show me your faith without your works, and I will show you my faith by my works" James 2:17, 18. "But will you know, O vain man, that faith without works is dead. Was not Abraham our father justified by works, when he had offered Isaac his son on the altar? See you how faith worked with his works and by works were faith made perfect" James 2:20-22. "You see then how that by works a man is justified, and not by faith only" James 2:24 "For as the body without the spirit is dead, so faith without works is dead also" James 2:26.

10. <u>Should be Inspired by God only:</u>

"That your faith should not stand in the wisdom of men, but in the power of God" I Corinthians 2:5. "This wisdom descends not from above, but is earthly, sensual, devilish" James 3:15. "For the kingdom of God is not in word, but in power" I Corinthians 4:20. "And my speech and my preaching was not with enticing words of man's wisdom, but in demonstration of the Spirit and of power:" I Corinthians 2:4. "Thus said the LORD; 'Cursed be the man that trusts in man, and makes flesh his arm, and whose heart departs from the LORD" Jeremiah 17:5. "With him is an arm of flesh; but with us is the LORD our God to help us, and to fight our battles. And the people rested themselves on the words of Hezekiah king of Judah" II Chronicles 32:8. "You need not fight in this battle; station yourselves, stand and see the salvation of the LORD on your behalf, O Judah and Jerusalem.' Do not fear or be dismayed; tomorrow go out to face them, for the LORD is with you." II Chronicles 20:17. "Do not trust in princes, in mortal man, in whom there is no salvation" Psalms 146:3. "Stop regarding man, whose breath of life is in his nostrils; for why should he be esteemed??" Isaiah 2:22. "Woe to the rebellious children," declares the LORD, "Who execute a plan, but not Mine, And make an alliance, but not of My Spirit, In order to add sin to sin;" Isaiah 30:1 "Now the Egyptians are men and not God, And their horses are flesh and not spirit; So the LORD will stretch out His hand, And he who helps will stumble and he who is helped will fall, and all of them will come to an end together." Isaiah 31:3. "When they took hold of you with the hand, you broke and tore all their hands; and when they leaned on You, You broke and made all their loins quake" Ezekiel 29:7. It is an abomination to put your trust in man and lean on the arm of the flesh. Trust and put you faith in God only.

11. <u>The End of Faith:</u>

"For you are obtaining/receiving the goal or the end of your faith, even the salvation of your souls" I Peter 1:9. "Looking to Jesus the author and finisher of our faith;" Hebrews 12:2. Faith begins where the Will of God is known: Search Him out for yourself!

Have Faith in God

Chapter 21

Gatherers Vs. Scatterers

This topic is rampant in the church today and it remains a hot topic as it touches on spiritual authority and the roles they play in people's lives. Careful to point out the problem without touching God's anointed but unfortunately I've been victim with a burning desire to talk about it rather than avoiding the subject. Shepherds are people that watch over souls as the bible says 'Obey them that have the rule over you, and submit yourselves: for they watch for your souls, as they that must give account, that they may do it with joy, and not with grief: for that is unprofitable for you" Hebrews 13:17. The key phrase is 'they must give an account.' Meaning they are entrusted with the souls of men/women but they do not own these souls. Someone paid a price and bought these souls with His own blood. It has been observed among shepherds of today (it's an epidemic) that the church has been turned into their personal property.

I've been going to this church I called home and one day shock waves went through my system when this preacher stood up and gave an ultimatum to members who according to her weren't bearing fruit; enough fruit for that matter; she was preaching about bearing fruit.

"Then he told this parable: "A man had a fig tree, planted in his vineyard, and he went to look for fruit on it, but did not find any. So he said to the man who took care of the vineyard, 'For three years now I've been coming to look for fruit on this fig tree and haven't found any. Cut it down! Why should it use up the soil?' 'Sir,' the man replied, 'leave it alone for one more year, and I'll dig around it and fertilize it. If it bears fruit next year, fine! If not, then cut it down "Luke 13:6-9. This is what disturbed me, the Person that gave the parable is the Head of the church and He was talking to one of his caregivers, a steward. Whether she meant it literally or allegorically isn't really important to me. There is nowhere in the ministry of Jesus where He excluded someone or anyone. Jesus ministry included people from all walks of life. This particular preacher's ministry was reaching out to certain types of people who were able to give and support her and those that weren't at the place in the lives she needed them to be were simply 'occupying space' and needed to make room for other more qualified potential members based on the subject of 'bearing fruit' who would potentially support the ministry. And of course my heart and mind had a rebuttal for that based on the books of Luke 19:13. She knows not what manner of spirit she is of, Luke 9:55, "For the Son of man is not come to destroy men's lives, but to save them" Luke 9:56. There has always been that king Saul spirit of envy and jealousy of upcoming David's among and within the church. And what's more interesting is that God will always raise up someone after His own heart to continue His work. Jesus said that "I will build my church and the gates of hell will not prevail against it" Matthew 16:18. And even though King David was submissive, he remained a threat to Saul and the kingdom. This is to encourage someone suffering persecution in the hands of a shepherd because of the gifts, talents and anointing God has bestowed that sparks envy to your spiritual parents. Take heart the lies that have been told about you are about to be silenced.

"You are hidden from the scourge of the tongue" Job 5:21 and "iniquity stoppeth her mouth" Job 5:16, Psalms 107:42. Your assignment is not dependent on their headship. Church is a big hospital where people go for various spiritual needs. Remember Jesus said "he that is well needeth not a physician but the sick do" Matthew 9:12. You did your part and went through the spiritual processing to get you to where you are. So do not feel guilty about your exit. If they cannot provide spiritual support the way you ought to receive it because of their prejudice and if their love for you has grown cold then there's no need to stay. These are the last days and the love of many will grow cold (Matthew 24:12). Your time there has been up and God is sending you to other avenues with and in

Him. If it is God's will for you to remain because the timing isn't right for you to leave, then He'll provide the grace sufficient for the circumstance. Serve without being enslaved if you can avoid it. Jesus himself instructed this "because we are bought with a price, do not become slaves of men" I Corinthians 7:23.

There are faithful (Hellenistic) Stevens in the church that have served faithfully that are full of wisdom and the Holy Spirit. "And Stephen, full of faith[b] and power, did great wonders and signs among the people. Then there arose some from what is called the Synagogue of the Freedmen (Cyrenians, Alexandrians, and those from Cilicia and Asia), disputing with Stephen. And they were not able to resist the wisdom and the Spirit by which he spoke. Then they secretly induced men to say, 'We have heard him speak blasphemous words against Moses and God.' And they stirred up the people, the elders, and the scribes; and they came upon him, seized him, and brought him to the council. They also set up false witnesses who said, 'This man does not cease to speak blasphemous words against this holy place and the law; for we have heard him say that this Jesus of Nazareth will destroy this place and change the customs which Moses delivered to us.' And all who sat in the council, looking steadfastly at him, saw his face as the face of an angel" Acts 6:8-15. My advice to you is with the discerning gift that you have, it is wise to flee peacefully than to tempt God by waiting around until they finally kill you. You have to know when the cloud is moving, discern when the cloud of God's covering on your life is moving so that you can move along with it and remain covered. If at all you get exposed because of failing to discern when the cloud has moved, you are jeorpidising you and your ministry. The place of instruction is a very risky and sensitive as you have to be very sensitive to the voice of God and act when He asks of you. Fear not, "blessed are you when men revile you, and persecute you, and shall say all manner of evil against you falsely, for my sake. Rejoice, and be exceeding glad: for great is your reward in heaven: for so persecuted they the prophets which were before you" Matthew 5:11-12. I've been shunned from a bible school because of this same reason but God kept me. I increased in wisdom and knowledge, and I have never been forsaken or unloved, Psalms 37:25. The lies they told about me were stopped by God. I was and still I'm engraved in the palm of His hand and my walls are continuously before Him, Isaiah 49:16. My success was not hidden in them but in God. All I had to do is found in Josh 1:8, "This book of the law shall not depart out of thy mouth; but thou shalt meditate therein day and night, that thou mayest observe to do according to all that is written therein: for then thou shalt make thy way prosperous, and then thou shalt have good success." Faithful is He that called you, and though they may try and manipulating you into fear of breaking apart, telling you that you will never succeed without them because of the spiritual covering, fear not your victory and success is hidden in the Words of the Bible. They are not your God!!

Little to nothing is told about Elijah's early life from birth, like Jesus there are bits and pieces of their lives missing from the Bible but we know that God was their ultimate authority, didn't answer to anyone but God and both fulfilled their assignment on this earth and left gloriously, and visibly in the clouds. Ministry/ Kingdom business is God's business not man's. No man can claim to own their ministry. Christ is the head of the church and that is who you answer to not the self-proclaimed gods that try to take His place. Your loyalty to them (shepherds) shouldn't be questioned. God called us to serve, but being slaves of them is an abomination because you were bought with a price. So if you suffer rejection and persecution from your spiritual mentors/authority, find a way of escape, and escape in God. God didn't intend for abuse to take place even though God could use that for His glory. Do not wait until they kill you. David understood this truth when he dodged the bullet/ arrow. He had a divine destiny ahead of him and wasn't about to let the king slay him. He escaped and steered clear of the king in order for him and his destiny to stay alive. Discord is hated by God Proverbs 6:19. You are valuable.

Jesus had the same problem with his disciples when they noticed someone operating in the same gift but not following them. "Master," said John, 'we saw a man driving out demons in your name and we tried to stop him, because he is not one of us" Luke 9:49 "And Jesus said unto him, Forbid him not: for he that is not against us is for us." Don't let them manipulate you or stop you, it is God who called you, "He who is not with me is against me, and he who does not gather with me, scatters" Luke 11:23. It's as simple as that. If they're trying to hinder you then you know why, they are not of God. Find you another mentor if you can, if not then rest assured that The Lord is your shepherd and you shall not be in want! (Psalms 23:1). God will lead, guide and instruct you in the way that you should go (Psalm 32:8) and learn a very valuable lesson. Moses reproduced himself and his legacy continued. Joshua did not raise up a mentor and the people backslid as a result and everyman did what was right in his own eyes. Even though the work needed to continue it was crippled by that failure to raise and mentor a leader. His legacy ended. The difference; Moses gathered and Joshua scattered. The destiny of Israel was not only to conquer and enter but they also needed to observe God's law even after settling down.

There are those that don't believe in your calling, gifts or talent. They have Nathanael's mentality and attitude, "Nathanael said to him, 'Can any good thing come out of Nazareth?'" Christ being the head of the church desires that all be gathered unto Him like a hen does its chicks "O Jerusalem, Jerusalem, you who kill the prophets and stone those sent to you, how often I have longed to gather your children together, as a hen gathers her chicks under her wings, but you were not willing" Matthew 23:37 and that none lost and all be one John 17:1-26. If you feel like an outcast, always remember The Lord is your shepherd and if they austrocized you rejoice and be glad for blessed art thou . . . "Blessed are they which are persecuted for righteousness' sake: for theirs is the kingdom of heaven. Blessed are ye, when men shall revile you, and persecute you, and shall say all manner of evil against you falsely, for my sake. Rejoice, and be exceeding glad: for great is your reward in heaven: for so persecuted they the prophets which were before you" Matthew 5:10-12. It is the anointing upon you that destroys and will continue to destroy the yoke, Isaiah 10:27. Tobias and Sanballats will always be there to pick on you, bully you and mock at your gifts, talents and anointing and will try to hinder the work of God ahead of you, Nehemiah 2:10-19; Nehemiah 4:1. 'He that began a good work in you will be faithful to complete it,' Philippians 1:6. No one will be able to stand against you all the days of your life if you observe to do according to all the laws and commandments of God. "No weapon fashioned against you shall prosper and every tongue that rises against you in judgment, thou shall condemn it because it is the heritage of the servants of the Lord and their righteousness is of me" Isaiah 54:17. God is your shield and defense. We all know that 'Jesus cursed the fig tree' (Mark 11:20) because it did not bear fruit in its season, don't be lazy, laziness is a curse. "Diligent hands shall bear rule," Proverbs 12:24. Be faithful and multiply that which you have so that you can be entrusted with someone else's too, Matthew 25:14-30. "Let no man despise your youth; but be you an example of the believers, in word, in conversation, in charity, in spirit, in faith, in purity" I Timothy 4:12. "Your gift will (always) make room for you and bring you before great men" Proverbs 18:16 always remember that!

Faithful Is He That Called You

CHAPTER 22

The Conviction of Integrity for Excellence

An unshakable or steadfast belief in something without need for proof or evidence that allows and enables for the steadfast adherence to a strict ethical code and being unimpaired, sound and complete, whole or undivided in order to attain the quality of a person's life in direct proportion to the commitment to the state, quality or condition of distinguishing oneself based on superior performance and surpassing others. Undoubtedly, there are rewards (blessings) and consequences (curses) of living above or beneath the standards. There are three words that we'll explore today, (i.) conviction (ii.) integrity and (iii.) excellence. Somehow I can't seem to pull them apart. They are enjoined together to obtain a desired result for a desired destination. It is written that He will give us the desires of our hearts Psalms 37:4-5 only live with the conviction of integrity for excellence; can't say it any other way.

David was one among the many that was chosen by God because according to scripture, (i). he was a man after God's own heart therefore God gave him the ability (Power) to perform above and beyond his peers and experienced people as well. David said that because of this relationship with God "I understand more than the ancients or have more wisdom than those with many years of experience, because I keep and have obeyed your precepts" Psalms 119:100. He was gifted in music, and used his gift to capture the heart of God therefore God empowered him with the ability to handle, manage and maintain power. His love roots for His God ran deep because it was out of the pain of rejection he received from his brothers . . . "When Eliab, David's oldest brother, heard him speaking with the men, he burned with anger at him and asked, 'Why have you come down here? And with whom did you leave those few sheep in the desert? I know how conceited you are and how wicked your heart is; you came down only to watch the battle'" I Samuel 17:28 . . . and him being the youngest of eight brothers that brought him closer to God. "Now David was the son of an Ephrathite named Jesse, who was from Bethlehem in Judah. Jesse had eight sons, and in Saul's time he was old and well advanced in years. Jesse's three oldest sons had followed Saul to the war: The firstborn was Eliab; the second, Abinadab; and the third, Shammah. David was the youngest. The three oldest followed Saul, but David went back and forth from Saul to tend his father's sheep at Bethlehem" I Samuel 17:12-15. "One day, David's father, Jesse, sent him to check on his brothers I Samuel 17:17 and an opportunity presented itself to outperform not only those that belittled him but those that had years of experience as well. As a result ". . . David triumphed over the Philistine with a sling and a stone; without a sword in his hand he struck down the Philistine and killed him" I Samuel 17:50. Here's the core of this passage in line with today's message "Whatever Saul sent him to do, David did it so successfully that Saul gave him a high rank in the army. This pleased all the people, and Saul's officers as well" I Samuel 18:5.

The Conviction of Integrity for Excellence is all tied up in this portion of scriptures:

David said to the Philistine, (Integrity) "You come against me with sword and spear and javelin, but I come against you in the name of the LORD Almighty, the God of the armies of Israel, whom you have defied. (Excellence because of his Conviction and Integrity) This day the LORD will hand you over to me, and I'll strike you down and cut off your head. Today I will give the carcasses of the Philistine army to the birds of the air and the beasts of the earth, and the whole world will know that there is a God in Israel. (Conviction) All those gathered here will know that it is not by sword or spear that the LORD saves; for the battle is the LORD's, and he will give all of you into our hands." (Excellence) As the Philistine moved closer to attack him, David ran quickly toward the battle line to meet him. Reaching into his bag and taking out a stone, he slung it and struck the Philistine on the forehead. The stone sank into his forehead, and he fell face down on the ground. (Excellence) So David triumphed over the Philistine with a sling and a stone; without a sword in his hand he struck down the Philistine and killed him" I Samuel 17:45-50.

The story of Isaac and Rebecca and their miraculous set up. Isaac was in pain. He had lost his mother not too long ago due to old age and was about to lose his father as well. Pain has a way of bringing you closer to God. Apparently He is the only One that can understand it all. Isaac was at his lowest point and the Bible records that after he married Rebecca and went in unto her, he was comforted. Ref: "And the servant told Isaac all the things that he had done. Then Isaac brought her into his mother Sarah's tent; and he took Rebekah and she became his wife, and he loved her. So Isaac was comforted after his mother's death" Genesis 24:66-67. "And it happened, before he had finished speaking, {Conviction: (that streams from her Lineage and Covenant)} that behold, Rebekah, who was born to Bethuel, son of Milcah, the wife of Nahor, Abraham's brother, came out with her pitcher on her shoulder. (Integrity) Now the young woman was very beautiful to behold, a virgin; no man had known her. And she went down to the well, filled her pitcher, and came up. And the servant ran to meet her and said, "Please let me drink a little water from your pitcher." So she said, "Drink, my lord." Then she quickly let her pitcher down to her hand, and gave him a drink. And when she had finished giving him a drink, she said, (Excellence) "I will draw water for your camels also, until they have finished drinking." Then she quickly emptied her pitcher into the trough, ran back to the well to draw water, and drew for all his camels. And the man, wondering at her, remained silent so as to know whether the LORD had made his journey prosperous or not. So it was, when the camels had finished drinking, that the man took a golden nose ring weighing half a shekel, and two bracelets for her wrists weighing ten shekels of gold, and said, "Whose daughter are you? Tell me, please, is there room in your father's house for us to lodge?" (Conviction and Excellence) So she said to him, "I am the daughter of Bethuel, Milcah's son, whom she bore to Nahor." Moreover she said to him, "We have both straw and feed enough, and room to lodge" Genesis 24:15-25

Points to Ponder:

We are going to look at the 'D' word because without it we're wasting precious unredeemable time talking about today's subject. It is the training and control of oneself and conduct usually for personal improvement expected to produce a specific character or pattern of behavior, especially training that produces moral or mental improvement. That word is discipline. A lot of people overlook the amount of discipline that is needed to make the mark. It is written that it is easy to miss the mark and without the discipline for preparation and endurance. "Strive with earnestness and keep on striving to enter in through the narrow door; for I tell you many will seek to enter and will not be able to" Luke 13:24. Another translation reads "But the narrow gate and the road that lead to life are full of trouble. Only a few people find the narrow gate" Matthew 7:14 "Enter through the narrow gate; for the gate is wide and the way is broad that leads to destruction, and there are many who enter through it; because strait is the gate, and narrow is the way, which leads to life, and few there be that find it" Matthew 7:13-14.

". . . But whoever slaps you on your right cheek, turn the other to him also. If anyone wants to sue you and take away your tunic, let him have your cloak also. And whoever compels you to go one mile, go with him two. Give to him who asks you, and from him who wants to borrow from you do not turn away" Matt 5:39-42

Endeavor to go the extra mile

CHAPTER 23

Finding Strength in Weakness

"And lest I should be exalted above measure by the abundance of the revelations, a thorn in the flesh was given to me, a messenger of Satan to buffet me, lest I be exalted above measure. Concerning this thing I pleaded with the Lord three times that it might depart from me. And He said to me, 'My grace is sufficient for you, for My strength is made perfect in weakness.' Therefore most gladly I will rather boast in my infirmities, that the power of Christ may rest upon me. Therefore I take pleasure in infirmities, in reproaches, in needs, in persecutions, in distresses, for Christ's sake. For when I am weak, then I am strong" (II Corinthians 12:7-10).

Every now and then we are faced with situations or people that we have no control over that bring discomfort to our lives and Paul was no exception. Thorns as we continue with this study can come in different forms, but it is the attitude when dealing with these thorns that matter. It could come as a person that keeps pushing those buttons and have no other choice but to endure. It could be a circumstance beyond your control involving finances, an illness or anything else that challenges your existence and threatens to take you out. In I Peter 5:7 we are reminded to "cast all your Care and anxiety on Him, because He cares for you" and of course His strength is made perfect in weakness! II Corinthians 12:8. Our attitude when going through or dealing with something always determines the intensity or pain of the thorn and can sometimes magnify the discomfort. We ought to learn how to control and let God handle those impossibilities we face instead of losing control of our peace. Let go and let GOD have His way. Our faith and faithfulness to Him often gets tested and we ought not come undone.

God uses thorns as a way to bring humility where pride has taken root. Paul said that lest he exalts himself because of the amount of revelations we was getting from God, God brought something he could not overcome to keep him abased, and assured him that he could handle the pain because His grace was sufficient enough for the problem. God will not give us more than we can bear, "no temptation has overtaken you that is not common to man. God is faithful, and he will not let you be tempted beyond your ability, but with the temptation he will also provide the way of escape, that you may be able to endure it" I Corinthians 10:13. God is in control of all things because "all things are from God" I Corinthians 11:12. "He must increase, but I must decrease" John 3:30, that ought to be our profession and lifestyle.

Something happens when people hit rock bottom and know for a fact that nobody can do a thing about it. Jesus described this a scenario about not having control of your life and having someone else call the shots on your behalf because of your incapability "Truly, I tell you with certainty, when you were young, you would fasten your belt and go wherever you liked. But when you get old, you will stretch out your hands, and someone else will fasten your belt and take you where you don't want to go" John 21:18. having to put your life in someone else's hands can be stressful because you don't know if they have your best interest at heart, and you're the only one that can take you to your destiny. Everyone else is concerned about their own dreams and goals. But here is a situation of weakness, and God assures us that He is in control and would show Himself strong if you would put your trust in Him. God brings us to a place where we're totally reliant upon Him and nobody else and no one else can deliver out of His hand. King David preferred to fall at the mercy of God when he had yet again sinned against God and was troubled. "Then David said to Gad, 'I am in great distress. Let us now fall into the hand of the LORD for His mercies are great, but do not let me fall into the hand of man" II Samuel 24:14 and "because His loving-kindness is better than life" Psalms 63:3. "The sacrifices of God are a broken spirit: a broken and a contrite heart, God will not despise" Psalms 51:17

". . . and be clothed with humility, for God resists the proud, but gives grace to the humble. Therefore humble yourselves under the mighty hand of God, that He may exalt you in due time," I Peter 5:5-6. Paul said lest he should be exalted above measure, a thorn was given to him to keep him humble (II Corinthians 12:7). So if and when you feel backed up into a corner of your circumstances don't let your helplessness and weakness get the better of you fall into the arms of God. He is the only one who can deliver you. Deliverance may not happen overnight but He'll show up on time. Thorns come as a result of;

1.   PRIDE AND ARROGANCE

As a child of God, humility is a virtue that you must wear. "God resists the proud, but gives grace to the humble" I Peter 5:5. Pride will demote you but humility will exalt you. "Pride goeth before destruction and a haughty spirit before a fall" Proverbs 16:18. Nebuchadnezzar king of Babylon was humiliated by God and reduced to an animal because of his pride and arrogance. "The king spake, and said, is not this great Babylon, that I have built for the house of the kingdom by the might of my power, and for the honor of my majesty? While the word was in the king's mouth, there fell a voice from heaven, saying, O king Nebuchadnezzar, to thee it is spoken; the kingdom is departed from thee. And they shall drive thee from men, and thy dwelling shall be with the beasts of the field: they shall make thee to eat grass as oxen, and seven times shall pass over thee, until thou know that the most High ruleth in the kingdom of men, and giveth it to whomsoever he will. The same hour was the thing fulfilled upon Nebuchadnezzar: and he was driven from men, and did eat grass as oxen, and his body was wet with the dew of heaven, till his hairs were grown like eagles' feathers, and his nails like birds' claws. And at the end of the days I Nebuchadnezzar lifted up mine eyes unto heaven, and mine understanding returned unto me, and I blessed the most High, and I praised and honored him that liveth forever . . . Now I Nebuchadnezzar praise and extol and honor the King of heaven, all whose works are truth, and his ways judgment: and those that walk in pride he is able to abase" Daniel 4:-30-37

2. REAPING THE FRUITS OF OUR DOING:

"Do not be deceived, God is not mocked; for whatever a man sows, this he will also reap" Galatians 6:7. Regardless of who we are in Christ "Of a truth I perceive that God is no respecter of persons:" Acts 10:34 ". . . and there is no partiality with God" Romans 2:11. "While the earth remains, Seedtime and harvest shall not cease" Genesis 8:22. King David is known for his greatness, and his love for God. He killed the bear, the lion and that giant that threatened Israel's existence and freedom. He was a man of God after God's own heart to the point where God established an everlasting (eternal) kingdom through his lineage but he wasn't perfect and God did not spare him. After he had taken Uriah's wife and orchestrated Uriah's death, God did not spare him. To whom much is given much is also required, (Luke 12:48). "Wherefore hast thou despised the commandment of the LORD, to do evil in his sight? Thou hast killed Uriah the Hittite with the sword, and hast taken his wife to be thy wife, and hast slain him with the sword of the children of Ammon. Now therefore the sword shall never depart from thine house; because thou hast despised me, and hast taken the wife of Uriah the Hittite to be thy wife. Thus saith the LORD, Behold, I will raise up evil against thee out of thine own house, and I will take thy wives before thine eyes, and give them unto thy neighbor, and he shall lie with thy wives in the sight of this sun. For thou didst it secretly: but I will do this thing before all Israel, and before the sun." II Samuel 12:9-12

3. TRIAL AND TEST OF OUR FAITH AND FAITHFULNESS

"There was a man in the land of Uz, whose name was Job; and that man was perfect and upright, and one that feared God, and turned away from evil." Job 1:1 "Now it came to pass on the day when the sons of God came to present themselves before God, that Satan also came among them. And God said unto Satan, Whence comest thou? Then Satan answered God, and said, 'from going to and fro in the earth, and from walking up and down in it.' And God said unto Satan, 'Hast thou considered my servant Job? for there is none like him in the earth, a perfect and an upright man, one that feareth God, and turneth away from evil.' Then Satan answered Jehovah, and said, 'doth Job fear God for nought? Hast not thou made a hedge about him, and about his house, and about all that he hath, on every side? thou hast blessed the work of his hands, and his substance is increased in the land. But put forth thy hand now, and touch all that he hath, and he will renounce thee to thy face?' . . . Then Job arose, and rent his robe, and shaved his head, and fell down upon the ground, and worshipped; and he said, naked came I out of my mother's womb, and naked shall I return thither: Jehovah gave, and Jehovah hath taken away; blessed be the name of Jehovah. In all this Job sinned not, nor charged God foolishly?" Job 1:6-22. It comes a time when out trust in God is shaken from its foundations and the truth about our faith and trust in God comes to light.

We are assured of one thing, as a child of God nothing will overcome us. He will not give us more than we can bear. God is always in control. "My brethren, count it all joy when ye fall into divers temptations; Knowing this, that the trying of your faith works patience" James 1:2-3 and patience is the key and ingredient to endure and glide through thorns whatever their shape or form.

Count it all Joy

CHAPTER 24

His Secret Place

Kingdom people, there is no better place to be than in His presence, there is fullness of joy and at His right hand are pleasures forevermore Psalms 16:11. He makes known to you the path of life (Psalms 16:11); according to His perfect will. For You make him a source of blessing forever and You make him glad with the joy of your presence Psalms 21:6. David experienced this completeness when he said that ". . . a day in your courts is better than a thousand. I had rather be a doorkeeper in the house of my God, than to dwell in the tents of wickedness" Psalm 84:10. "One thing have I desired of the LORD, that will I seek after; that I may dwell in the house of the LORD all the days of my life, to behold the beauty of the LORD, and to inquire in his temple" Psalms 27:4. "O LORD, I love the habitation of Your house And the place where Your glory (and honor) dwells" Psalms 26:8.

Everyone has a yearning for that spiritual connection with a supreme being. Depending on the authenticity of whoever it is they find, i.e. whether the one and only true God or a counterfeit, there's a feeling of completeness or fulfillment. It is unreal if it is founded on a spirit other than the one and only true God because it is only God (Elohim) that can bring this wholeness to a person. God created man to have fellowship with Him and that is why man will forever seek after, whether they find Him or not, they'll be emptiness inside that only God can fill. "But from there you will seek the LORD your God, and you will find Him if you search for Him with all your heart and all your soul" Deuteronomy 4:29. "Seek the LORD while He may be found; Call upon Him while He is near" Isaiah 55:6. "You will seek Me and find Me when you search for

Me with all your heart" Jeremiah 29:13. God demanded this of us because He knew how He made us and what was out there . . . "You shall love the LORD your God with all your heart and with all your soul and with all your might" Deuteronomy 6:5.

It's an indescribable feeling being in the presence of God, times of refreshing come from the presence of God Acts 3:19. The benefits of being in the Secret Place with God are that:

1. <u>God is past intriguing, mysterious and unsearchable.</u>

He is simply unfathomable. The curiosity of who He is can be breathtaking in trying to figure out more about Him. "O the depth of the riches both of the wisdom and knowledge of God! How unsearchable are his judgments, and his ways past finding out! Romans 11:33. "Listen to this, O Job, Stand and consider the wonders of God" Job 37:14. "Do you know about the layers of the thick clouds, the wonders of one perfect in knowledge," Job 37:16. "Who is this that hides counsel without knowledge?' "Therefore I have declared that which I did not understand, Things too wonderful for me, which I did not know" Job 42:3. "But as for me, I would seek God, and I would place my cause before God; who does great things, unsearchable miracles past finding out, unfathomable, Yea, marvelous things and wondrous works without number Job 9:10.

2. <u>God protects you from slander and the effects of it.</u>

Faith cometh by hearing and hearing by the word of God, Fear cometh by hearing, and hearing an evil report . . . whose report will you believe Isaiah 53:1. "You shall hide them in the secret of your presence from the pride of man: you shall keep them secretly in a pavilion from the strife of tongues" Acts 31:20. "You will be hidden from the scourge of the tongue, and you will not be afraid of violence when it comes" Job 5:21. "But he saves [other people] from their slander and the needy from the power of the mighty" Job 5:15. "The upright see it and are glad; But all unrighteousness shuts its mouth" Psalms 102:42. "So the poor man has hope, and the mouth of the unrighteous evil-doer is stopped" Job 5:16.

3. <u>God offers protection from our enemies and negative circumstances.</u>

"For in the day of trouble He will conceal me in His tabernacle; in the secret place of His tent He will hide me; He will lift me up on a rock" Psalms 27:5. "He that dwells (lives) in the secret place of the Most High shall abide under the shadow of the Almighty God. I will say of the LORD, 'He is my refuge and my fortress; My God, in Him I will trust.' Surely He shall deliver you from the snare of the fowler and from the perilous pestilence. He shall cover you with His feathers, and under His wings you shall take refuge; His truth shall be your shield and buckler. You shall not be afraid of the terror by night, nor of the arrow that flies by day, nor of the pestilence that walks in darkness, nor of the destruction that lays waste at noonday. A thousand may fall at your side, and ten thousand at your right hand; but it shall not come near you. Only with your eyes shall you look, and see the reward of the wicked. Because you have made the LORD, who is my refuge, Even the Most High, your dwelling place, No evil shall befall you, nor shall any plague come near your dwelling; For He shall give His angels charge over you, to keep you in all your ways. In their hands they shall bear you up, lest you dash your foot against a stone. You shall tread upon the lion and the cobra, the young lion and the serpent you shall trample underfoot. Because he has set his love upon me, therefore I will deliver him; I will set him on high, because he has known My name. He shall call upon Me, and I will answer him; I will be with him in trouble; I will deliver him and honor him" Psalm 91:1-15. "From six troubles He will deliver you, even in seven evil will not touch you" Job 5:19. "You will laugh at violence and famine, and you will not be afraid of wild beasts for you will be in league with the stones of the field, and the beasts of the field will be at peace with you." Job 5:22-23. "And the wolf will dwell with the lamb, and the leopard will lie down with the young goat, and the calf and the young lion and the fatling together; and a little boy will lead them" Isaiah 11:6. "The wolf and the lamb will graze together, and the lion will eat straw like the ox; and dust will be the serpent's food. They will do no evil or harm in all My holy mountain," says the LORD" Isaiah 65:25. "You will know that your tent is secure, for you will visit your abode and fear no loss Job" 5:24. "If you are pure and upright, surely now He would rouse Himself for you and restore your righteous estate" Job 8:6.

4. God promises long life.

"With long life will I satisfy him, and show him my salvation" Psalm 91:16. "He asked life of You, You gave it to him, Length of days forever and ever" Psalms 21:4. "You will prolong the king's life: and his years as many generations." Job 5:8. "You shall come to your grave in a full age, like as a shock of corn comes in his season" Job 5:26. ". . . and that you may cling to Him, for He is your life and the length of your days . . ." Deuteronomy 30:19. "For by Me your days will be multiplied, and years of life will be added to you." Proverbs 9:11.

5. God blesses your children and their children:

"You will know also that your descendants will be many, and your offspring as the grass of the earth" Job 5:25. His descendants will be mighty on earth; The generation of the upright will be blessed Psalms 112:2. For I will pour out water on the thirsty land and streams on the dry ground; I will pour out My Spirit on your offspring and My blessing on your descendants; And they will spring up among the grass Like poplars by streams of water.' Isaiah 44:3-44. "Your descendants would have been like the sand, and your offspring like its grains; their name would never be cut off or destroyed from My presence" Isaiah 48:19.

6. God gives clear direction in His presence:

I will instruct you and teach you in the way you should go; I will guide you with My eye. Do not be like the horse or like the mule, which have no understanding, which must be harnessed with bit and bridle, Else they will not come near you. Many sorrows shall be to the wicked; But he who trusts in the LORD, mercy shall surround him Psalms 32:8-10.

God is Love and "Whoever does not love does not know God, because God is love" I John 4:8. He is in love with His creation "but to Israel he said, All day long I have stretched forth my hands to a disobedient and gainsaying people" Romans 10:21. "I have spread out My hands all day long to a rebellious people, Who walk in the way which is not good, following their own thoughts" Isaiah 65:2. "The LORD has appeared of old to me, saying: 'Yes, I have loved you with an everlasting love; Therefore with loving kindness I have drawn you" Jeremiah 31:3. And you will seek Me and find Me, when you search for Me with all your heart Jeremiah 29:13. 'Now as they went on their way, he entered a certain village, where a woman named Martha welcomed him into her home. She had a sister named Mary, who sat at the Lord's feet and listened to what he was saying. But Martha was distracted by her many tasks, so she came to him and asked "Lord, do you not care that my sister has left me to do all the work by myself? Tell her then to help me." But the Lord answered her "Martha, Martha, you are worried and distracted by many things. There is need of only one thing. Mary has chosen the better part, which will not be taken away from her" Luke 10:38-42. Mary chose the right thing, to sit at his feet, in His presence, Martha got preoccupied, and she went about doing the right thing the wrong way at the wrong time. It wasn't important to serve Jesus as it was to be in His presence, loving and learning him. This is a picture of today's Christians; too busy to be in His presence.

Repent you therefore, and be converted, that your sins may be blotted out, when the times of refreshing shall come from the presence of the Lord. And he shall send Jesus Christ, which before was preached to you: Acts 3:19-20.

It's an honor and a privilege to be in His Presence

CHAPTER 25

STEWARDISE/STEWARDSHIP

"Moreover, it is required in stewards that a man is found faithful." I Corinthians 4:2. We've talked about the relationship between God (being owner of everything) and man's position as it relates to overseeing God's stuff. Gen, God did not create the garden until there was a man to till/work or manage it. God handed creation over to man so that man can be caretaker. The story of the prodigal son is a good illustration as it relates to possessions. When the prodigal son returned home to his father, his older brother was displeased at the way he was treated and the Grande welcome he received from their father. He confronted his father at the way he handled his younger brother's behavior as seen here, ". . . he was angry and would not go in (to the feast). Therefore his father came out and pleaded with him. So he answered and said to his father, 'Lo, these many years I have been serving you; I never transgressed your commandment at any time; and yet you never gave me a young goat that I might make merry with my friends. But as soon as this son of yours came, who has devoured your livelihood with harlots, you killed the fatted calf for him.' he replied to him and said to him, 'Son, you are always with me, and all that I have is yours" Luke 15:28-31.

Jesus confirms this communal property ownership, "All that is mine is yours, and what is yours is mine, and I have been glorified through them;" "All that the Father has is mine" John 16:15. The same correlation between the father and son has been extended to us in that "In that day you will know that I am in My Father, and you in Me, and I in you" John 14:20. Bottom line is whatsoever the

Father has is yours but it's a question of how we handle what has been awarded that we'll determine our end, glory or shame.

1. Acknowledgement:

God owns it all, He is the great creator. "The earth is the Lord's, and the fullness thereof; the world, and they that dwell therein. He has founded it upon the seas and established it upon the rivers." Psalms 24:1-2. "All things were made by him; and without Him was nothing made that was made" John 1:3. "For every beast of the forest are mine, and the cattle upon a thousand hills. I know every bird of the mountains, and everything that moves in the field is Mine" Psalms 50:10-11. Acknowledge that even though God has granted us an enormous opportunity to rule and reign, to have and hold, to own and manage, He owns it all and we answer to Him no matter where it is we're placed on this earth or what it is we have. "With good will render service, as to the Lord, and not to men" Ephesians 6:7, "and whatever you do, do it heartily, as to the Lord, and not to men;" Colosians 3:23

2. Management:

God is a giver. He created all things that He could share it with His creation. He loved the world sooo much that He gave, John 3:16. He hates it when man becomes stingy and selfish and pronounces judgment if the poor are neglected and great blessing if you give to the poor. "The kingdom of heaven is like a man going on a trip. He called his servants and entrusted some money to them. To one he gave five talents, to another, two, and to another, one, each according to his own ability; and he went on his journey. Immediately the one who had received the five talents went and traded with them, and gained five more talents. In the same way, the one who had two talents earned two more. But he who received the one talent went away, and dug a hole in the ground and hid his master's money.

Now after a long time the master of those servants came and settled accounts with them. The one who had received five talents came up and brought five more talents, saying, 'Master, you gave me five talents. See, I've earned five more talents. His master said to him, 'well done, you good and faithful servant: you have been faithful over a few things, I will make you ruler over many things: enter you into the joy of your lord.' Also the one who had received the two talents came up and said, 'Master, you entrusted two talents to me. See, I have gained two more talents.' His master said to him, 'well done, good and faithful servant; you have been faithful over a few things, I will make you ruler over many things: enter you into the joy of your lord.' And also the one that had received the one talent came and said, 'Lord, I knew that you are a hard man, reaping where you did not sow, and gathering where you did not scatter; And I was afraid, and went and hid your talent in the earth: see, there you have that is yours.' But his master answered and said to him, 'you wicked, lazy slave, you knew that I reap where I did not sow and gather where I scattered no seed. Then you should have invested my money with the bankers. When I returned, I would have received my money back with interest.' 'Therefore take away the talent from him, and give it to the one who has the ten talents. Because to everyone who has, more will be given and he will have more than enough, but to him that has not, even that which he has will be taken away from him' and cast the unprofitable servant into outer darkness where there shall be weeping and gnashing of teeth" Matthew 25:14-30. People should think of us as servants of Christ and managers or stewards who are entrusted with God's mysteries I Corinthians 4:1. There you have it your attitude to what God entrusts you with determines your destiny.

3. Responsibility:

"Whoever is faithful with very little is also faithful with a lot, and whoever is dishonest with very little is also dishonest with a lot. So if you haven't been faithful with unrighteous wealth, who will trust you with true wealth?" Luke 16:10-11. The true test of trust doesn't take place at the top of your game but at the bottom when you have little to nothing. God entrusts you with wealthy based on how you handled the little He gave you when you had nothing or very little. The measure of a person shines forth when going through struggles, hardships and in crises. "His master said to him, Well done, you good and faithful servant; because you have been faithful over a few things, I will make you ruler over many things: enter you into the joy of your lord" Matthew 25:21. Being faithful unto death with small things qualifies or disqualifies you to greatness. Taking responsibility for our actions is crucial. Remember at the garden, when Adam handed over his kingship to the devil, instead of taking responsibility, he blamed someone else for his failures. These were his exact words, "The woman whom You gave to be with me, she gave me from the tree, and I ate" Genesis 3:12 and was thrown out as a result. The way you handle money goes along way. Here is an illustration of a steward that didn't handle stewardship as he should but because of his attitude, he was able to deliver himself. "There was a certain rich man who had a steward, and an accusation was brought to him that this man was wasting his goods. So he called him and said to him, 'What is this I hear about you? Give an account of your stewardship, for you can no longer be steward.' Then the steward said within him, 'What shall I do? For my master is taking the stewardship away from me. I cannot dig; I am ashamed to beg. I have resolved what to do, that when I am put out of the stewardship, they may receive me into their houses.' So he called every one of his master's debtors to him, and said to the first, 'How much do you owe my master? And he said, 'A hundred measures of oil.' So he said to him, 'Take your bill, and sit down quickly and write fifty.' Then he said to another, 'And how much do you owe?' So he said, 'A hundred measures of wheat.' And he said to him, 'Take your bill, and write eighty.' So the master commended the unjust steward because he had dealt shrewdly. For the sons of this world are shrewder in their generation than the sons of light" Luke 16:1-8. He took responsibility for his actions and even though he used some shady methods in trying to fix his mess, his mess was fixed and he saved himself.

4. Accountability:

"Consequently, every one of us will give an account of himself to God" Romans 14:12 and . . . "give an account of your stewardship or management" Luke 16:2. "For we must all appear before the judgment seat of Christ; that every one may receive the things done in his body, according to that he has done, whether it be good or bad" II Corinthians 5:10. "When he returned, after receiving the kingdom, he ordered that these slaves, to whom he had given the money, be called to him so that he might know what business they had done. Then came the first, saying, Lord, your pound has gained ten pounds. And he said to him, 'Well done, good slave, because you have been faithful in a very little thing, you are to be in authority over ten cities" Luke 19:15-17. There is no exception to this rule, small and great will all stand before God and give an account. Even on earth we have seen great men of power prosecuted and indicted for their abuse of power. It happens and here on earth as it will happen in heaven. "Thy Kingdom come, Thy will be done on earth as it is in Heaven" Matthew 6:10.

As we aspire and pursue greatness, let's keep these truths with all our hearts. A faithful steward/manager will be rewarded; an unfaithful steward/manager will face the consequences.

Faithfulness is always superior; Unfaithfulness inferior

CHAPTER 26

The BLOOD

1. Life in the Blood:

"**B**ut flesh with the life thereof, which is the blood thereof," Genesis 9:4. "The LIFE of the flesh is in the BLOOD" Leviticus17:11, 14; Deuteronomy 12:23. To understand the direction of this study, we have to start from the beginning. Genesis records the first time blood had to be used in order to make a correction. Our first parents, Adam and Eve, signed their own death row by violating God's command and brought judgment on all their descendants after them in that all of creation was sentenced to death. God our (Heavenly Father) stepped in and through the shed blood of an animal made them fur and drove them out of the garden (Genesis 3:21-24). There was life in the blood enough for the remission of their sin. The bible does not directly point out how he got the furry coats, we fill in the blanks. God had to have killed an animal to make them coats for their covering. They didn't have the understanding of taking responsibility for their wrong doing especially when dealing with God, instead of blame shifting as it's clearly revealed (Genesis 3:12-13), but God made the sacrifice for the and life had to go on. They pronounced death and God showed them how to make it right but they didn't get it as we see in the case of Cain. Life is in the blood, and the only way to reverse their curse was through the blood and restore life through the blood. "For the life of the flesh is in the blood: and I have given it to you upon the altar to make atonement for your souls: for it is the blood that maketh an atonement for the soul" Leviticus 17:11

First siblings Cain and Abel had different professions, one tilled the ground and Abel kept the sheep (Genesis 4:2). ". . . in process of time it came to pass, that Cain brought of the fruit of the ground an offering to the LORD and Abel, also brought of the firstborn of his flock and of the fat thereof. And the LORD had respect to Abel and to his offering:" Genesis 4:3-4. There is no blood in the fruit of the ground and God would not accept his offering unless blood (and the life in it) was shed. Abel received remission for his sin because God accepted it but God rejected Cain and his offering. Who knows his motives might have been right BUT you got to do it right. Perfect example of how right and perfect things have to be done when dealing with God is found here; "And when they came to the threshing-floor of Nacon, Uzzah put forth his hand to the ark of God, and took hold of it; for the oxen stumbled. And the anger of Jehovah was kindled against Uzzah; and God smote him there for his error; and there he died by the ark of God" II Samuel 6:6-7. It doesn't matter how right your motives are it just has to be done the right way or you face the consequences. Abel received acceptance and Cain rejection all because of handling God with faulty mechanisms and not following instructions and not following through with instructions regardless whether instructions were given or not. There is an established format for everything when dealing with God. God is a God of ORDER!

"The God of peace brought the great shepherd of the sheep, our Lord Jesus, back to life through the blood of an eternal promise" Hebrews 13:20. This revelation of using the blood started back at the Garden of Eden, which in order for sacrifice to be acceptable blood had to be shed. This ultimate price was paid and God the Father sacrificed his only son in order to regain control and the rightful place of authority and hand it back to man who lost it at the Garden of Eden, and win some more sons because many had been lost through deceit and Satan's rule on earth all those years. Through the shed blood of Jesus Christ we can now receive forgiveness of sin and obtain the promise of life ever after. "Much more then, being now justified by his blood, we shall be saved from wrath through him" Romans 5:9. "Neither by the blood of goats and calves, but by his own blood had he entered in once into the holy place, having obtained eternal redemption for us. for if the blood of bulls and of goats, and the ashes of an heifer sprinkling the unclean, sanctifies to the purifying of the flesh: How much more shall the blood of Christ, who through the eternal Spirit offered himself without spot to God, purge your conscience from dead works to serve the living God?" Hebrews 9:12-14. So we are now free form guilt of sin. "For this is my blood of the new testament, which is shed for many for the remission of sins" Matthew 26:28. "In whom we have redemption through his blood, the forgiveness of sins, according to the riches of his grace" Ephesians 1:7. "In whom we have redemption through his blood, even the forgiveness of sins:" Colossians 1:14. "Neither by the blood of goats and calves, but by his own blood he entered in once into the holy place, having obtained eternal redemption for us" Hebrews 9:12. "And they sung a new song, saying, Thou art worthy to take the book, and to open the seals thereof: for thou wast slain, and hast redeemed us to God by thy blood out of every kindred, and tongue, and people, and nation" Revelation 5:9. And we now live because of His blood.

2. Power in the Blood:

". . . feed the church of God, which he hath purchased with his own blood" Acts 20:28. This is what power the ultimate sacrifice had. In this age wealth, status and power is determined by the numbers. It's a numbers game and here we see ultimate power portrayed. Instead of money, blood was used to purchase the entire church of Jesus Christ. That's power! Without blood, no covenant could be possible between God and man. "And Moses took the blood, and sprinkled it on the people, and said; behold the blood of the covenant, which the LORD hath made with you concerning all these words" Exodus 24:8 "Whereupon neither the first testament was dedicated without blood. For when Moses had spoken every precept to all the people according to the law, he took the blood of calves and of goats, with water, and scarlet wool, and hyssop, and sprinkled both the book, and all the people, Saying, This is the blood of the testament which God hath enjoined unto you" Hebrews 9:18-20. "How much more shall the blood of Christ, who through the eternal Spirit offered Himself without spot to God, cleanse your conscience from dead works to serve the living God?" Hebrews 9:14

Without this covenant we would be in the eternal state of death, living only for a moment and all mankind sentenced to eternal doom and destruction because the prince of this world (Satan) still had authority stolen from Adam. "The thief cometh not but to kill steal and destroy but I am come that you might have life and have it more abundantly" John 10:10. "And they overcame him by the blood of the Lamb and by the word of their testimony; and they loved not their lives unto the death" Revelation 12:11. Power in the blood causes us to triumph against the forces of darkness, "But if we walk in the light, as he is in the light, we have fellowship one with another, and the blood of Jesus Christ his Son cleanse us from all sin cleanses us from all sin" 1 John 1:7. Power in the blood enough to cleanse and sanctify and make us holy and acceptable before God ". . . the blood of the covenant, wherewith he was sanctified . . ." Hebrews 10:29. "And from Jesus Christ, who is the faithful witness, and the first begotten of the dead, and the prince of the kings of the earth, unto him that loved us, and washed us from our sins in his own blood," Revelation 1:5. The blood has power to usher us into the holiest of God "Brothers and sisters, because of the blood of Jesus we can now confidently go into the holiest place" Hebrews 10:19 and meet with God, "but now in Christ Jesus you who once were far off have been brought near by the blood of Christ" Ephesians 2:13 Before this privilege of approaching God was taken away because of sin. "In him we have redemption through his blood, the forgiveness of sins, in accordance with the riches of God's grace" Ephesians 1:7. God will not stand sin!

Power to be in fellowship: "The cup of blessing which we bless, is it not the communion of the blood of Christ? The bread which we break, is it not the communion of the body of Christ?" I Corinthians 10:16. "For this is My blood of the covenant, which is poured out for many for forgiveness of sins" Matthew 26:28; Power to justify: "being justified freely by His grace through the redemption that is in Christ Jesus, whom God set forth as a propitiation by His blood, through faith, to demonstrate His righteousness, because in His forbearance God had passed over the sins that were previously committed" Romans 3:24-25 "Much more then, being now justified by his blood, we shall be saved from wrath through him" Romans 5:9; Power to be at peace with God and man: ". . . and by Him, to reconcile all things to Himself, by Him, whether things on earth or things in heaven, having made peace through the blood of His cross" Colossians 1:20; Power for divine protection" "And the blood shall be to you for a token upon the houses where ye are: and when I see the blood I will pass over you, and the Plague shall not be upon you to destroy you" Exodus 12:13; Power to heal: "who Himself bore our sins in His own body on the tree, that we, having died to sins, might live for righteousness; by whose stripes you were healed" I Peter 2:24.

3. <u>WORD in the Blood:</u>

"And He said, 'What have you done? The voice of your brother's blood cries out to Me from the ground" Genesis 4:10. Blood speaks, because of the life in it only the giver of the life in the blood hears the cries when blood is shed. Because of the nature and cause of Abel's life loss, it is safe to say that Abel's blood cried out to God in complaint of the injustice he received form his brother Cain and vengeance. "To Jesus the Mediator of the new covenant and to the blood of sprinkling that speaks better things than that of Abel" Hebrews 12:24. The blood of Jesus speaks too. It speaks of things pertaining to the covenant. On the contrary we know that the blood of Abel cried out to God for vengeance and the reason why Jesus blood speaks better things, is because of His mission on earth to redeem, offer remission of sins/forgiveness of sins, healing, protection, and life" judgment and vengeance was not in the package or commission therefore the blood of Jesus speaks better things about us than that of Abel's blood which spoke vengeance and judgment. Every time blood is shed, blood speaks. Depending on the condition of the heart of the blood/life lost, it can speak of anything, love mercy vengeance, and it speaks to God. That's why God cautions people not to take a life and let nature take its course or you will be held accountable for the life you took.

His Blood is all you need.

CHAPTER 27

To Him That Overcometh

Today I'll touch on a difficult subject, one that involves stretching out your faith so far out and taking it to another level until you almost or do reach your breaking point (pop). I've been there a time or two and that's how I got to find out that demons are real and they love to dwell in this realm we're about to walk through and explore. "And not only so, but we glory in tribulations also: knowing that tribulation works patience;" Romans 5:3. "But they that wait for the Lord shall renew their strength; they shall mount up with wings as eagles; they shall run, and not be weary; they shall walk, and not faint" Isaiah 40:31. The fruit of the Spirit that is so needed in the body of Christ and in the life of every Christian is the fruit of patience and waiting on the Lord and being patient to the last hopeless moment. The remedy "Rejoicing in hope; patient in tribulation; continuing steadfastly (instantly) in prayer" Romans 12:12. Throughout the history of bible we have seen great patriarchs, God's generals, prophets and faithful pilgrims have had their faith and faithfulness to God tested and tried. "That the trial of your faith, being much more precious than of gold that perishes, though it be tried with fire, might be found to praise and honor and glory at the appearing of Jesus Christ" I Peter 1:7

Letting patience have her perfect work, that ye may be perfect and entire, wanting nothing (James1:4). The one thing that patience (waiting on the Lord) is guaranteed to produce is perfection. Jumping the gun has always brought disaster as seen in the case of Abraham and Ishmael. According to Genesis 16 Ishmael was Abraham's fist born son, in Israel the firstborn son was given twice as much of the inheritance as the rest of the sons. In Exodus 13:1-2

"The LORD said to Moses, 'consecrate to me every firstborn male. The first offspring of every womb among the Israelites belongs to me, whether man or animal." This was not supposed to be if Abraham had fully obeyed God and waited for THE PROMISE, the covenant child, because Ishmael was a quick fix to their doubt and unbelief. And for generations because of the blessing upon the Ishmaelite found in Genesis 21:13 "And also of the son of the bondwoman will I make a nation, because he is thy seed" being the one that carried the birthright of a super blessed friend of God we have reaped the fruits of their doing. Abraham produced two sons primarily. One suffered and endured the pain of rejection from his father, and to this day we see him (Ishmael) exhibit the fruits of rejection, and the other (the chosen one) paid the price of acceptance and we see the two in constant war with each other. God again in Judges ordered the Israelites to destroy them all but that didn't happen, they ended up coexisting and intermarrying and have suffered the consequences since; Sibling hatred based on destiny and purpose. One was chosen and one rejected all because of the simple fruit of Patience or the lack of it.

Patience births perfection. For us to see the perfect will of God unfold and fulfilled accordingly it is a must for patience to come to fruition! Wait on the LORD: be of good courage, and he shall strengthen thine heart: wait, I say, on the LORD. Even when it seems impossible because it will look impossible, wait on the Lord. David said in Psalms "I would have fainted or despaired unless I had believed that to see the goodness of the LORD In the land of the living? Psalms 27:13 "For evildoers shall be cut off: but those that wait upon the LORD, they shall inherit the earth" Psalms 37:9. "Wait on the LORD, and keep his way, and he shall exalt you to inherit the land: when the wicked are cut off, you shall see it" Psalms 37:34.

There is a promised reward to them that will wait on the Lord. As hard as it is God made sure that your labor of waiting be not in vain? And to him that overcometh shall be bestowed with all these blessings. Being faithful unto death is a privilege, and a gift. Jesus said because the world hated Him we too will be hated (Mark 13:13). Out of the book of Revelation God spells out His the promise of reward. His Word does not return unto Him void (Isaiah 55:11), in the fullness of time . . .

- To him that overcometh will I give to eat of the tree of life, which is in the midst of the paradise of God. Revelation 2:7
- He that overcometh shall not be hurt of the second death. Revelation 2:11
- To him that overcometh will I give to eat of the hidden manna, and will give him a white stone, and in the stone a new name written, which no man knoweth saving he that receiveth it. Revelation 2:17
- And he that overcometh, and keepeth my works unto the end, to him will I give power over the nations: And he shall rule them with a rod of iron; as the vessels of a potter shall they be broken to shivers: even as I received of my Father. And I will give him the morning star. Revelation 2:26-28
- He that overcometh, the same shall be clothed in white raiment; and I will not blot out his name out of the book of life, but I will confess his name before my Father, and before his angels. Revelation 3:5
- Him that overcometh will I make a pillar in the temple of my God, and he shall go no more out: and I will write upon him the name of my God, and the name of the city of my God, which is new Jerusalem, which cometh down out of heaven from my God: and I will write upon him my new name. Revelation 3:12
- To him that overcometh will I grant to sit with me in my throne, even as I also overcame, and am set down with my Father in his throne. Revelation 3:21
- He that overcometh shall inherit all things; and I will be his God, and he shall be my son. Revelation 21:7

Be vigilant and overcome, let patience have her perfect work.

CHAPTER 28

Six Days Shalt Thou Work

God in scripture has always associated unfruitfulness to wickedness and often called an unfruitful, lazy person wicked and worthy of damnation (Matthew 25:26). An idle mind is the devil's workshop they say and "in the multitude of business dreams are born" Ecclesiastes 5:3, "he who is slothful in his work is a brother to him who is a great destroyer" Proverbs 18:9. God worked for six days recreating this universe and rested on the seventh (Genesis 2:2), man is made in His image and is not an exception to this rule. "Six days shalt thou work, but on the seventh day thou shalt rest" Exodus 34:21, again it says "Six days thou shalt work: the seventh day thou shalt cease" Exodus 23:12. Before God created Adam in the flesh, it is written "The LORD God took the man and put him in the Garden of Eden to work it and take care of it" Genesis 2:15. He didn't plant the garden until there was a man to work it, and there's no better way to say than this "If a man is lazy, the rafters sag; if his hands are idle, the house leaks" Ecclesiastes 10:18. There are so many scriptures in the bible that condemns laziness and unfruitfulness.

"He spake also this parable; A certain man had a fig tree planted in his vineyard; and he came and sought fruit thereon, and found none. Then said he unto the dresser of his vineyard, Behold, these three years I come seeking fruit on this fig tree, and find none: cut it down; why cumbereth it the ground? And he answering said unto him, Lord, let it alone this year also, till I shall dig about it, and dung it: And if it bear fruit, well: and if not, then after that thou shalt cut it down" Luke 13:6-9. Jesus was speaking in parables about a tree that wouldn't bear fruit; it was to be cut down. Unfruitfulness is as unpopular today as it was yesterday and nobody wants a lazy anybody. "Every branch in Me that does not bear fruit, He takes away; and every branch that bears fruit, He prunes it so that it may bear more fruit" John 15:2. "For whoever has, to him shall be given, and he shall have more abundance: but whoever has not, from him shall be taken away even that he has" Matthew 13:12; Matthew 25:29; Mark 4:25 all these talk about increase, progress and bearing fruit.

God put His deposit in every person in order for it not to go to waste but to work "because the one who is in you is greater than the one who is in the world" I John 4:4. So there's really no excuse for any Christian, you have been given the mind of Christ (I Corinthians 2:16), "and do not be conformed to this world, but be transformed by the renewing of your mind, so that you may prove what the will of God is, that which is good and acceptable and perfect" Romans 12:2, redeeming the time (making the most of your time and opportunities) for the days are evil Ephesians 5:16. It is worldly to sit idly by, time wasted cannot be redeemed. We were created to be creative just like God, tilling the land was a command and work is a must. "Lazy hands bring poverty, but hard-working hands bring riches" Proverbs 10:4; "The soul of the sluggard craves and gets nothing, but the soul of the diligent is made fat" Proverbs 13:4. "The hand of the diligent shall bear rule: but the slothful shall be under tribute (forced labor)" Proverbs 12:24. Laziness brings the curse of poverty, lack and scarcity and that does not glorify God or reflect on His character "He owns a cattle and a thousand hills" Psalms 50:10 ". . . for the world is Mine, and the fullness thereof" Psalms 50:12 . . . "and the silver is Mine (God's) and gold is Mine (God's)" Haggai 2:8 ". . . you know the grace of our Lord Jesus, the Messiah. Although he was rich, for your sakes he became poor, so that you, through his poverty, might become rich" II Corinthians 8:9 and not just from winning the lottery but through diligence, work. "He became a curse for us . . . cursed is He that hangs on a tree" Galatians 3:13.

It isn't God's will for anyone not to work . . . "If a man will not work, he shall not eat." II Thessalonians 3:10. God loves the poor but hates slothfulness.

"A little sleep, a little slumber, a little folding of the hands to rest, so shall your poverty come upon you like a robber, and want like an armed man" Proverbs 6:10-11; Proverbs 24:33-34. "So I saw that there is nothing better than for a man to have joy in his work; for that is his portion . . ." Ecclesiastes 3:22. "The sluggard will not plow by reason of the cold; therefore shall he beg in harvest, and have nothing" Proverbs 20:4; "Love not sleep, lest thou come to poverty; open thine eyes, and thou shalt be satisfied with bread" Proverbs 20:13; "The desire of the slothful killeth him; for his hands refuse to labor. He coveteth greedily all the day long: but the righteous giveth and spareth not" Proverbs 21:25-26. "The slothful man roasteth not that which he took in hunting: but the substance of a diligent man is precious" Proverbs 12:27. I could go on and on. "Whatsoever your hand finds to do, do it with all your might; for there is no work (activity) or planning (device) or knowledge or wisdom in the grave (Sheol) where you are going" Ecclesiastes 9:10.

Let Not Your Hands Be Slack

CHAPTER 29

Reigning In Your Domain

"But also some of the Jewish exorcists, who went from place to place, attempted to name over those who had the evil spirits the name of the Lord Jesus, saying, "I adjure you by Jesus whom Paul preaches. And there were seven sons of one Sceva, a Jew, and chief of the priests, which did so. And the evil spirit answered and said, Jesus I know, and Paul I know; but who are you? And the man, in whom was the evil spirit, leaped on them and subdued all of them and overpowered them, so that they fled out of that house naked and wounded. And this was known to all the Jews and Greeks also dwelling at Ephesus; and fear fell on them all, and the name of the Lord Jesus was magnified. And many that believed came, and confessed, and showed their deeds. Many of them also which used curious arts brought their books together, and burned them before all men: and they counted the price of them, and found it fifty thousand pieces of silver. So mightily grew the word of God and prevailed" Acts 19:13-20.

This is exactly what happens to Christian believers that play games with God. So many times I have been with Christians who claim to be for the most part Christians but always getting whooped (whipped) by some circumstance and not really seeing the fruits of their labor. It is dangerous to sit on the fence, claiming one thing in public and living a lie in private. No one can ever get complete victory in their life while sitting on the fence like that, just like "no man can serve two masters: for either he will hate the one, and love the other; or else he will hold to the one, and despise the other. You cannot serve God and mammon" Matthew 6:24. ". . . He that wavereth is like a wave of the sea driven with the wind and tossed.

For let not that man think that he shall receive any thing of the Lord. A double minded man is unstable in all his ways" James 1:6-8. Bible rules must be obeyed for the blessing of God to flow and for you to experience total victory and experience wholeness in God. It is possible to live in total victory. God has promised but those promises flow only if those guidelines (God's Laws) are not being violated. "For whosoever shall keep the whole law, and yet offend (stumble) in one point, he is guilty of all" James 2:10. "And such as do wickedly against the covenant shall he corrupt by flatteries: but the people that do know their God shall be strong, and do exploits" Daniel 11:32

Here's how to gain complete control and have complete power, dominion and authority, complete victory in every area of your life, and have the peace of God that passes all understanding keep your heart and mind through Christ Jesus (Philippians 4:7): Right Standing With God!!. "He has showed you, O man, what is good; and what does the LORD require of you, but to do justly, and to love mercy, and to walk humbly with your God?" Micah 6:8. "And you shall do that which is right and good in the sight of the LORD: that it may be well with you, and that you may go in and possess the good land which the LORD swore to your fathers" Deuteronomy 6:18. No and's, if's or but's about this, spiritual forces are real and that's what we wrestle against on a daily basis either through people or circumstances, and more so if you bear the name of Jesus. God sees the hearts of every person: "But the LORD said to Samuel, "Do not consider his appearance or his height, for I have rejected him. The LORD does not look at the things man looks at. Man looks at the outward appearance, but the LORD looks at the heart" I Samuel 16:7. "But be you doers of the word, and not hearers only, deceiving your own selves" James 1:22

Here's another incident of people that had been walking with God and applying what they'd heard. After being with Jesus, listening, watching and understanding his heart for the ministry, they were given an opportunity and proved to be faithful and victorious. "And the seventy returned again with joy, saying, Lord, even the devils are subject unto us through thy name. And he said unto them, I beheld Satan as lightning fall from heaven. Behold, I give unto you power to tread on serpents and scorpions, and over all the power of the enemy: and nothing shall by any means harm you" Luke 10.17-19. For thou hast made him a little lower than the angels, and hast crowned him with glory and honor. Thou madest him to have dominion over the works of thy hands; thou hast put all things under his feet Psalms 8:5-6. God has entrusted every believer with His Power and authority . . . USE IT!! "You are of God, little children, and have overcome them: because greater is he that is in you, than he that is in the world" I John 4:4. There is no excuse for anyone that understands who they are in Christ to be defeated. "These things I have spoken to you, that in me you might have peace. In the world you shall have tribulation: but be of good cheer; I have overcome the world" John 16:33. And because He has overcome then you will overcome, If He failed like Adam did, then we'd be doomed to failure "BUT thanks be to God, which always causes us to triumph in Christ, and makes manifest the aroma of his knowledge by us in every place" II Corinthians 2:14. I'm glad He couldn't be a failure. His Father (The God of all creation), who is now your father were and are ONE.

Believer there is no excuse for if you do not rule and reign in your domain. "Every place on which the sole of your foot treads, I have given it to you, just as I spoke to Moses" Joshua 1:3 "Every place where on the soles of your feet shall tread shall be yours: from the wilderness and Lebanon, from the river, the river Euphrates, even to the uttermost sea shall your coast be" Deuteronomy 11:24. "God is not a man, that he should lie; neither the son of man, that he should repent: has he said, and shall he not do it? Or has he spoken, and shall he not make it good?" Numbers 23:19; "So shall my word be that goes forth out of my mouth: it shall not return to me void, but it shall accomplish that which I please, and it shall prosper in the thing whereto I sent it" Isaiah 55:11. "Keep therefore the words of this covenant, and do them, that you may prosper in all that you do" Deuteronomy 29:9. That's the antidote for ruling and reigning because ". . . ye are the elect race (chosen generation), a royal priesthood, a holy nation, a people for God's own possession (peculiar people), that ye may show forth the excellences of him who called you out of darkness into his marvelous light:" I Peter 2:9

It's time to reign in your Domain!!

CHAPTER 30

Marriage Holy, bed undefiled!!

This goes out to all. I have been serving in ministries that didn't give credit where credit was due based on this topic we're about to explore. I wasn't recognized for the gift God bestowed on me because I didn't have a spouse. It was the pastor's conviction, message and belief that "two are better than one" (Ecclesiastes 4:9) "because they have a good reward for their labor; for if they fall, one will lift up his companion; but woe to him who is alone when he falls, for he has no one to help him up. Again, if two lie down together, they will keep warm; but how can one be warm alone? Though one may be overpowered by another, two can withstand him. And a threefold cord is not quickly broken." That was his argument according to scripture that ruled us single ministers at that time and made us feel guilty about why we weren't married at the time, in spite of my convictions to serve God as a single woman. And of course his favorite scripture in support of this dogmatic thinking was that "God said it is not good for the man to be alone" Genesis 2:18 and a suitable helper was needed for him.

There is a woman in every man, and woman is made complete: God said it is not good for the man (Adam) to be alone (Genesis 2:18) and Eve was made for Adam. "God caused the man to fall into a deep sleep; and while he was sleeping, he took one of the man's ribs and closed up the place with flesh. Then the LORD God made a woman from the rib he had taken out of the man and he brought her to the man. The man said, 'This is now bone of my bones and flesh of my flesh; she shall be called 'woman, for she was taken out of man" (Genesis 2:21-23. Apostle Paul backs this up even though his main motive and intention (if you read all his letters) is to enlighten readers about the roles each gender are to play as far as ranking is concerned. For generations it was believed that women were created to be servants or slaves and for generations that's exactly how women were portrayed. In I Corinthians 11:8-9 it is written "For the man is not of the woman: but the woman of the man. Neither was the man created for the woman; but the woman for the man." If you decide to get married, you'll be marrying the earth, dust of the ground according to Genesis 2.7 and will have to put up with what comes with it, i.e. earthly, fleshy sensual worldly things of this world.

"Turn, O backsliding children, says the LORD; for I am married unto you: and I will take you one of a city, and two of a family, and I will bring you to Zion" Jeremiah 3:14: Let's dig a little deeper. This is not about forbidding you to marry; I Timothy 4:3, but according to scripture bring enlightenment of who God is and the love He has for all, but mankind in the quest and longing for control use only some portions of scripture to manipulate their congregation into getting the kind of results they're looking for from their congregation. Once you enter into covenant with God, you become married to God . . . and you ought to care for the things of God and that becomes the primary will of God for your life.

Now about what you asked: "Is it advisable for a man not to marry?" I Corinthians 7:1-2 (NIV), the same scripture reads like this according to the New American Standard version "now concerning the things about which you wrote, it is good for a man not to touch a woman, but, because of fornications {a worldly act done by children of the world who will not inherit the kingdom of God, ref: 'neither fornicators, nor idolaters, nor adulterers, shall inherit the kingdom of God' I Corinthians 6:9-10} . . . let each man have his own wife, and let each woman have her own husband." "The unmarried woman cares for the things of the Lord, that she may be holy both in body and in spirit: but she that is married cares for the things of the world, how she may please her husband." I Corinthians 7:34. "And Jesus answering said unto them, the children of this world marry, and are given in marriage: But they which shall be accounted worthy to obtain that world, and the resurrection from the dead, neither marry, nor are given in marriage:" Luke 20:34 "know ye not that the friendship of the world is enmity with God. Whosoever therefore will be a friend of the world is the enemy of God" James 4:4.

There's just no better way to say it. God loves us all whether you have the strength to control yourself or not, so if you choose to marry, you're saving yourself from the fires of hell, if you choose not to marry, celibacy is a command, a requirement and an eternal lifestyle till Jesus returns. "So it's fine for a father to give his daughter in marriage, but the father who doesn't give his daughter in marriage does even better" I Corinthians 7:38, "So I say to those who are not married, especially to widows: It is good for you to stay single like me. But if they do not have self-control, let them marry; for it is better to marry than to burn with passion" I Corinthians 7:8-9. "But if you do get married, you have not sinned. If a virgin gets married, she has not sinned. However, these people will have trouble, and I would like to spare them from that" I Corinthians 7:28 "The wife is bound by the law as long as her husband lives; but if her husband be dead, she is at liberty to be married to whom she will; only in the Lord: But in my opinion she is happier if she remains as she is; and I think that I also have the Spirit of God." I Corinthians 7:39-40

God is God of all; He is unbiased and would rather if you were single. It can be as sensitive as this "But I say to you, That whoever looks on a woman to lust after her has committed adultery (for married folk) with her already in his heart" Matthew 5:28 so in order to avoid fornication then marry, and if you're married be faithful to the letter! For the singles I say . . . "I will lift up mine eyes unto the hills, from whence cometh my help. My help cometh from the LORD, which made heaven and earth" Psalms 121:1-2. Don't worry if you fall and there's no one to help . . . Ecclesiastes 4:9, "for a righteous man falls seven times, and rises again, But the wicked stumble in time of calamity" Proverbs 24:16. The steps of a good man and woman are ordered by the LORD: and he delighteth in his way. Though he fall, he shall not be utterly cast down: for the LORD upholdeth him with his hand. I live you with word to ponder: "Better one handful with tranquility [peace] than two handfuls with toil and chasing after the wind." Eccl 4:6.

The choice is yours, to marry or not to marry

Chapter 31

Music for the Heavenlies

"Son of man, take up a lamentation on the king of Tyrus, and say unto him, thus said the Lord GOD; Thou sealest up the sum, full of wisdom, and perfect in beauty. Thou hast been in Eden the garden of God; every precious stone wast thy covering, the sardius, topaz, and the diamond, the beryl, the onyx, and the jasper, the sapphire, the emerald, and the carbuncle, and gold: the workmanship of thy tabrets and thy pipes wast prepared in thee in the day that thou wast created. Thou wast the anointed cherub that covereth: and I set thee,'so that thou wast upon the holy mountain of God; thou hast walked up and down in the midst of the stones of fire. Thou wast perfect in thy ways from the day that thou wast created, till unrighteousness was found in thee. By the abundance of thy traffic (merchandise) they filled the midst of thee with violence, and thou hast sinned: therefore have I cast thee as profane out of the mountain of God; and I have destroyed thee, O covering cherub, from the midst of the stones of fire. Thy heart was lifted up because of thy beauty; thou hast corrupted thy wisdom by reason of thy brightness: I have cast thee to the ground; I have laid thee before kings, that they may behold thee. By the multitude of thine iniquities, in the unrighteousness of thy traffic (merchandise), thou hast profaned thy sanctuaries; therefore have I brought forth a fire from the midst of thee; it hath devoured thee, and I have turned thee to ashes upon the earth in the sight of all them that behold thee. All they that know thee among the peoples shall be astonished at thee: thou art become a terror, and thou shalt nevermore have any being" Ezekiel 28:12-19.

Today's topic is a sensitive one and about to strike a cord and mess with a nerve. The second person in command (back in the day) was created with the gift of music as seen above. The reason why God created the angel Lucifer with such a musical gift and ability was so that God could be magnified and glorified in worship. He was the covering cherub that dwelt in the Heavenlies, he beheld God and his commission was that through that awesome gift of music he would worship God and no other angel was bestowed with this ability. Therefore Music was initially intended for worship to GOD! That's how it was and that's how it will be forever!

There's a very fine line between the spiritual realms and as we see in Job 1, when the angels of God arrayed themselves before God, Satan was there with them, explains one thing, that he is allowed to roam freely. That's the bottom line. Music is very spiritual and based on these facts:

- Music was planted in a spiritual being . . . Ref: Psalm 104:1-4 "Bless the LORD, O my soul. O LORD my God, thou art very great; thou art clothed with honour and majesty. Who coverest thyself with light as with a garment: who stretchest out the heavens like a curtain: Who layeth the beams of his chambers in the waters: who maketh the clouds his chariot: who walketh upon the wings of the wind: Who maketh his angels spirits; his ministers a flaming fire:
- Music originated from God:
- Music was orchestrated in the Spiritual realm, Ref: John 4:24 "God is a Spirit: and they that worship him must worship in spirit and truth."

The prophet Elisha understood the power of music, when Israel was faced with another crisis and Jehosphat went to Elisha for a Word from the Lord. Elisha ordered a musician to be brought to him, Ref: "But now bring me a minstrel. And it came to pass, when the minstrel played, that the hand of The Lord came upon him. And he said, Thus saith the LORD . . ." II Kings 3:15-16. The atmosphere became conducive for prophesy because the music that was played changed the spiritual atmosphere and ushered the presence of God. It had to begin in the unseen (spiritual realm) and then a manifestation was revealed in the seen (natural realm). Here's another illustration on how powerfully spiritual music is . . . "And it came to pass, when the evil spirit from God was upon Saul, that David took an harp, and played with his hand: so Saul was refreshed, and was well, and the evil spirit departed from him" I Samuel 16:23. God loves music that much and humans like God love music. It speaks volumes and touches to the soul from the spirit in ways that cannot be explained.

Tragedy is when Lucifer was expelled from Heaven and cast down to the earth. God did not take away the gift from him, it was still engrafted in him . . . Ref: "And he (Jesus) said unto them, I beheld Satan fall as lightning from heaven" Luke 10:18. Up until this point music was solely intended for worship. Since the fall of Satan music became corrupted and the intent twisted that music has been used for other purposes other than worship to the one true God. God also put the gift in man after Satan lost his crown to replace what was lost and just like Adam deviated from his purpose so do the people of this age with this musical ability. Many of them have yielded to seducing spirits and corrupted the intention . . . (Ref: "Now the Spirit speaketh expressly, that in the latter times some shall depart from the faith, giving heed to seducing spirits, and doctrines of devils; Speaking lies in hypocrisy; having their conscience seared with a hot iron;" I Timothy 4:1-2). Songs are composed just about anything and everything other than the originator of music and its purpose because the prince of this world has blinded them Ref: "In whom the god of this world hath blinded the minds of them which believe not" II Corinthians 4:4 and ". . . their minds were hardened; for until this very day at the reading of the old covenant the same veil remains unlifted, because it is removed in Christ" II Corinthians 3:14 and they have never come to the knowledge of the truth (II Timothy 3:7).

Another truth based on scripture; musically speaking or not, just by the fact that words are used in most songs unless we're dealing with an instrumental piece which is no exception to the rule, and words have power, ". . . and calls those things which be not, as though they were" Romans 4:17 . . . "death and life are in the power of the tongue; and they that love it shall eat the fruit thereof" Proverbs 18:21; "an evil man is ensnared by the transgression of his lips, but the righteous will escape from trouble; a man shall be satisfied with good by the fruit of his mouth . . ." Proverbs 12:13-14; "He who keeps watch over his mouth and his tongue keeps his soul from troubles" Proverbs 21:23; A man's belly shall be satisfied with the fruit of his mouth; and with the increase of his lips shall he be filled Proverbs 18:20: ". . . by your words you shall be justified, and by your words you shall be condemned" Matthew 12:37. So you might find yourself cursing yourself depending on what the message in the music is projected.

"For I am the LORD, I change not" Malachi 3:6 "Jesus Christ the same yesterday, and today, and forever" Hebrews 13:8. King David understood the purpose of his gift. He honored God with it and God honored him back and established an everlasting (eternal) kingdom through his lineage in spite of his failures and shortcomings. You can't go wrong with this truth . . .

Let Music Return To Worship.

CHAPTER 32

Nothing's For Nothing; Something's For Something

"In the beginning God . . ." Genesis 1:1; ". . . The world and all it contains, You have founded them" Psalms 89:11, def. for founded—to set up; to launch; to institute; use as a basis for; grounded on; having a basis ; "In the beginning was the Word, and the Word was with God, and the Word was God" John 1:1. Someone was there in the beginning, not something or nothing according to scripture. God created something out of something and not something out of nothing. The fact fact that He was there from everlasting (past eternity) to everlasting (future eternity) gives us an idea that, He (God) started something, out of Himself but there was something to work on. "You send forth your spirit, they are created: and you renew the face of the earth" Psalms 104:30. "And the earth was without form, and void; and darkness was upon the face of the deep. And the Spirit of God moved upon the face of the waters" Genesis 1:2.

God is a God of vision, perception, purpose, journey (requires setting goals, planning and preparation) accomplishments of those goals, a successful, prosperous destination, beauty and perfection. Anything other than that is not a reflection of God but that of a wonna be. The standards He sets for Himself are unattainable to man based on the fall of man, not even the angels have the capacity to reach those standards because He is God all by Himself and there is none beside Him. From Genesis to Revelation God speaks . . . of a beginning, a journey (processing) and a destination. When God created Adam and Eve, He had a vision, plan and a purpose for them. They were created in the image of God Himself; they were a reflection of God to be exact. According Genesis 1:1 the world was indeed perfect, between Genesis 1:1 and Genesis 1:2, there is no scripture directly explaining where the commotion and destruction came from or a story that connects the two verses. My explanation is found in Luke 10:18, "And he said unto them, I beheld Satan as lightning fall from heaven," why ". . . Because your heart is lifted up and you have said, "I am a god, I sit in the seat of gods in the heart of the seas:" Yet you are a man and not God. You were in Eden, the garden of God; every precious stone was your covering: The ruby, the topaz and the diamond; the beryl, the onyx and the jasper; the lapis lazuli, the turquoise and the emerald; and the gold, the workmanship of your settings and sockets, were in you. On the day that you were created they were prepared. "You were the anointed cherub who covers, and I placed you there. You were on the holy mountain of God; you walked in the midst of the stones of fire. You were blameless in your ways from the day you were created until unrighteousness was found in you. By the abundance of your trade you were internally filled with violence, and you sinned; therefore I have cast you as profane from the mountain of God. And I have destroyed you, O covering cherub, from the midst of the stones of fire. Your heart was lifted up because of your beauty; you corrupted your wisdom by reason of your splendor. I cast you to the ground; Ezekiel 28:1-17.

Before Adam was created Satan had already been thrown to the earth! He existed as a fallen angel; dethroned because he wanted to be like God and God already declared that there was none like Him and there will never be another in Heaven above or in earth below. As a fallen angel he didn't like the idea of being replaced by a creature who looked like God himself that would ultimately defeat all of his purpose and existence. He (Satan) spent time observing what plan of action to use until he found something that could work. In the Spiritual realm Adam and Eve were created at the same time Genesis 1:26 and the blessing was spoken into their lives without any restrictions . . . Genesis 1:28-31 "And God blessed them, and God said unto them, Be fruitful, and multiply, and replenish the earth, and subdue it: and have dominion over the fish of the sea, and over the fowl of the air, and over every living thing that moveth upon the earth And God said, Behold, I have given you every herb bearing seed, which is upon the face of all the earth, and every tree, in the which is the fruit of a tree yielding seed; to you it shall be for meat. And to every beast of the earth, and to every fowl of the air, and to everything that creepeth upon the earth, wherein there is life, I have given every green herb for meat: and it was so. And God saw everything that he had made, and, behold, it was very good. And the evening and the morning were the sixth day."

"And every plant of the field before it was in the earth, and every herb of the field before it grew: for the LORD God had not caused it to rain upon the earth, and there was not a man to till the ground" Genesis 2:5 but they existed in Genesis 1:26 because God created them. Ironic. "And the LORD God formed man of the dust of the ground, and breathed into his nostrils the breath of life; and man became a living soul. And the LORD God planted a garden eastward in Eden; and there he put the man whom he had formed. Out of the ground made the LORD God to grow every tree that is pleasant to the sight, and good for food; the tree of life also in the midst of the garden, and the tree of knowledge of good and evil." Genesis 2:2-10 "And the LORD God took the man, and put him into the Garden of Eden to dress it and to keep it. And the LORD God commanded the man, saying, of every tree of the garden thou mayest freely eat: but of the tree of the knowledge of good and evil, thou shalt not eat of it: for in the day that thou eatest thereof thou shalt surely die. And the LORD God said it is not good that the man should be alone; I will make him a help meet for him" Genesis 2:15-17. "And the LORD God caused a deep sleep to fall upon Adam, and he slept: and he took one of his ribs, and closed up the flesh instead thereof; And the rib, which the LORD God had taken from man, made he a woman, and brought her unto the man" Genesis 2:21-22.

Eve wasn't there when God gave the commands about the forbidden trees in the garden, she hadn't been created yet. All the dos and don'ts were given to Adam. By the time Eve came around, Satan through observation floating in space (a spiritual realm unseen to the natural) noticed the emotional reaction and connection Adam expressed when interacting with Eve. He found a loophole . . . God is not imperfect, His plan for our lives works if we work it. This thing called a free will was given to man when God created man in His image and because God is not bound by anything or anybody, man was also not bound by anything or anyone but GOD. He was given dominion, the power and authority to rule over all! ". . . and subdue it: and have dominion over the fish of the sea, and over the fowl of the air, and over every living thing that moveth upon the earth Genesis 1:28. Our plans are faulty without God. When Adam exercised his freewill and ate the fruit, proved that when man violates God imperfection and destruction begin to take a toll. God is all about perfection. If you walk the line and follow His will you will be okay. He tried to protect man, He knew what was out there but man turned his back on God on his own free will!

Understanding God will take an eternity but the model that He has set before us to use has shed some light about His ways, nothing's for nothing, and something's for something . . . There was a plan for those trees being in the midst of the garden. Timing was of the essence. When they ate the fruit of the knowledge of good and evil, God removed the tree of life to preserve what was left of His plan for their lives in and for His timing. Adam's timing interfered with God's timing. If God says wait, then wait. "To everything there is a season, and a time to every purpose under the heaven:" Ecclesiastes 3:1.

Timing is everything

CHAPTER 33

Unlimited Possibilities

"I returned, and saw under the sun, that the race is not to the swift, nor the battle to the strong, neither yet bread to the wise, nor yet riches to men of understanding, nor yet favor to men of skill; but time and chance happeneth to them all" Ecclesiastes 9:10. Today I'll talk about possibilities. For those who are faced with challenges in whatever they endeavor to do . . . me included there is nothing impossible. We are responsible for how high we want to go. Those barriers of doubt, fear and unbelief, unpreparedness and lack of planning, not being adequately equipped, are stumbling blocks that can easily be turned into stepping stones if you have the understanding of who you really are as a Christians. "Now faith is the substance of things hoped for, the evidence of things not seen" another version explains it better "Now faith is the assurance that what we hope for will come about and the certainty that what we cannot see exists" better yet, I'll post another version of the same scripture with a different interpretation carrying the same meaning "Faith assures us of things we expect and convinces us of the existence of things we cannot see" and "Now faith is the assurance of things hoped for, the proving of things not seen." I could go on and on posting different versions of this scripture found in Hebrews 11:1.

It speaks of possibilities, existing facts that there is no hindrance accept the hindrance in our minds created but fear and doubt and the corresponding action of our lips. We belong to an unlimited God, He resides inside of us and His Holy Spirit engulfs us. We have a model to emulate and a map to follow that clearly spells out instructions on how to get there, what Spiritual foods to eat so that we don't go hungry and yet we find ourselves stuck every now and then. Let me remind you of how powerful we are . . . 1 Corinthians 15:27 "For he hath put all things under his feet. But when he saith all things are put under him, it is manifest that he is excepted, which did put all things under him." We're talking about your BIG Brother Jesus Christ . . . Psalm 8:6 "You make him to rule over the works of Your hands; You have put all things under his feet," Matthew 11:27 "All things have been handed over to Me (Jesus Christ) by My Father; and no one knows the Son except the Father; nor does anyone know the Father except the Son, and anyone to whom the Son wills to reveal Him" Matthew 28:18 "And Jesus came up and spoke to them, saying, "All authority has been given to Me in heaven and on earth" Ephesians 1:22 "And He put all things in subjection under His feet, and gave Him as head over all things to the church", Hebrews 2:8 "YOU HAVE PUT ALL THINGS IN SUBJECTION UNDER HIS FEET." For in subjecting all things to him, He left nothing that is not subject to him. But now we do not yet see all things subjected to him.

"Enlarge the place of your tent, and let them stretch forth the curtains of your habitations: spare not, lengthen your cords, and strengthen your stakes;" Isaiah 54:2 why? "For you shall break forth on the right hand and on the left; and your seed shall inherit the Gentiles, and make the desolate cities to be inhabited." If this is to take place in the natural then your mind has to be the starting point. Here God commands us to stop putting limits on Him and dare to expand our vision without fear. God created man to have no boundaries, only the trees at the center of the garden in Genesis 2. It takes strategy, planning and preparation, wisdom and knowledge, strength of a unicorn "God brought him forth out of Egypt; he hath as it were the strength of a unicorn" . . . it can be done. "Though your beginning was small, yet your latter end should greatly increase" Job 8:7 so" . . . who has despised the day of small things? For they shall rejoice" Zechariah 4:10. "For I am confident of this very thing, that He who began a good work in you will perfect it until the day of Christ Jesus" Philippians 1:6.

Matthew 11:27 "All things have been handed over to Me by My Father; and no one knows the Son except the Father; nor does anyone know the Father except the Son, and anyone to whom the Son wills to reveal Him" Matthew 28:18 "And Jesus came up and spoke to them, saying, "All authority has been given to Me in heaven and on earth" Jesus was given all power and authority in Heaven and earth and that same power and authority has been handed over to us and "Behold, I give to you power to tread on serpents and scorpions, and over all the power of the enemy: and nothing shall by any means hurt you" Luke 10:19. "Every place that the sole of your foot shall tread, that have I given to you, as I said to Moses," Joshua 1:3. "There shall not any man be able to stand before you all the days of your life: as I was with Moses, so I will be with you: I will not fail you, nor forsake you, be strong and of a good courage: for to this people shall you divide for an inheritance the land, which I swore to their fathers to give them. Only be you strong and very courageous, that you may observe to do according to all the law, which Moses my servant commanded you: turn not from it to the right hand or to the left that you may prosper wherever you go. This book of the law shall not depart out of your mouth; but you shall meditate therein day and night, that you may observe to do according to all that is written therein: for then you shall make your way prosperous, and then you shall have good success. Have not I commanded you? Be strong and of a good courage; be not afraid, neither be you dismayed: for the LORD your God is with you wherever you go" Joshua 1:5-9.

There is your recipe for total success. There are no limits whatsoever . . . what might seem to be impossible to you is actually an opportunity to reexamine watchfully, carefully. Life is a journey and success is too. "For precept must be upon precept, precept upon precept; line upon line, line upon line; here a little, and there a little:" Isaiah 28:10. It's a learning process, correct what's wrong and keep on going there is no limit to your success. You are an unlimited being, possessing an unlimited potential to complete your purpose because of the Unlimited God who resides in you and "being confident of this very thing, that he who began a good work in you will perfect it until the day of Jesus Christ:" Philippians 1:6. Walk the line, be patient and you will be over the top. It's your heritage. "Verily, verily, I say unto you, he that believeth on me, the works that I do shall he do also; and greater works than these shall he do; because I go unto the Father" John 14:12.

Embrace Your Unlimited Possibilities.

CHAPTER 34

Temple for Merchandise??
How low will you go?!!

"**D**o you not know that your body is a temple of the Holy Spirit, who is in you, whom you have received from God? You are not your own; you were bought at a price. Therefore honor God with your body" I Corinthians 6:19-20. This is very complicated especially in today's society. I'm about to tread stormy waters but at least I dropped my heart open and left guiltless. If what you do with your body does not bring honor to God according to the Will and Testament, honey you erreth! Satan is the mastermind of this deception and author of all confusion when it comes to what's right and wrong. In Matthew 4:1-11, Jesus Himself was no exception to this rule. With all the power He had on earth, bowing down to a good idea didn't derail Him from his mission and plainly unacceptable. If He traded the glory His Heavenly Father had waiting for Him if He followed through for a glory that would last him his 33 years on earth and pay bitterly in the end would have been a disaster for Himself and the human race He was on quest to save.

Adam and Eve hadn't been exposed to devils and principalities, their world was perfect with no interference, and disturbance or deceit until the master of deception sneaked in turned their whole life around. Genesis 3.1 records that ". . . the serpent was more crafty (and subtle) than any of the wild animals the LORD God had made. He said to the woman, "Did God really say, 'You must not eat from any tree in the garden'?". And I say unto you yeah did God really say . . . think about that for a minute. Every time you get fabulous money making scheme that violates scripture in some form do you jump on it without really thinking saying that God will get the glory or what? The will for your life is in the Will and Testament that you ought to spend more time reading (The Bible) and in order to withstand the wiles of the devil, you need to put on the Whole Armor of God (Ephesians 6:10-11). How can you guard yourself if you do not know how?

I have had many opportunities to do modeling but turned them down for one reason only . . . that at some point I would be required to be parsley clothed and array myself on an isle in order to get a garment sold. Here's the problem, according to scripture "whoever loves his brother lives in the light, and there is nothing in him to make him stumble" (I John 2:10), and "It is good neither to eat flesh, nor to drink wine, nor any thing whereby thy brother stumbleth, or is offended, or is made weak" Romans 14:21. "Therefore, if food causes my brother to stumble, I will never eat meat again, so that I will not cause my brother to stumble" 1 Corinthians 8:13. I know that my semi-naked body has the ability to make someone lust for my body that would potentially drive them to sin against their bodies and against God so it would be a violation and against the Will of God for my life if I took on modeling in today's world. Jesus was speaking into the future when He said these words ". . . to them that sold doves, take these things hence; make not my Father's house a house of merchandise." John 2:16. We all know that we (the body of Christ have been bought with a price and we're no longer our own). The warning here was not turn the temple (which is the father's) where the Holy Spirit resides and dwells into a soliciting object. Use the brain and the hands. The bible says in Ecclesiastes 9:10 "Whatsoever thy hand (not your sensual body) findeth to do, do it with thy might; for there is no work, nor device, nor knowledge, nor wisdom, in the grave, whither thou goest."

You would think that only the weak would fall into this trap but this takes it to another level. This is a man that walked with Jesus all through His ministry up until this point in Matthew 26:14-16 "Then one of the twelve, called Judas Iscariot, went unto the chief priests, And said unto them, What will ye give me, and I will deliver him unto you? And they covenanted with him for thirty pieces of silver. And from that time he sought opportunity to betray him."

Greed was his master and he succumbed to it like a baby to its milk. He was easily tempted of the devil because he had a preexisting problem and Satan capitalized on this problem of greed and ended up killing himself out of guilt. Even though Jesus allowed to it in order to fulfill scripture Judas ended up in the world's hall of shame for trading the ultimate Temple of the Holy Spirit for 30 pieces of silver . . . much like we do today. It made him rich sure enough for a season and paid for it with his life for The Life he traded. He traded the Temple for Merchandise!

God condemns harlotry. Time and time again He judged the Israelites for their unfaithfulness to Him. That tells us one thing; He made a woman for a man! polygamy was not designed by God as a matter of fact HE only allowed it because of man's fallen nature and the ignorance that came with it. God built the one woman for the one man He created. Prostitution, polygamy and adultery are not of God. They are an abomination and should not be performed, encouraged or tolerated. If He approved of it, Adam would have had Eve, Evelyn and add Steve to the list.

This subject transcends all scopes and spheres when talking about trading humans for money or slavery. "Then there passed by Midianites merchantmen; and they drew and lifted up Joseph out of the pit, and sold Joseph to the Ishmaelites for twenty pieces of silver: and they brought Joseph into Egypt" Genesis 37:28. Need I remind you that "You were bought with a price; do not become slaves of men" I Corinthians 7:23 if you can help it! Plain and simple Father's house and your body (if a born again Christian) have one thing in common . . . both house the Holy Spirit and referred to as temples, hence temples of the Holy Spirit therefore total care needs to be taken when dealing with the Father's House. Remember "for ye are bought with a price: therefore glorify God in your body, and in your spirit, which are God's" I Corinthians 6:20. "And Jesus said unto her, neither do I condemn thee: go, and sin no more" John 8:11. "He that is without sin cast the first stone" John 8:7. With this I leave you with this to ponder "for what shall it profit a man, if he shall gain the whole world, and lose his own soul?" Mark 8:36

Glorify God in your bodies the Godly Way!!

Chapter 35

Who told you you're not gifted? Woman??!

I am daring to go there. For centuries men have had control over women and women have been put on the same level as children, and in some cultures they still do. The only credit women get get is child bearing and in some modern societies is still considered a curse. Blame it on the ego (a clear disillusion on superiority); in later decades women have fought (some shed blood) for equality (another clear indication of disillusion) and broken free from masculine dictatorship. The mind we now know is a powerful organ; an organ that on its own cannot be controlled. It can be influenced by ideas, opinions, doctrines and/or philosophies but not controlled. You can get the illusion and your mind can make you think you're controlling another adult being but every person was created to possess a free will and the ability to make decisions independently, individually and own an opinion without and apart from interference, intrusion or influence. And when I talk about the mind, I mean the grown up mind.

The form of punishment for BOTH men and women who commit sexual sins in the Old Testament was death by stoning. BUT In John 8: 1-11 ". . . Jesus went to the Mount of Olives. Early in the morning he came again to the temple; all the people came to him, and he sat down and taught them. The scribes and the Pharisees brought a woman who had been caught in adultery, and placing her in the midst they said to him, 'Teacher, this woman has been caught in the act of adultery. Now in the law Moses commanded us to stone such. What do you say about her?" It has never been recorded in the bible that the men was just as guilty but preachers tell of this incident emphasizing on the woman who was caught in the act.

"Zelophehad son of Hepher had no sons; he had only daughters, whose names were Mahlah, Noah, Hoglah, Milcah and Tirzah" Numbers 26:33. "The daughters of Zelophehad son of Hepher, belonged to the clans of Manasseh son of Joseph. The names of the daughters were Mahlah, Noah, Hoglah, Milcah and Tirzah. They approached the entrance to the Tent of Meeting and stood before Moses, Eleazar the priest, the leaders and the whole assembly, and said, our father died in the desert. He was not among Korah's followers, who banded together against the LORD, but he died for his own sin and left no sons. Why should our father's name disappear from his clan because he had no son? Give us property among our father's relatives. So Moses brought their case before the LORD and the LORD said to him, What Zelophehad's daughters are saying is right. You must certainly give them property as an inheritance among their father's relatives and turn their father's inheritance over to them" Numbers 27:1-7. Need not to explain this passage it's self-explanatory. These women placed a demand based on their right to inherit their father's property and God said that they were right!! Women need to do the same thing. God does not discriminate, people do, you too have an inheritance with your Heavenly Father and sometimes based on your right to inherit your portion, have to place a demand regardless of what people (society at large) thinks or says!!!

Single moms I feel for you because this society has had a tendency to punish women who have had babies before they got married. Single moms in positions of authority raise questions of morality, integrity and character. Some have been mistaken for solicitors while the men who fathered these children walk as free men. They should be a law in place that says these men be given the same treatment if not worse than the women they impregnated, in fact they should be mutilated Bobbit style, ". . . if your right eye causes you to sin, tear it out and throw [it] from you! For it is better for you that one of your members be destroyed than your whole body be thrown into hell" Matthew 5:29. This might sound harsh to you but society shows no mercy on these women in passing judgment and GOD has literally provided a solution. "Judge not and thou shalt not be judged . . ." Matthew 7.1 and Luke 6.37). I do not like to use the words "out of wedlock" because really these children had no control of their existence and they do not deserve to be referred to as children born out of wedlock. In II Corinthians 3:6 we know that "the letter killeth" and since a most governance and houses of law are based on the letter hence judgment or judging is inevitable. "Children are a heritage of the LORD: and the fruit of the womb is his reward. As arrows in the hand of a mighty warrior, so are the children of one's youth. Happy is the man or woman whose quiver is filled with them, they will speak to the adversaries at the gate" Psalms 127:3-5 and especially not when there's an indiscriminate, unbiased promise from God found in Isaiah 54:13 "And all your children shall be taught of the LORD; and great shall be the peace of your children". According to John 1:12-13 sheds light and reveals what preachers {male chauvinistic dogmatic preachers ignore (deliberately I believe)}. It reads "but as many as received him, to them gave the power to become the sons of God, even to them that believe on his name: Which were born, *not of blood, *nor of the will of the flesh, *nor of the will of man, but of God. There you have it. There were and still have been babies born of blood (artificial insemination?), will of the flesh (fornication and adultery?) and thirdly will of man (cloning?). It blows my mind! BUT God will accept all who will accept Jesus Christ!!

"There is one body, and one Spirit, even as ye are called in one hope of your calling; one Lord, one faith, one baptism, one God and Father of all, who is above all, and through all, and in you all (hear this woman). But unto every one of us (woman included) is given grace according to the measure of the gift of Christ. Wherefore he saith, when he ascended up on high, he led captivity captive, and gave gifts unto men . . ." (If this same statement was owned or spoken by Prophetess Deborah of Judges or Mary Magdalene, the wording would have been different, inclusive, but since a man called Apostle Paul is responsible for that kind of language (I call it Paul's doctrine), then we have to put up with the exclusivity in the passage as it only mentions gifts to men) but this does not exclude the woman! ". . . And he gave some, apostles; and some, prophets; and some, evangelists; and some, pastors and teachers; for the perfecting of the saints, for the work of the ministry, for the edifying of the body of Christ: Ephesians 4:4-12. I'll go deeper The same God (who was a man) through the mouth Moses His servant ordered capital punishment on both genders if caught in the act (depending on the circumstances), and it was the same God (a man) who (did not abolish but fulfilled the law) justified the woman caught in the act . . . thank God for the dispensation of Grace. So now both the man and the woman can be free and not judged!

"This I say therefore, and testify in the Lord, that ye henceforth walk not as other Gentiles walk, in the vanity of their mind, Having the understanding darkened, being alienated from the life of God through the ignorance that is in them, because of the blindness of their heart: Who being past feeling have given themselves over unto lasciviousness, to work all uncleanness with greediness. But ye have not so learned Christ; If so be that ye have heard him, and have been taught by him, as the truth is in Jesus: That ye put off concerning the former conversation the old man, which is corrupt according to the deceitful lusts; And be renewed in the spirit of your mind; And that ye put on the new man, which after God is created in righteousness and true holiness" Ephesians 4.17-24.

"This is what the LORD Almighty says: Consider now! Call for the wailing women to come; send for the most skillful of them. Let them come quickly and wail over us till our eyes overflow with tears and water streams from our eyelids" Jeremiah 9:17-18. If women were totally useless and could not be used of God then God would have called the men to accomplish this task. And the place of women is where God has called them to not neglecting their responsibilities of course. "As for you, O watchtower of the flock, O stronghold of the Daughter of Zion, the former dominion will be restored to you; kingship will come to the Daughter of Jerusalem" Micah 4:8. "Rise and thresh, O Daughter of Zion, for I will give you horns of iron; I will give you hoofs of

Bronze and you will break to pieces many nations." You will devote their ill-gotten gains to the LORD, their wealth to the Lord of all the earth. Micah 4:13. "Deborah, a prophetess, the wife of Lappidoth, was leading Israel at that time. She held court under the Palm of Deborah between Ramah and Bethel in the hill country of Ephraim, and the Israelites came to her to have their disputes decided" Judges 4:4. If she thrived in Old Testament times, then you have nothing to be afraid of, accept for not fulfilling the call of God on your life.

Rule in the midst of thine enemies

CHAPTER 36

Rebuilding Thy Walls

Every time I meditate on this subject/topic I couldn't think of a better person to write about than Job. His story by far surpasses a lot if not all of the stories I've read in the Bible on repentance, repositioning, replenishing, restoration, renewing, and rebuilding. He was a righteous man that loved God with all his heart and eschewed evil, (Job 1.1). He was perfect, and perfectly in line with the phrase in the Bible where God commanded the ninety nine year old Abraham to "walk before me and be thou perfect" in Genesis 17.1. He followed all the rules and laws laid down in the Torah that even God recommended him to Satan in Job 1.8, but even that didn't stop adversity from invading his life. (Confirms what Jesus said in John 16.33 "These things I have spoken unto you, that in me ye might have peace. In the world ye shall have tribulation: but be of good cheer; I have overcome the world)." Matter of fact, he paid so much attention to the rules of sanctification and consecration just in case one of his sons or daughters misbehaved and said a bad word while they were out partying (Job 1.5).

A very profound discovery of God's divine protection on his own is stated in Job 1.10. Satan himself couldn't penetrate God's hedge of protection around Job without God's permission. He was safe from harm just as God promised to his covenant people. Psalm 91, God has His shield/hedge/fortress/wall of protection around His people! People of God everybody needs this. If there wasn't a real threat somewhere in and from cosmos there wouldn't be any need for protection and the Bible wouldn't mention it. There is danger lurking in the shadows in a realm unseen by our natural eyes and God protects His own from the wiles of the devil Ephesians

6.11. "Be sober and vigilant because your adversary the devil as a roaring lion, walketh about seeking whom he may devour" I Peter 5.8. As the sons of God (angels) came to present themselves before God, guess who was there along with them? the devil (Job 1.6). He is allowed to roam freely, there are some he can touch and others he can't.

Getting back to this wall of protection so desperately needed by all Christians, depending on how you live some need to constantly keep repairing breaches and cracks. Job had to constantly sanctify his sons and daughters (Job 1.5) because apparently he had a revelation (in my opinion) about cracks, crevices, windows and doorways that we create every time we violate scripture believe it or not, but thank God for the blood of Jesus and the work on Calvary. His perfect life brought protection but there was a loophole and the devil seized the moment. Another time his sons and daughters went out partying because of the fact that their lives weren't as holy as their father's was they lost their lives in a vicious attack from the enemy the devil (Job 1.13-19). In an instant, in one day everything he worked so hard for all his life was gone including all his children and those that were left lived to tell, they were the messengers of doom . . . faith cometh by hearing, and hearing by the word of God (Romans 10.17) . . . fear cometh by hearing, hearing doom and destruction. That's why the Bible commands us to fear not 365 times, one for each day! God released the Hand of Protection He had around Job just to prove a point to Satan. He bragged on the faithfulness of Job but it cost him everything and in the end turned out to be worth it (Job 42.12) and his hedge of protection was restored because he remained faithful in tribulation . . . "though he slay me, yet will I trust in him: but I will maintain mine own ways before him" Job 13.15.

Nehemiah 1.2-3 describes the horrible condition of the city of Jerusalem after it had been raided and taken captive by their adversaries (Babylon). It reads "the remnant Jews that had escaped which were left of the captivity there in the province are (were) in great affliction and reproach: the wall of Jerusalem also is broken down; and the gates thereof are burned with fire." Sounds like a repeat performance of what's going on in the world and especially in the U.S. today and a total reflection of what was going on in

Jerusalem at the time of Nehemiah. As opposed to Job's situation where his was a case of faithfulness to His God on the contrary, Jerusalem in Nehemiah's time was as a result of their infidelity and unfaithfulness to God that brought them that judgment. Even after the prophet Jeremiah warned them of this outcome, they did not return to God. They invited the judgment of God by provoking God to His face with detestable abominations which were unacceptable in the sight of God. Their wall of protection was destroyed and they were totally to blame and the way to rebuild the walls was to return to God with their whole heart!

These are two extreme cases of loyalty and disloyalty, faithfulness (fidelity) and unfaithfulness (infidelity to God). Whether you live Holy as the Lord Himself or live like a spiritual tyrant and rebellion's your first and last name, there will be times when the enemy of our souls will penetrate the walls of protection either by Divine permission or by invasion. Rebuilding our walls of protection is certain. Our lifestyle dictates how long our adversity lasts. According to Theologians Job's pain lasted only nine (9) months (42 chapters of Job), Israel's captivity to Babylon seventy (70) years. It's inevitable; there will be a rebuilding in everyone's life. The responsibility of how long adversity lasts falls on our shoulder. The more we comply to His statutes the less the time, the more we revolt and rebel the more the time it will take for a rebuilding. I say we comply and expedite the process.

Enjoy the rebuilding process!

CHAPTER 37

Angels and Ravens

In the Old Testament Ravens, though associated with predatory feeding activity were used by God to meet a need in the book of I Kings 17.1-6. Ravens in nature were created by God as birds; peaceful in nature (they chirped, or tweeted to each other) but after the fall of man (Adam), they became scavenging flesh eating birds of prey. In Genesis 15.10-11 these birds of prey appear again as it's written "so Abram took all these for him and then cut them in two and placed each half opposite the other, but he did not cut the birds (of sacrifice) in half. When birds of prey came down on the carcasses, Abram drove them away."

Yet in spite of their ravening, devouring, predatory nature God decided to use a Raven to sustain Elijah in time of famine and sent its very meal; meat and bread: the stable meal intended for these creatures. "Now Elijah the Tishbite, from Tishbe in Gilead, said to Ahab, 'as the LORD, the God of Israel, lives, whom I serve, and there will be neither dew nor rain in the next few years except at my word.' Then the word of the LORD came to Elijah: 'Leave here, turn eastward and hide in the Kerith Ravine, east of the Jordan. You will drink from the brook, and I have ordered the ravens to feed you there.' So he did what the LORD had told him. He went to the Kerith Ravine, east of the Jordan, and stayed there. The ravens brought him bread and meat in the morning and bread and meat in the evening, and he drank from the brook."

Angels on the other hand possess an ability to communicate with Word/s to humans. Example Abram again before his name was changed to Abraham had such an encounter with three angels . . ." And the LORD appeared unto him in the plains of Mamre: and he sat in the tent door in the heat of the day; And he lift up his eyes and looked, and, lo, three men stood by him: and when he saw [them], he ran to meet them from the tent door, and bowed himself toward the ground, And said, My Lord, if now I have found favor in thy sight, pass not away, I pray thee, from thy servant" Genesis 18.1-3.

Such is the case with Manoah, who like Abram (Abraham) had the pleasure of interacting with an angel in Judges 13.9; it reads "God heard Manoah, and the angel of God came again to the woman while she was out in the field; but her husband Manoah was not with her." He had asked for a visitation because the angel appeared to Manoah's wife while he was not with her and gave instructions and he asked for a repeat visitation in Judges 6-8. "Then the woman went to her husband and told him, "A man of God came to me. He looked like an angel of God, very awesome. I didn't ask him where he came from, and he didn't tell me his name. But he said to me, 'You will conceive and give birth to a son. Now then, drink no wine or other fermented drink and do not eat anything unclean, because the boy will be a Nazirite of God from birth until the day of his death. Then Manoah prayed to the LORD: "O LORD, I beg you, let the man of God you sent to us come again to teach us how to bring up the boy who is to be born." There are endless stories of angels sent by God and having conversations and interactions with humans including Jacob and the angel he wrestled with in Gen 32.24-28.

My point is for generations God has promised provision to His children as seen in Matthew 6.25-26 "Therefore I say unto you, take no thought for your life, what ye shall eat, or what ye shall drink; nor yet for your body, what ye shall put on. is not the life more than meat, and the body than raiment? Behold the fowls of the air: for they sow not, neither do they reap, nor gather into barns; yet your heavenly Father feedeth them. Are ye not much better than they?" Je-ho'-va-Ji'-re (yahweh yir'-eh, "Yahweh sees"): The name given by Abraham to the place where he had sacrificed a ram provided by God, instead of his son Isaac (Gen 22:14). The meaning plainly is that the Lord sees and provides for the necessities of His servants. King David said in Psalms 37.25 that "I have been young, and now am old; yet have I not seen the righteous forsaken, nor his seed begging bread."

Now the differences between Ravens (allegorically) and Angels are:

1. Ravens are scavenging birds of prey, they are predatory, and Angels are not!

2. Angels were sent with 'WORD' from the Lord (in season or out of season i.e they can talk and Ravens are birds, they chirp, or tweet . . . do not have 'WORD' (seasoned or not)

3. Angels can interact with humans WORD from the Lord, Ravens cannot

The similarities between Ravens and Angels are:

1. They were sent from God

2. They both have wings (they can fly)

3. They both had a specific assignment to specific individuals.

Human beings are interdependent and not independent of one another; no man's an island. Christians have had a tendency to confuse angels for ravens or vice versa. Unless armed with the gift of discerning of spirits (I Corinthians 12.10), it is difficult and almost impossible to differentiate angels from ravens (allegorically or metaphorically characteristically categories). The only difference is the outcome of events because we know the content of their characters by the fruit they bear. "Beware of false prophets, who come to you in sheep's clothing, but inwardly they are ravenous wolves. You will know them by their fruits. Do men gather grapes from thorn bushes or figs from thistles? Even so, every good tree bears good fruit, but a bad tree bears bad fruit. A good tree cannot bear bad fruit, nor can a bad tree bear good fruit. Every tree that does not bear good fruit is cut down and thrown into the fire. Therefore by their fruits you will know them." Matthew 7:15-20

People with ravenous, scavenging behaviors are for your ultimate demise. They may seem to possess godly character "having a form of godliness, but denying the power thereof: BUT from such turn away" II Timothy 3.5 but because they are imposters, they're simply deceitful in character. Cultivate no friendships or any types of interaction with these types of messages, it'll lead to abuse of whatever relationship created between us and the raven even though God does tend to send these people our way to meet a need, and that's it!! They possess no ability to edify, because it's not in them to edify or encourage us, remember they are birds of prey, they're scavengers and predatory, and the very meat (answer from God) they bring us, they can turn around and eat it themselves: they're cut-throat, let them deliver and cut them loose!! "Oh give us help against the adversary, For vain is the help of man!!." Psalms 108:12.

Angels however are there for your good, their will for you is the Father's will and they would not harm you unless commanded by God Himself to carry out a harmful or hurtful act against us because of your rebellion as seen in Numbers 22:22-23 "Then God's anger was aroused because he went, and the Angel of the Lord took His stand in the way as an adversary against him. And he was riding on his donkey, and his two servants were with him. Now the donkey saw the Angel of the Lord standing in the way with His drawn sword in His hand." They (Angels) come with WORD of the Lord in season and out of season so what comes out of their mouth are to encourage, edify and build us up. They can not only provide for the need as commanded by God but they fend off the ravens in our lives by looking out for us as well. "After all, the message that the angels brought was reliable, . . ." Hebrews 2:2. "Be not forgetful to entertain strangers: for thereby some have entertained angels unawares." Hebrews 13:2.

Collaborate with Angels not Ravens

CHAPTER 38

Re-Membering, Re-positioning for Re-storing (Increase)

Thankfulness

Deuteronomy 8.18-19 brings the best intro to this message . . . after it's all said and done, and all is well never forget where you came from . . . "But thou shalt remember the LORD thy God: for it is he that giveth thee power to get wealth, that he may establish his covenant which he sware unto thy fathers, as it is this day. And it shall be, if thou do at all forget the LORD thy God, and walk after other gods, and serve them, and worship them, I testify against you this day that ye shall surely perish." While chasing your dream it is important that you don't get lost in it, but to take a moment and smell the roses. An attitude of gratitude goes a long way and "while you continue in prayer, watch in the same with thanksgiving" Colosians 4.2

But thou shalt remember that thou wast a bondman in Egypt, and the LORD thy God redeemed thee thence: therefore I command thee to do this thing. Deuteronomy 24.18. In Luke 17.11-18 records the story of the ten lepers, "and it came to pass, as he went to Jerusalem, that he passed through the midst of Samaria and Galilee. As he entered into a certain village, there met him ten men that were lepers, which stood afar off: And they lifted up their voices, and said, Jesus, Master, have mercy on us, when he saw them, he said unto them, Go show yourselves unto the priests. And it came to pass, that, as they went, they were cleansed. One of them, when he saw that he was healed, turned back, and with a loud voice glorified God, fell down on his face at his feet, giving him thanks: and he was a Samaritan. Jesus answering said, were there not ten cleansed? But where are the nine? There are not found that returned to give glory to God, save this stranger.

Ungratefulness more often than not is associated with pride and arrogance and closes the doors to more opportunities for growth and increase and if it's done unconsciously doesn't change a thing, gratefulness opens the door to increase always. "Being careful for nothing, in everything by prayer and supplication with thanksgiving let your requests be made known to God" Philippians 4.6. Always remember where you came from and; "O give thanks to the LORD; for he is good: because his mercy endures forever" Psalms 118:1; 107:1. That alone is a good enough reason to stop and give thanks unto God and

Always Maintain an Attitude of Gratitude

CHAPTER 39

War of the Knees

InterSession: Intensely enter a session with the Holy Spirit

Believe it or not, our victories and failures *as Christians* is tied into this concept of tapping into the third Heaven into the throne room of God with boldness (Hebrews 4.16). There are some achievements that are unattainable without prior planning and preparation primarily because even though "the heavens declare the glory of God;" Psalms 19.1 and ". . . God created the heaven and earth" Genesis 1.1, since the fall of man, there is a realm that is dominated by principalities, powers, rulers of the darkness of this world and spiritual wickedness in high places Ephesians 6.12. In Daniel 10.1-20, that even though Daniel had been praying and fasting for twenty four days, the angel of God was released with his answer on the very first day of his prayer but some spiritual force prince of Persia ({symbolic} ruler in the time of Daniel that was dominating the spiritual and natural realm in that region) withstood him for twenty one days.

In Matthew 17, describes the story of Jesus' disciples who were sent out to minister and they came across a young man disturbed, bound, oppressed and tormented by demonic forces living inside his body and Jesus said to them when they couldn't cast the demon out in Matthew 17:21 that "this kind of devils—goeth not out but by prayer and fasting" Ephesians 6.13 and being ". . . able to take unto you/us the whole armor of God, that ye/we may be able to withstand in the evil day, and having done all, to stand" because "we wrestle not against flesh and blood, but against principalities, against powers, against the rulers of the darkness of this world, against spiritual wickedness in high places" Ephesians 6.12. The prophet Daniel understood this phenomenon and applied the principle known to him, the Israelites in prophet Jeremiah's time also understood spiritual forces as recorded in Jeremiah 44.25 "thus saith the LORD of hosts, the God of Israel, saying; Ye and your wives have both spoken with your mouths, and fulfilled with your hand, saying, We will surely perform our vows that we have vowed, to burn incense to the queen of heaven, and to pour out drink offerings unto her: ye will surely accomplish your vows, and surely perform your vows" and the consequence follows, God's anger burned and in Jeremiah 44:27 reads "behold, I will watch over them for evil, and not for good: and all the men of Judah that are in the land of Egypt shall be consumed by the sword and by the famine, until there be an end of them . . . and all the remnant of Judah, that are gone into the land of Egypt to sojourn there, shall know whose words shall stand, mine, or theirs."

This is a very wide errie topic that deals solely on the Spiritual realm and even though every Christian is called to pray that they fall not into temptation (Matthew 26:41), there is a category/ hierarchy of watchmen . . . people who have been assigned by God to be spiritual watchmen. As it is written ". . . I have set thee a watchman unto the house of Israel; therefore thou shalt hear the word at my mouth, and warn them from me" Ezekiel 33:7; "I have set watchmen upon thy walls, O Jerusalem, which shall never hold their peace day nor night: ye that make mention of the LORD, keep not silence" Isaiah 62:6. This category requires a level of dedication, discipline and commitment that only the Holy Spirit can provide. Often times we find ourselves empty, not knowing what to pray But Thank God for the Holy Spirit for "likewise the Spirit also helpeth our infirmities: for we know not what we should pray for as we ought: but the Spirit itself maketh intercession for us with groanings which cannot be uttered" Romans 8.26.

". . . the weapons of our warfare are not carnal, but mighty through God to the pulling down of strong holds;" II Corinthians 10:4. By definition a stronghold is a strongly fortified defensive structure or a fortress; a place of refuge, survival or domination by a particular group or idea. If I was to use these definitions of strongholds, in order for a total demolition to take place it would take an arrangement, preparation, strategy, plan and a force/power much like the military. This is layman's illustration of what we need to do with spiritual strongholds. But thanks be to God who leads us into triumph . . . II Corinthians 2:14. The greatest weapon our spiritual adversary uses to detour us from the straight and narrow is temptation and Jesus warned us in Matthew 26:41 "watch and pray, that ye enter not into temptation: the spirit indeed is willing, but the flesh is weak." This is for every believer; in order to live a successful Christian life, unpolluted and sturdy, unmovable and unshakable the remedy is prayer; "with all prayer and petition pray at all times in the Spirit, and with this in view, be on the alert with all perseverance and petition for all the saints," Ephesians 6:18.

"But ye beloved, building up yourselves on your most holy faith (ought to be or by) praying in the Holy Ghost," Jude 1:20. God delights and desires to see us in constant communication with Him. The sad reality is that "there is none that understandeth, there is none that seeketh after God. They are all gone out of the way, they are together become unprofitable; there is none that doeth good, no, not one" Psalms 53:3 "every one of them is gone back: they are altogether become filthy; there is none that doeth good, no, not one. Romans 3:11. Psalms 14:2 (2 Chronicles 16:9) "The Lord looked down from heaven upon the children of men, to see if there were any that did understand, that did seek God." Ezekiel 22:30 "And I sought for a man among them, that should make up the hedge, and stand in the gap before Me for the land, that I should not destroy it: but I found none." But II Chronicles 7:14 reveals a God that has not given up on His people and gives a remedy and solution to societal and global problems, urges "if my people, which are called by my name, shall humble themselves, and pray, and seek my face, and turn from their wicked ways; then will I hear from heaven, and will forgive their sin, and will heal their land."

Heed and Boldly Enter In

CHAPTER 40

Spiritual Pollution

The state of being polluted in our soul causing contamination in our spirit man is brought about by earthy, sensual, worldly desires or lusts and actions of our bodies. According to James 1:14 pollution, takes root and brings forth fruit in form of actions when we take heed or yield to doctrines, philosophies, beliefs that form our culture. This state of contamination deeply penetrates into our minds and in our souls causing us to be a person, people or a nation "tossed to and fro, having no roots therefore ". . . carried about by every wind of doctrine, and by the sleight of men, and cunning craftiness, whereby they lie in wait to deceive;" Ephesians 4:14 who "speak lies in hypocrisy; and their conscience seared with a hot iron;" I Timothy 4:2. This causes us to become ineffective lacking the power in this walk with Christ, thus polluting the whole being, and . . . "as a man thinketh in his heart so is he" (Proverbs 23:7). God sternly warns about this state of lukewarmness, this weak condition that even though we keep that ". . . a form of godliness, we still "denying the power thereof: from such (we ought to) turn away" II Timothy 3:5. We become a "people that draweth nigh unto (GOD) with our mouths, and honor HIM with our lips, but our hearts become far from GOD" Matthew 15:8. And if we don't turn away and repent in time we become ". . . lukewarm, and neither cold nor hot, (the ultimate consequence is that) God spews us out of His mouth" Revelation 3:16. We are further warned in scripture that ". . . even as they did not like to retain God in their knowledge, God gave them over to a reprobate mind, to do those things which are not convenient;" in Romans 1:28 the breaking ground for judgment and cleansing!

It is a dangerous place to be in a state of rebellion or complacency (lukewarm). As it's written ". . . rebellion is as the sin of witchcraft, and stubbornness is as iniquity and idolatry. Because thou/we (in this generation) rejected the word of the LORD, HE hath also rejected thee/us from being king" (Royalty through Christ) I Samuel 15:23. But "the Lord is slow to anger and abounding in steadfast love, forgiving iniquity and transgression, but he will by no means clear the guilty, visiting the iniquity of the fathers on the children, to the third and the fourth generation." Numbers 14:18; Exodus 34:6-7; Exodus 20:5-6 See not only does it bring judgment on us but our children and their children and their children after them until the cycle of rebellion is broken and then light will shine through, but we lose our inheritance (destiny) and the place of promise that had been promised by God becomes shall be as a dream of a night vision.

"Be ye not unequally yoked together with unbelievers: for what fellowship hath righteousness with unrighteousness? And what communion hath light with darkness?" II Corinthians 6:14. In order to remain pure and free from spiritual pollution it's important to bring about a separation which can sometimes feel like isolation from unbelieving people . . . "what harmony exists between the Messiah and Belial, or what do a believer and an unbeliever have in common?" II Corinthians 6:15 another version of this same scripture says that "what concord hath Christ with Belial? Or what portion hath a believer with an unbeliever?" There has to be hedge a line or defining separation between you/us and they of ". . . he works of the flesh which manifest, which are these; adultery, fornication, uncleanness, lasciviousness, Idolatry, witchcraft, hatred, variance, emulations, wrath, strife, seditions, heresies, envyings, murders, drunkenness, revellings, and such like: of the which I tell you before, as I have also told you in time past, that they which do such things shall not inherit the kingdom of God" . . . and cling to people that have ". . . the fruit of the Spirit which is love, joy, peace, longsuffering, gentleness, goodness, faith, meekness, temperance: against such there is no law, and they that are Christ's have crucified the flesh with the affections and lusts. If we live in the Spirit, let us also walk in the Spirit (of Christ). (Galatians 5:19-25).

I have heard some say that the place of the greatest raw, untapped and unrealized potential is not the work place, but the grave yard. Millions of lives cut short and people not able to fully tap into, explore and exploit their full potential and this is a sadness of the reality, "but the people that do know their God shall be strong, and do exploits." Daniel 11:32

"Beloved, believe not every spirit, but try the spirits whether they are of God: because many false prophets are gone out into the world. Hereby know ye the Spirit of God: Every spirit that confesseth that Jesus Christ is come in the flesh is of God: And every spirit that confesseth not that Jesus Christ is come in the flesh is not of God: and this is that spirit of antichrist, whereof ye have heard that it should come; and even now already is it in the world. Ye are of God, little children, and have overcome them: because greater is he that is in you, than he that is in the world." 1 John 4:1-4

"See then that ye walk circumspectly, not as fools, but as wise, redeeming the time, because the days are evil" Ephesians 5:15-16. "I therefore, the prisoner of the Lord, beseech you that ye walk worthy of the vocation wherewith ye are called, with all lowliness and meekness, with longsuffering, forbearing one another in love; endeavoring to keep the unity of the Spirit in the bond of peace" Ephesians 4:1-3. For we brought nothing into this world, and it is certain we can carry nothing out; having food and raiment let us be therewith content. But they that will be rich fall into temptation and a snare, and into many foolish and hurtful lusts, which drown men in destruction and perdition for the love of money is the root of all evil: which while some coveted after, they have erred from the faith, and pierced themselves through with many sorrows. But thou, O man/woman/child of God, flee these things; and follow after righteousness, godliness, faith, love, patience, meekness. Fight the good fight of faith, lay hold on eternal life, whereunto thou art also called, and hast professed a good profession before many witnesses . . ." 1 Timothy 6:7-12

"I give you charge in the sight of God, who quickens all things, and before Christ Jesus, who before Pontius Pilate witnessed a good confession; that you keep this commandment without spot, unrebukeable, until the appearing of our Lord Jesus Christ: which in his times he shall show, who is the blessed and only Potentate, the King of kings, and Lord of lords; who only has immortality, dwelling in the light which no man can approach unto; whom no man has seen, nor can see: to whom be honor and power everlasting. Amen" I Timothy 6:13-16. "Flee also youthful lusts: but follow righteousness, faith, charity, peace, with them that call on the Lord out of a pure heart. But foolish and unlearned questions avoid, knowing that they do gender strifes. And the servant of the Lord must not strive; but be gentle unto all men, apt to teach, patient, in meekness instructing those that oppose themselves; if God peradventure will give them repentance to the acknowledging of the truth; and that they may recover themselves out of the snare of the devil, who are taken captive by him at his will.!!" I Timothy 2:22

Be Pure and Unpolluted

Chapter 41

Indestructibility

"For the weapons of our warfare are not carnal but mighty through God to the pulling down of strongholds," II Corinthians 10:4. Time and time and time again I have been faced with life threatening situations that could have taken me out but because of the covenant and promise as seen in Genesis 17:7 the threats have been diffused. "And I will establish my covenant between me and thee and thy seed after thee in their generations for an everlasting covenant, to be a God unto thee," through Jesus Christ, God has kept me alive. Destiny and purpose have everything to do with why I am still alive and I'm sure you're witness to this in your own way in your own life and you certainly have a story to tell of how good God has been to you.

There are many examples I could use in this study about how God preserved the apples of His eye for an intended purpose. That's why it is very important to understand the will of God for your life. I have heard people say in their opinion if you're looking for untapped, unrealized, raw or unused potential, the best place to find this is the graveyard, where goals, dreams and ambitions never really came to be realized or fruition. Ecclesiastes 9:10 reads that "whatsoever your hand finds to do, do it with your might; for there is no work, nor device, nor knowledge, nor wisdom in the grave wither thou goest." Ecclesiastes 9:11, ". . . the race is not to the swift, nor the battle to the strong, neither bread to the wise, nor riches to men of understanding, nor yet favor to men of skill; BUT time and chance happened to them all."

Paul recorded that ". . . We are troubled on every side, yet not distressed; perplexed, but not in despair; persecuted, but not abandoned or forsaken; cast down and struck down, but not destroyed. Always bearing about in our body the dying of the Lord Jesus, that the life also of Jesus might be made manifest in our body. For we which live are always delivered unto death for Jesus' sake, that the life also of Jesus might be made manifest in our mortal flesh" (II Corinthians 4:8-11). Another illustration of Apostle Paul's indestructibility is shown in Acts 28:1-6 ". . . when they were escaped, then they knew that the island was called Melita. And the barbarous people shewed us no little kindness: for they kindled a fire, and received us every one, because of the present rain, and because of the cold. And when Paul had gathered a bundle of sticks, and laid them on the fire, there came a viper out of the heat, and fastened on his hand. When the barbarians saw the venomous beast hang on his hand, they said among themselves, no doubt this man is a murderer, whom, though he hath escaped the sea, yet vengeance suffereth not to live. And he shook off the beast into the fire, and felt no harm. Howbeit they looked when he should have swollen, or fallen down dead suddenly: but after they had looked a great while, and saw no harm come to him, they changed their minds, and said that he was a god.

Another illustration of indestructibility as a result of God's favor because of the covenant and is found in the book of Genesis 37:2-5 And . . . "Joseph being seventeen years old was feeding the flock with his brethren . . . : and Joseph brought unto his father their evil report. Now Israel loved Joseph more than all his children, because he was the son of his old age: and he (Jacob) made him a coat of many colors, and when his brothers saw that their father loved him more that all his brothers, they hated him, and could not speak kindly to him. And Joseph dreamed a dream, and he told it to his brethren and they hated him yet more . . ." he was the figure of authority over of his parents and his brothers to the point where his parents and brothers made obeisance to him. Genesis 37.11 "And his brothers envied him; BUT (Jacob) his father observed the saying"

In verse 13 of Genesis 37, Jacob (Israel) sent Joseph to check on his brothers . . . Genesis 37:18-19 "and when they saw him afar off, before he came near to them, they conspired against him to slay/kill him . . . saying to one another here comes the dreamer." They ended up throwing him in a pit and then later sold him to some

Midianite merchants. Genesis 39:1 "And Joseph was brought down to Egypt; and Potiphar an officer of Pharaoh, captain of the guard, an Egyptian bought him of the hands of the Ishmaelites, which had brought him down thither." Genesis 37:31-36 records his brothers returned to his father after soiling Jacob's coat with animal's blood to make it look like an animal had devoured him and Jacob believed them and grieved over his son Joseph. Genesis 39:2-4 BUT ". . . the Lord was with Joseph, and he was a prosperous man; (even though reduced to a slave by his own brothers), and he was in the house of his master the Egyptian. And his master saw that the Lord was with him, that the Lord made all that he did to prosper in his hand . . . Joseph found grace in his sight, and he served him: and he made him overseer over his house, and all that he had he put it into his hand."

He was so blessed that Potiphar's wife wanted to sleep with him but he escaped leaving his coat behind later accusing him of rape and she used Joseph's coat as evidence so he ended up in Jail. "BUT the Lord was with Joseph, and showed him mercy, and gave him favor in the sight of the keeper of the prison. And the keeper of the prison committed to Joseph's hand all the prisoners that were in the prison ; . . . (to manage them) . . . and whatsoever they did there, he was the doer of it. The keeper of the prison looked not to anything that was under his hand; because the Lord was with him, and that which he did, the LORD made it to prosper" Genesis 39:7-23. "No weapon that was formed against Joseph ever prospered; and every tongue that rose against him in judgment was condemned. That was the heritage of Joseph the servants of the LORD, and his righteousness is of me, saith the LORD" Isaiah 54:17.

He was indestructible because of his destiny and his purpose for living. To cut the long story short, Joseph with gift of interpretation of dreams made way for him as scripture says in Proverbs 18:16 that "a man's gift maketh room for him, and bringeth him before great men." Joseph was promoted to prime minster of Egypt for the preservation of his people Israel and God used his lemons and turned them to lemonade, a phrase I like to use. Joseph's wisdom and spiritual gift sustained his family and cities surrounding Egypt when the famine hit and Egypt was the only place to find food in that region at that time all because of Joseph the dreamer.

"Who shall separate us from the love of Christ? Shall tribulation, or distress, or persecution, or famine, or nakedness, or peril, or sword? As it is written, for thy sake we are killed all the day long; we are accounted as sheep for the slaughter. Nay, in all these things we are more than conquerors through him that loved us." Romans 8:35-37 "These things I have spoken unto you, that in me ye might have peace. In the world ye shall have tribulation: but be of good cheer for I have overcome the world." John 16:33 and ". . . in all these things we are more than conquerors through Him who loved us." Romans 8:37 and "If the world hates you, you know that it has hated Me before it hated you" John 15:18.

In II Corinthians 11:24-33 Records that, five times he received from the Jews thirty-nine lashes. Three times he was beaten with rods, once he was stoned, three times he was shipwrecked, a night and a day he spent in the deep. He has been on frequent journeys, in dangers from rivers, dangers from robbers, dangers from his own countrymen, dangers from the Gentiles, dangers in the city, dangers in the wilderness, dangers on the sea, dangers among false brethren; He has been in labor and hardship, through many sleepless nights, in hunger and thirst, often without food, in cold and exposure. Apart from such external things, there is the daily pressure on him (Paul) of concern for all the churches . . . The God and Father of the Lord Jesus, He who is blessed forever, knows that he is not lying. In Damascus the ethnarch under Aretas the king was guarding the city of the Damascenes in order to seize him, and he was let down in a basket through a window in the wall, and so escaped his hands. There you have it. Many times Paul's very own life was threatened but for the virtue of the fact that he was on a mission, had a destiny and purpose, and he was fulfilling the will of God he became indestructible until his work on was finished.

Jesus in Luke 10:19 "Behold, I give unto you power to tread on serpents and scorpions, and over all the power of the enemy: and nothing shall by any means hurt you." Psalms 91:7-16 "A thousand shall fall at thy side, and ten thousand at thy right hand; but it shall not come nigh thee . . . there shall no evil befall thee, neither shall any plague come nigh thy dwelling. For he shall give his angels charge over thee, to keep thee in all thy ways. They shall bear thee up in their hands, lest thou dash thy foot against a stone. Thou shalt tread upon the lion and adder: the young lion and the dragon shalt thou trample under feet."

It is my prayer and hope that you remain patient in tribulation (because you are indeed indestructible), continuing steadfastly in prayer (Romans 12:12) "And not only so, but we glory in tribulations also: knowing that tribulation worketh patience; (Romans 5:3) and able to quench the fiery darts of the enemy (Ephesians 6:16), and when the enemy comes in like a flood, the Spirit of the Lord will raise/lift up a standard against him (Isaiah 59:19). Fear Not!

Remain INDESTRUCTIBLE

Chapter 42

Holiness 101

"The god of this age has blinded the minds of unbelievers, so that they cannot see the light of the gospel of the glory of Christ, who is the image of God" (II Corinthians 4:4). Generations X's and the Millennials have been the generation that have enjoyed the prosperity of their parents and grandparents. Even though they have had it easier than the generations before them and the generations after them, we see the effects of prosperity without God, as seen in James 1:14 . . . a generation that is tempted, when he/they is/they drawn away of his/their own lust, and enticed and though prosperity originates from God Himself, James 1:13 records "Let no man say when he is tempted, I am tempted of God: for God cannot be tempted with evil, neither tempteth he any man:"

According to Luke 16:15 "You/We are those (the generation) who justify ourselves in the sight of men, but God knows our hearts; for that which is highly esteemed among men is detestable in the sight of God." Too many provocative, sensual, uncensored, explicit and graphic images or materials have flashed before their/ our eyes and what's worse is parents allow too much freedom to kids than their brains can handle. With much freedom and liberty is much responsibility and they are barely able to take responsibility for what they're exposed to. Ever heard of this saying "garbage in garbage out", well this kind freedom and exposure to the ungodly has brought about SIN and now we're reaping the fruits thereof. Be not deceived God is not mocked! Galatians 6:7. It is written in James 1:15, that ". . . when lust hath conceived, it bringeth forth sin: and sin, when it is finished, bringeth forth death" and the judgment we're experiencing now . . . (with the global economy and other all these other global problems) will not cease until we get back to the grassroots. Judges 17:6 reflects this scenario as it reads that "In those days there was no king in Israel, but every man did that which was right in his own eyes," we know now based on scripture that "there is a way which seemeth right unto a man, but the end thereof are the ways of death (and destruction)." Proverbs 14:12

God never spared Israel (the apple of His eye) and He won't spare this generation either. Even though we're not under the law but living under the dispensation of His Grace (Romans 6:14) we cannot afford to "worship any other god for the LORD, whose name is Jealous." Exodus 34:14 reads "the God that we serve is a jealous God among us" Deuteronomy 6:15, "visiting the iniquity of the fathers upon the children unto the third and fourth generation of them that hate me." Exodus 20:5 records that He " . . . is the same yesterday today and forever more" Hebrews 13:8; "lest the anger of the LORD our God be kindled against us, and destroy us from off the face of the earth . . . Deuteronomy 6:15, the same values cherished yesterday are the same values cherished today. "Righteousness exalts a nation but sin is a reproach to ANY people." In Proverbs 14:34 we see that of all the kingdoms and nations that ever came to be, were either exalted by righteousness or destroyed by sin and brought them to oblivion, desolation, destruction and disintegration. Examples of such the cities are Sodom and Gomorrah in the time of Abraham (Genesis 19:24). Israel's fall to the Babylonians in 586 BC as prophesied in Daniel 9, Jeremiah 50:46 gave a glimpse of the prophesy on the fall of Babylon to Cyrus of Persia because Belteshazah refused to acknowledge God unlike his father Nebuchadnezzah who amended his ways. The writing on the wall was a warning of the end of his reign and shortly after that Babylon was taken! "For thus says the LORD of hosts, the God of Israel: 'As My anger and My fury have been poured out on the inhabitants of Jerusalem, so will My fury be poured out on you when you enter Egypt" in disobedience/rebellion Jeremiah 42:18

"For I am the LORD your God: . . . He which hath called you is holy, so ye shall therefore sanctify yourselves, and ye shall be holy; for I am holy" (Leviticus 11:44; I Peter 1:15-16) and "be ye therefore perfect as I your Father which is in Heaven am perfect," Matthew

5:48; this is not a debate; it is a command from Elohim. There is no middle ground. I kings 18:21 reads "If the LORD is God, follow Him; but if Baal, follow him." In Matt 6:24 Jesus said "No man can serve two masters: for either he will hate the one, and love the other; or else he will hold to the one, and despise the other. Ye cannot serve God and mammon." "Behold, I set before you this day a blessing and a curse; A blessing, if ye obey the commandments of the LORD your God, which I command you this day: And a curse, if ye will not obey the commandments of the LORD your God, but turn aside out of the way which I command you this day, to go after other gods, which ye have not known." Deuteronomy 11:26-28.

"I call heaven and earth to record this day against you, that I have set before you life and death, blessing and cursing: therefore choose life, that both thou and thy seed may live:" Deuteronomy 30:19 and Jesus in II Peter 1:3-4 "according as his divine power hath given unto us all things that pertain unto life and godliness, through the knowledge of him that hath called us to glory and virtue: Whereby are given unto us exceeding great and precious promises: that by these ye might be partakers of the divine nature, having escaped the corruption that is in the world through lust!" "So shall my word be that goeth forth out of my mouth: it shall not return unto me void, but it shall accomplish that which I please, and it shall prosper in the thing whereto I sent it" Isaiah 55:11, knowing as written in II Corinthians 1:20 . . . that "all the promises of God in him are yea, and in him Amen, unto the glory of God by us," and last but not least John 10:10 reads "I am come that they might have life, and have it more abundantly." See Numbers 23:19 "God is not a man, that he should lie, nor a son of man, that he should change his mind. Does he speak and then not act? Does he promise and not fulfill?" The Choice is yours, choose life!

More Life to you

CHAPTER 43

Attitude is Everything . . .

To give a small illustration, I went to pick my kids up from daycare today and yes I parked on the wrong spot and the only reason I did that is because I saw a bunch cars parked in front of me (mind you there is not one no parking sign at that spot!); I was not blocking traffic but parked along the curb. The senior pastor of that church saw me come out of my car and yelled at me to move my car because I had parked in the wrong place . . . (he could probably make a sermon out of that encounter come Sunday morning) but he was ticked that I dared parked my car in that area . . . (and believe me it won't happen again after that experience) but my point is there would have been a better way to convey that message which would make him look a little more Christ like than the way he did but I was convinced that he was not going to ruin the rest of my evening and that inspired today's lesson.

The book of Colossians 4:6 couldn't say it better . . . "Let your conversation be always full of grace, seasoned with salt, so that you may know how to answer everyone." We never know when the angel might decide to show up without warning. Hebrews 13:2 reads "Being not forgetful to entertain strangers: for thereby some have entertained angels unawares." The most perfect example in my opinion was when Jesus was being persecuted in Luke 13:34-35 clearly illustrates today's message . . . "O Jerusalem, Jerusalem, which killest the prophets, and stonest them that are sent unto thee; how often would I have gathered thy children together, as a hen [doth gather] her brood under [her] wings, and ye would not!

Behold, your house is left unto you desolate: and verily I say unto you, Ye shall not see me, until [the time] come when ye shall say, Blessed [is] he that cometh in the name of the Lord." Sad but true the hearts of the Jews in the time of Jesus was hardened and it cost them the moment they'd been waiting for for centuries and the next time they would see their Savior, Lord and King, their Messiah would be on His second coming.

I cannot begin to tell you how many times I have seen poor customer service skills involving the tongue emanating out of church officials, without knowledge or just because they have lost the true meaning of servitude. "The customer is always right" is a motto used among customer service reps. Scripture tells us in James 3:6-12 ". . . the tongue is a fire. The tongue is an unrighteous world among our members, staining the whole body, setting on fire the cycle of nature, and set on fire by hell. For every kind of beast and bird, of reptile and sea creature can be tamed and has been tamed by humankind, but no human being can tame the tongue-a restless evil, full of deadly poison. With it we bless the Lord and Father, and with it we curse men, who are made in the likeness of God. From the same mouth come blessing and cursing. My brethren, this ought not to be so. Does a spring pour forth from the same opening fresh water and brackish? Can a fig tree, my brethren, yield olives, or grapevine figs? No more can salt water yield fresh."

Therefore what we need to have is "grace poured into thy lips:" and as a result of it "therefore God hath blessed thee forever."(Psalms 45:2). "Death and life are in the power of the tongue: and they that love it shall eat the fruit thereof." (Proverbs 18:21), "An evil man is ensnared by the transgression of his lips, but the righteous will escape from trouble."(Proverbs 12:13), "From the fruit of a man's mouth he enjoys good, But the desire of the treacherous is violence. The one who guards his mouth preserves his life; the one who opens wide his lips come to ruin." (Proverbs 13:2-3). "A gentle answer turns away wrath, But a harsh word stirs up anger" Proverbs 15:1.

My greatest lesson on attitude is in the story of Moses, "And the people chode with Moses, and spake, saying, would God that we had died when our brethren died before the Lord! And why have ye brought up the congregation of the Lord into this wilderness, that we and our cattle should die there? And wherefore have ye made us to come up out of Egypt, to bring us in unto this evil place?"

Numbers 20:2. In the midst of total confusion, bickering and verbal assault coming from the Israelites at the Waters at Meribah, he their spiritual leader needed and was required to be cool calm and collected amidst the chaos. Luke 12:48 reads "For unto whomsoever much is given, of him shall be much required:" But he snapped, lost his temper and struck the rock when he was supposed to "speak unto the rock before their eyes that it may yield its water" (See Numbers 20:1-13). "Moses lifted up his hand, and with his rod he smote the rock twice: and the water came out abundantly" Numbers 20:12. "Then the LORD spoke to Moses and Aaron, "Because you did not believe Me, to hallow Me in the eyes of the children of Israel, therefore you shall not bring this assembly into the land which I have given them." That small act of disobedience cost him his promise. Your attitude does determine your altitude . . .

Blessings to you

CHAPTER 44

Gain and Godliness

We have come to an age of knowledge as predicted in Habakkuk 2:14 which states that "the earth shall be filled with knowledge" and ". . . because without it the people are destroyed" (Hosea 4:6). Even though its increase has brought about the increase of sorrow (Ecclesiastes 1:18), and though it is wise according to Proverbs 10:14 to lay up knowledge, the effects of it has made the rich richer and poorer poor, enlarging the gap between the poor and the rich because of one of the seven deadliest sins of greed.

Church sermons are flooded with this doctrine of gain whereby the haves are treated with respect and admiration . . . "put on a pedestal" and the have nots despised, disdained, ignored, austrocized and avoided like a plague, and yes this happens in the church, when the bible clearly reads in Deuteronomy 15:11 "For the poor will never cease to be in the land; therefore I command you, saying, 'You shall freely open your hand to your brother, to your needy and poor in your land." Pulpits are manipulating members to give, give until they have nothing left to live off of, and Christians are snared in this doctrine out of disparity and fear of what could happen if they don't "obey". . . Jeremiah 5:31 clearly reflects this . . . "The prophets prophesy falsely, and the priests bear rule by their means; and my people love to have it so: and what will ye do in the end thereof?."

The scripture clearly commands that the tithes and offerings be brought to the store houses (Malachi 3:10) . . . pure and simple, not grudgingly or under compulsion for God loveth a cheerful giver (II Corinthians 9:7). Casting thy bread upon the waters: for thou shalt find it after many days Ecclesiastes 11:1. Seed time and harvest will never cease (Genesis 8:22) so it is imperative to give BUT OUT OF A FREE WILL. Only IF out of the prophetic unction (if you're one of those that branched out of the prophetic and apostolic anointing) does a man or woman of God specifies an amount from the leading of the HOLY SPIRIT can you give what is specified. Here God guarantees that your seed will succeed in the thing it was sent to . . . "and blessed is she that believed: for there shall be a performance of those things which were told her from the Lord." (Luke 1:45)

God wants you to have Joy in your heart, live abundantly, have all your bills paid on time (building your credibility) and God wants you to invest and increase . . . "After these things the word of the LORD came to Abram in a vision, saying, "Do not be afraid, Abram. I am your shield, your exceedingly great reward" Genesis 15:1. God is a God of increase (I Corinthians 3:6 and Psalms 115:14), and the blessing of the Lord maketh RICH and addeth no sorrow to it (Proverbs 10:22. You will have all these things that your heart desires added unto you after seeking first His Kingdom (Luke 12:31), "Let no man seek his/her own, but every man another's wealth and or welfare," (I Corinthians 10:24). "For the earth is the Lords and it's fullness thereof" (I Corinthians 10:26) and "for you know the grace of our Lord Jesus Christ, that though He was rich, yet for your/our sake he became poor, so that by his poverty you/we might become rich" II Corinthians 8:9.

"Charge them that are rich in this world, that they be not high minded, nor trust in uncertain riches, but in the living God, who giveth us richly all things to enjoy; that they do good, that they be rich in good works, ready to distribute, willingly to communicate" I Timothy 6:17-18. Be wise now therefore, as God begins to bless you or if you're in that waiting mode never ever forget to always be content and happy with what you have . . . "not supposing that gain is Godliness . . . and from such as teach this kind of doctrine withdraw yourself, BUT Godliness with contentment is GREAT GAIN". (I Timothy 6:5, 6). Finally "let him that stole steal no more: (ref: Malachi 3:10) but rather let him labor, working with his hands the thing which is good, that he may have to give to him that needeth," Ephesians 4.28. "Not that I speak in respect of want: for I have learned, in whatsoever state I am, therewith to be content" Philippians 4:1.

BONUS CHAPTER:

The True Vine and His Branches by Prof. Khuram Shahzad of Flow of The Spirit Ministries, Pakistan

I am the true vine, and My Father is the gardener . . . . He prunes every branch that produces fruit—so that it will produce more fruit." John 15:1-2

Our Father is the gardener; we are branches under His care. He watches over our lives. The painful afflictions which cut into our very souls, the taking from us of objects that are dear to us, as when the gardener with his sharp knife removes luxuriant branches from the vine—are our Father's prunings! No hand but His—ever holds the knife! We are sure, then, that there is never any careless cutting, any unwise or mistaken pruning, any needless removing of rich branches or growths.

We really need to go no farther than this. A strong, abiding confidence that all the trials, sorrows and losses of our lives—are parts of our Father's prunings—ought to silence every question, quiet every fear and give peace and restful assurance to our hearts, in all their pain. We cannot know the reason for the painful strokes—but we know that He who holds the pruning-knife is our Father! That is all we need to know.

The other thought in the Lord's parable, is scarcely less full of comfort to a Christian. Jesus says, that it is the fruitful branches which the Father prunes: "He prunes every branch that produces fruit—so that it will produce more fruit."

Afflictions are not, then, a mark of God's anger or disapproval; rather, they are a mark of His favor. The branches into which

233

He cuts, from which he trims away the luxuriant growths—are fruit-bearing already. He does not prune the fruitless branches—He cuts them off altogether as useless, as mere cumberers, absorbing life and yielding nothing of blessing or good.

Some Christians have the impression that their many troubles indicate that God does not love them—that they cannot be true Christians, or they would not be so chastened. This teaching of Christ shows how mistaken they are. The much chastening shows that the Father is pruning His fruitful branch—to make it more fruitful! All whom the Father loves—He chastens!

It is the fruitless branch that is never pruned; the fruitful branch is pruned, and pruned—not by one without skill, not by an enemy—but by the wise Father! Thus we see how we may rejoice—even in our trials and afflictions!

One who was altogether ignorant of the art and purpose of pruning, who should see a man with a sharp knife cutting off branch after branch of a luxuriant vine, would at first suppose that the pruner was ruining the vine. So at the time it seems—but by and by, it appears that the prunings have made the vine more fruitful. In the season of vintage, the grapes are more luscious, with a richer flavor in them—because of the cutting away of the superfluous branches.

In like manner, if an angel who had never witnessed anything of human suffering, and who knew nothing of its object, were to see the Father causing pain and affliction to His children, it would seem to him that these experiences could be only destructive of happiness and blessing; but if the angel were to follow those chastened lives on to the end, he would see untold blessing coming out of the chastenings! The Father was but pruning the branches—that they might bear more and better fruit!

We should never lose sight of the divine purpose in all trials—to make our lives more fruitful.

ABOUT THE AUTHOR:

S is Grace M.R. Makau (Lee) Spiritual journey began before she was born as Jeremiah 1.5 confirms that "before I formed you in the belly I knew you, and before you came forth of the womb I sanctified you and I (the Lord) ordained you a prophet unto the nations." As a baby she was dedicated by Rev William Tuimising of Deliverance Churches of Kenya. She was born to very staunch born again Christian parents and from the very beginning she was initiated in the faith of Our Lord Jesus Christ. Her father Rev. Shadrack Makau was already firmly rooted and grounded in the ministry under Deliverance Churches of Kenya some 40 years ago even though accepted the Lord Jesus as his personal savior in 1959 (some 50 years ago), has never let go of his promise. Her father eventually retired from his engineering/telecommunications career/profession that he loved dearly ("Yea doubtless, and I count all things [but] loss for the excellency of the knowledge of Christ Jesus my Lord: for whom I have suffered the loss of all things, and do count them [but] dung, that I may win Christ," Philippians 3:8) for the sake of the call and the demands of the ministry and has been pioneer of 58 Deliverance Churches across Kenya from 1990 to present, earning him the title of overseer. Her mother (Mrs. Rophence Makau), was/is the daughter of an Anglican born again believer (Isaac Mwanjala), and her mother—an intercessor and prophetess filled with the Holy Spirit (Jemimah Mwanjala).

Her mother (Rophence Makau) accepted the Lord Jesus Christ when she was 8 years old, not only stood by her husband (Rev. Shadrack Makau) in ministry but also intercedes and stands in the gap for the believers in the body of Christ as it relates to the Kingdom of God to this day. She not only helped nurture and protect the gift that was in her daughter, Rev. Grace M.R. Lee {"When I call to remembrance the unfeigned faith that is in thee, which dwelt first in thy grandmother Lois, and thy mother Eunice; and I am persuaded that in thee also" II Timothy 1.5, given her by prophecy, with the laying on of the hands of the presbytery . . . (I Timothy 4.14),} but is and has been an educator, counselor, coach and mentor to countless women and men of all ages.

She accepted Jesus Christ as her Lord and savior as a young child and was filled with the Holy Spirit in March of 2000. She had accepted the call of God early in her life and though she felt challenges of modern day living and peer pressure in her teens she never let go. Not only was Rev. G.M.R. Makau (Lee) raised in the church but thrust in ministry early in her teens and was officially ordained into the Ministry of Jesus Christ in September 19th 2006. She recalls being bullied into ministry by her eldest brother in a nice way, who alongside her father started a string of churches in Kenya and Europe. They did their part in training up the child in the way that she should go, so that when Rev. got/gets old she would not depart from it (Proverbs 22.6).

She often prayed that God would give her a brain and spiritual transplant from her father because of the kind of spirit he possesses. He is very passionate, tenacious and undying pertaining to the things of God. She always said that she learned most of everything she needed to know about God, His kingdom and His work from the master himself (her father) and refusing to be affected by (MCS) Middle Child Syndrome (as she often called it), her parents' feet deeply firmly rooted in ministry, all her 3 older siblings followed suit, making ministry not only a part of her family's legacy, but a heritage in which she is privileged and proud to be a part of. She remembers her father decreeing time and time again the words of Joshua the son of Nun ". . . as for me and my house we will serve the Lord" (Joshua 24.15), and those words became established and true then as it is today . . . (Job 22.28).

Her love and devotion to her savior and Lord JESUS CHRIST is her greatest motivation. In HIM she lives, moves and has her being and gets her inspiration from The TEACHER The Holy Spirit.